THE CONTRACT ADVANTAGE™:

Contracts as a Business Asset™

Frederikke C.

ISBN:
eBook: 978-1-960346-62-9
Paperback: 978-1-960346-63-6
Hardback: 978-1-960346-64-3

DEDICATION

To my daughter, my only child, whose brilliance as a psychiatrist and wisdom have been my daily lessons in perspective, grace, and restraint.

You taught me long ago:

"If I don't look at Mum, she won't see me..."

And in moments of business heat, your reminder always echoes:

"Mum, just because you can say it, doesn't mean you should say it."

Our favorite remains timeless:

"Hmm... I'm sure it doesn't work that way..."

You've taught me more than you know, and I carry your wisdom into every room I enter.

And to my partner, my conscience, and my unwavering sense in this life: I love you and our daughter unconditionally. You are the quiet foundation beneath all my work. I am endlessly grateful for that.

ACKNOWLEDGMENTS

To the leaders and builders who believe businesses should serve life, not consume it.

To every visionary who dares to design freedom into their growth.

And to my clients, past, present, and future, whose trust has turned strategies into success stories.

Writing this book would not have been possible without the trust and collaboration of my clients, who inspire my work every day. Your commitment to building businesses that thrive while living fully has been my greatest motivation.

I am deeply grateful to my colleagues and advisors who continue challenging and elevating my thinking, helping me refine complex ideas into actionable strategies.

To the proponents behind CLM innovation and operational excellence, your dedication is reshaping the future of business.

My close circle of supporters and sounding boards deserves a special thank you. Your encouragement and belief in this mission have fueled every chapter.

Finally, to this book's readers:

May it guide, inspire, and empower you to scale smarter, grow stronger, and live more freely.

PREFACE

Welcome to *The Contract Advantage*™.

This series was born from a simple belief:

> Operational pain points are not inevitable burdens - they are untapped business assets.

> Across my career advising leaders around the world, from scaling SMBs to Fortune 500 giants, I've seen the same frustrations in boardrooms and project meetings: Contract chaos, vendor risks, compliance fears, and operational friction are slowing down growth.

However, I've also seen the transformational power of treating these areas not as isolated problems, but as levers for growth.

The Advantage Series™ is my battle-tested methodology and playbook for leaders like you - decision-makers ready to move beyond survival mode and design companies that scale with clarity, deliver measurable ROI, and create the freedom to focus on what m*atters most.*

In this volume, *"The Contract Advantage*™," we will explore how to transform contracts from cost centers into growth engines.

Each book in this series stands alone, yet together they form a powerful library for growth-minded leaders seeking lasting, sustainable success.

I've designed these pages to be more than insights. They

are frameworks, actionable strategies, and field-tested tools you can apply immediately to your organization.

Whether you are an executive, an owner, a leader of teams, or an architect of enterprise transformation, my hope is simple:

I hope this series empowers you to build a business that works brilliantly so that you can live brilliantly, too.

Let's begin.

— **Frederikke C.**, Trusted Growth Advisor & Author of *The Advantage Series™*

VOLUME I

THE THEORY

TABLE OF CONTENTS

INTRODUCTION

Imagine losing millions of dollars each year simply because contracts are mismanaged. With every decision mattering, overlooking a contract renewal or having a vague vendor agreement can drain resources and weaken your competitive edge. A real case study showed that inefficient contract processes may cost organizations as much as $1.7 million per 100 employees annually.

Case Study: Mid-Sized Technology Company (Anonymized – Client's Name Withheld)

A mid-sized technology company with approximately 500 employees relied on manual, fragmented contract management processes. The company stored contracts in disparate locations, handled approvals via email, and manually tracked deadlines. Over one fiscal year, the finance department estimated that delays in contract approvals, missed renewal opportunities, and time spent locating documents resulted in lost revenue and increased operational costs totaling $8.5 million. When normalized, this equated to $1.7 million per 100 employees. After implementing an automated contract management system, the company reduced these losses by over 60% within two years.

This statistic makes us question how many companies

unknowingly sacrifice revenue, stifle innovation, and jeopardize customer satisfaction. This book confronts these challenges head-on, offering a comprehensive framework to reimagine Contract Lifecycle Management (CLM) as a strategic engine for business growth.

Legal and administrative departments relegated contracts to their back offices for too long - a necessary but often cumbersome form of compliance. The common narrative treats these documents as static proofs of agreement rather than dynamic instruments that can drive strategic decisions. Because many managers fear risk and only deal with problems as they arise, they miss opportunities to use contracts to gain a competitive edge. The result is a disconnect: an organization might excel in product innovation or market penetration, yet struggle with an outdated process that continually undermines opportunities. This book challenges that division, arguing that a well-orchestrated contract management system is not merely an administrative function but a core element of growth strategy.

A careful examination of modern business practices reveals that the chaos in managing contracts does more than create operational delays - it breeds financial inefficiencies, undermines internal and external trust, and places companies at a distinct disadvantage against more agile competitors. Organizations with fragmented systems, manual processes, and isolated data risk more than short-term setbacks. They compromise long-term strategic planning, exposing themselves to revenue leakage, compliance issues, and diminished customer loyalty. The unmistakable contradiction is this: designing contracts to secure relationships and enforce commitments, but mishandling them fundamentally sabotages those objectives.

This reality becomes even more pronounced when considering the operational environment businesses now operate in. Contract management inefficiencies slow decision-making and impair responsiveness to customer needs in a market defined by relentless speed and an incessant demand for transparency. A delayed contract approval cycle is not simply a bureaucratic hiccup—it disrupts the entire customer experience and hampers the agility required for innovation. Tracking and quantifying each contractual misstep reveals a cost that exceeds lost revenue. It undermines an organization's reputation, weakens customer and supplier trust, and ultimately impacts market positioning.

This book will give detailed analyses of how contemporary contract management practices fall short and a roadmap to overcoming these limitations. One recurring theme is the urgent need for an integrated approach that aligns contract processes with the overall business strategy. A modern CLM framework transcends the regulatory box-checking mentality, instead positioning contracts as living, strategic assets. This perspective shift is essential because it transforms how organizations view contracts— from static obligations they must maintain at all costs into dynamic tools that forecast market trends, optimize resource allocation, and strengthen customer relationships.

This narrative does not rely solely on theory. A compilation of actual studies I have experienced over the years illustrates how companies have successfully reduced contract backlogs, increased accuracy in contract processing, and improved user satisfaction scores from less-than-promising levels to remarkable highs. These successes are not unique occurrences. They provide practical insights into how a re-engineered contract management system can create a multiplier effect across multiple facets of a business, from operational efficiency to strategic market positioning. The promise of such a transformation is tangible, and the potential return on investment is compelling.

It is essential to understand that the path to a customer-focused CLM system begins with a willingness to question long-held contract assumptions. Companies should view each contract as a potential cornerstone of a broader strategy, rather than perceiving it as a cumbersome legal artifact. This approach necessitates breaking down silos, integrating data, and adopting new technologies that can convert fragmented processes into cohesive systems. Such a transformation does not happen overnight but requires deliberate steps and continuous adjustments. Leaders must drive this change, transcending the limitations of traditional practices and setting a vision that positions CLM as integral to legal compliance and overall business success.

One of the most striking features of an updated contract management strategy is its direct impact on risk management. Organizations can anticipate potential issues with modern, automated systems before they escalate into costly problems. By continuously monitoring contract obligations and flagging discrepancies in real-time, companies can minimize regulatory risks and reduce the frequency of compliance breaches. This approach safeguards the organization and allows it to be flexible. With effective risk management, decision-makers can confidently pursue growth opportunities and be secure in knowing that their contractual frameworks will not become a stumbling block.

In parallel, a modern CLM system transforms how companies interact with their customers. Today's market segments demand speed, accuracy, and personalized experiences. A streamlined contract process that connects intelligently with customer relationship management systems can deliver these attributes consistently. A proactive approach to contract management ensures that contractual terms meet customer needs and provides timely notifications for renewals and adjustments, thus powerfully enhancing customer trust and loyalty. Ultimately, every improved contract interaction contributes to an enhanced brand perception that signals reliability, professionalism, and a commitment to excellence.

This book also sets a clear strategic agenda for those ready to confront the status quo. It offers a step-by-step guide to transforming fragmented and reactive CLM into a robust, forward-looking system that delivers value on multiple fronts. Please consider the possibility that every contract in your organization is not merely an obligation but a potential resource that, if managed properly, can open new avenues for revenue and improve operational resilience. With carefully constructed frameworks, actionable checklists, and true-to-life detailed implementation projects, case studies, this book maps out the journey from a state of reactive contract management to one that is integrated, efficient, and strategically aligned with growth objectives.

By engaging with this material, you take the first step toward redefining a crucial aspect of your business operations. This material offers more than just an abstract critique of current practices; Leaders in every industry will find value in the practical strategies and empirical evidence provided. The economic imperatives are clear, the strategic benefits substantial, and the call to action undeniable.

To compete effectively, you cannot afford to ignore the importance of good contract management. The promise of a re-engineered CLM system lies in its ability to convert operational chaos into systematic, measurable performance improvements. With the right blend of technology, integrated workflows, and cultural change, organizations can turn contract management into an advantage that distinguishes them from the competition. Contracts will help us grow and become more reliable by improving our processes and prioritizing customer needs.

This book presents a balanced synthesis of rigorous analysis and field-tested practices. This book challenges conventional wisdom, urging readers to question why contract processes have remained so resistant to change and what it will take to reorient them toward a more proactive, customer-focused future. As you progress through these pages, you will encounter compelling arguments supported by data, illustrative success stories, and clear, actionable guidelines for transforming your contract management processes. Every chapter builds on the last, weaving the varied elements of finance, operations, risk management, and customer engagement into a unified vision of contract-driven growth.

The actual value of effective contract management ultimately lies not just in avoiding losses and ensuring compliance, but in leveraging a decisive strategic advantage that benefits the entire organization. The insights offered here challenge perspectives, inspire change, and provide a pragmatic roadmap for turning what was once a routine administrative task into a cornerstone of business innovation – rethinking, rethinking, rethinking, and re-engineering contract management positions you to secure current operations and capture emerging opportunities in a competitive, ever-changing market.

The journey ahead may be complex, but the rewards are clear—a robust contract management system is vital in today's fast-paced, data-driven business environment. You can transform an essential process into a dynamic advantage with a thoughtful approach that integrates modern technologies and strategic imperatives. This book sets the stage for that transformation, inviting you to shift your perspective and harness the true potential hidden within your contracts.

CHAPTER 1:

INTRODUCTION TO CUSTOMER-CENTRIC CLM

Contracts underpin every facet of modern business, yet too many organizations persist with disjointed, outdated management practices that waste resources and hinder growth and innovation. When contract processes lack cohesion and strategic insight, companies expose themselves to revenue loss, operational risk, and missed opportunities that directly impact their competitive standing. This discussion centers on the widespread shortcomings in contract management systems. It makes the case for reimagining contract lifecycle management with a customer-oriented philosophy—a move that promises to turn an administrative necessity into a core driver of business expansion.

The challenge is familiar to those who command complex operations: a sprawling archive of outdated agreements, labor-intensive manual processes, and a pervasive sense that contractual oversight is more a burdensome formality than a source of strategic value. In many organizations, contract management remains reactive and fragmented, a state that undermines confidence among senior decision-makers and leaves reservoirs of opportunity untapped. Despite increasing pressures from executive leadership to achieve operational clarity, the continued reliance on archaic practices results in an incessant cycle of missed renewals, unfavorable vendor terms, and significant revenue leakage.

Quantitative data support what many leaders already suspect. Studies indicate that organizations with inefficient contract processes risk substantial financial drain, figures reaching millions of dollars annually relative to their operational scale. For instance, even mid-sized enterprises with relatively moderate staffing levels can see annual resource losses that, when calculated on a per-employee basis, amount to tens of thousands of dollars squandered. Beyond direct revenue losses, there exists a secondary cost in the form of eroded customer trust and diminished market reputation, consequences that prove even more damaging over time. This numerical reality accentuates the urgency of transitioning from fragmented, risk-prone contract management to a system designed to support and accelerate business performance.

As markets evolve and customer expectations grow ever more sophisticated, companies can no longer afford to treat their contracts as static legal documents. Instead, contracts must be reconceived as dynamic instruments capable of adapting to the demands of modern commerce. A renewed approach recognizes contracts as living embodiments of business relationships, each serving as a platform for long-term customer engagement. When contract management transcends its traditional administrative role, organizations gain the ability to manage risk more effectively and capture value hidden within the agreed terms.

This discussion is driven by a recognition that the current state of many contract management systems represents a strategic vulnerability. This blind spot compromises agility in times of rapid change. The events of recent years have underscored the pitfalls of an inflexible contract infrastructure. Global disruptions, unexpected market down-turns, and supply chain interruptions further expose the insidious costs of inadequate contract oversight. Documented incidents reveal that organizations struggle with fulfilling contractual obligations during periods of stress, leading to delayed project launches, suboptimal pricing arrangements, and an overall disjointed customer experience. These shortcomings are a stark reminder that a reactive stance toward contract management is no longer viable for companies determined to secure a leading edge.

The call for change is not merely an administrative update but a strategic pivot - a reorientation that integrates customer needs directly into the heart of contract processes. Viewing contracts solely as legal instruments robs them of their potential to drive relationship-building and operational agility. A reconfigured approach prioritizes active customer engagement, emphasizes solution-focused contract design, and promotes a framework of accountability that aligns with business growth objectives. Such transformation requires a fundamental shift in how companies view their contracts: not as burdens that must be managed, but as opportunities to reinforce trust, create enduring partnerships, and generate measurable value for the organization and its stakeholders.

This shift in perspective begins with understanding that the existing model is not working. Consider the multifaceted risks of relying on fragmented contract management systems. Resource misallocations due to inefficient manual reviews, misinterpretation of contract terms, and lost opportunities hidden among volumes of paperwork are commonplace. The cumulative effect of these factors does more than just reduce efficiency—it directly curtails a company's ability to capitalize on market trends and position itself as a proactive, agile player in a competitive landscape.

One of the most tangible metrics demonstrating the cost of current practices is the significant revenue loss resulting from poor contract oversight. Revenue leakage may arise in various forms: agreements with unfavorable pricing that fail to adapt to market changes, overpaying for goods or services due to rigid contract terms, or missing renewal opportunities where renegotiation could yield enhanced benefits. These issues are compounded by a lack of visibility into contract performance and an absence of robust tracking mechanisms that could otherwise alert organizations to upcoming milestones or renegotiation windows. Such visibility, when well executed, reduces risks and paves the way for new revenue streams.

Furthermore, the operational inefficiencies intrinsic to the traditional contract management paradigm often lead to significant backlogs, placing an undue burden on teams already stretched thin. The crisis of contract overload—wherein the sheer volume of necessary contract reviews and approvals overwhelms available resources—creates a self-reinforcing loop: delays in processing hamper decision-making, which delays valuable customer interactions and stalls business initiatives. A streamlined, consolidated approach integrating technological support and redefining process ownership can break this cycle, allowing companies to direct resources toward more strategic, value-generating activities.

Examining the interplay between contracts and customer experience reveals an additional opportunity. Contracts have long been viewed as a necessary evil, a function that must be endured for the sake of regulatory compliance or legal protection. However, the relationship suffers when customers perceive contract interactions as overly burdensome or unresponsive to their needs. An organization that proactively incorporates customer feedback into contract design and ensures contract terms evolve with changing client requirements will be rewarded with improved satisfaction, deeper loyalty, and a stronger competitive position. When paired with robust internal processes to manage contractual risk, this customer-focused approach creates an environment where business and customer success reinforce one another.

Enhancing the oversight of contractual agreements also plays a crucial role in risk management. Poorly structured contracts can conceal significant liabilities and expose an organization to penalties or operational surprises, derailing long-term strategy. When contracts are drafted with a mindset that anticipates change, accommodates evolving customer relationships, and embeds clear governance mechanisms, the organization is better insulated against regulatory fines, litigation risks, and compliance failures. This protective function does not operate in isolation—risk management, when integrated with a customer-conscious approach, contributes directly to the sustainable competitiveness of the business.

The benefits of reinventing contract management extend far into operational realms. Resource allocation improves when teams move from labor-intensive, manual processes toward a system that capitalizes on automation and intelligent data analysis. By instituting rigorous and responsive workflows, companies can reduce cycle times and accelerate the moment when contracts begin generating value. This acceleration is beneficial from an operational standpoint and underpins a strategic advantage that echoes through the entire organization. Faster contract turnaround times mean quicker reactions to market opportunities, shaping a company's trajectory and leading to stronger financial performance.

Central to this reimagined contract management system is the role of technology. Modern platforms with the latest advancements in artificial intelligence and machine learning offer capabilities that far exceed traditional systems. These technologies provide granular insights into contract performance, automatically flag potential discrepancies, and suggest improvements based on historical data. Yet, the promise of technology is best realized when it works in concert with a clear, strategically oriented vision—one that places customer needs and business outcomes at the fore. When precision data analytics meets an unwavering commitment to customer service, contract management transforms from a legacy function into a central pillar of business strategy.

This strategic evolution does not come without challenges. Adopting a customer-oriented model requires new processes and technologies and a shift in organizational culture. Senior leaders must move beyond the constraints of linear thinking and embrace a more dynamic perspective that sees contracts as inherently linked to every facet of business performance. Such a transformation demands honest introspection about legacy practices and a willingness to disrupt entrenched approaches in favor of a model that prioritizes future growth.

The path forward involves a comprehensive reexamination of contract management processes. Decision-makers must systematically identify the limitations of existing systems, pinpoint the areas where inefficiencies have taken root, and redesign workflows to highlight operational efficiency and customer value. Expanding the discussion beyond mere compliance or administrative control, the focus shifts to how contracts can catalyze enhanced business relationships and measurable performance improvements. This holistic framework is designed to support various initiatives—from reducing administrative burdens and streamlining renewals to unlocking hidden revenue potential and managing risk with greater foresight.

Persistent inefficiencies in contract management also translate into a competitive disadvantage. In an era where the pace of business demands agility and responsiveness, companies that cling to outdated practices place themselves at a tangible disadvantage relative to peers who have adopted more integrated, customer-focused strategies. The failure to innovate how contracts are managed impacts the bottom line and shifts market perceptions, ultimately diminishing the organization's stature and credibility. Leaders who recognize this reality are compelled to act decisively, investing in transforming contract processes to secure a competitive edge that goes far beyond cost reduction.

The renewed contract management model under discussion is more than a reconfiguration of procedures; it reinvents a core business function. Its success hinges on integrating cross-functional teams, adopting advanced technologies, and, most critically, an unwavering commitment to placing customer interests at the center. When implemented effectively, the transformation yields benefits that ripple through every enterprise area, from improved governance and reduced risk to enhanced partner relationships and an overall uplift in performance. This approach is not merely theoretical. Organizations that have successfully reengineered their contract management systems report dramatic improvements: near-elimination of processing backlogs, more agile responsiveness to market changes, and a marked increase in customer satisfaction scores.

Disruptions in contract management are symptomatic of broader organizational challenges, yet they also present a unique opportunity for radical improvement. By confronting the realities of inefficient processes, leadership can unlock many benefits that trickle down through every layer of the business. Streamlined workflows and improved oversight help reclaim lost revenue and fortify the company's reputation. Such meaningful changes transform contracts from stagnant documents into living frameworks that drive strategic decision-making and sustained growth.

What emerges from this analysis is a clear call for change—a mandate for companies to reexamine, reorganize, and reinvigorate their approach to managing contracts. The need for a profound transformation is undeniable, and the benefits of doing so touch every aspect of the enterprise. Clear operational improvements, enhanced risk mitigation, and the ability to align contract terms directly with customer expectations ultimately lead to improved market performance.

This discussion offers a detailed exploration of how organizations can transition from disjointed, reactive contract practices to systems that mitigate risk, protect the enterprise, and generate significant competitive advantage. The following discussion will present a step-by-step guide to realizing this vision, outlining the key components necessary to transform contract management into a dynamic instrument supporting growth, operational excellence, and superior customer service.

Emphasizing real-world case studies, practical frameworks, and actionable insights throughout, the analysis provides a robust roadmap for transforming a critical yet often overlooked function into a strategic asset. Through rigorous data analysis, illustrative examples, and a clear-eyed look at both the challenges and opportunities, the discussion seeks to empower decision-makers to take decisive action.

The considerations shared here are not based solely on theoretical constructs; they represent tangible outcomes observed in organizations that have rethought their approach to managing contracts. These enterprises have reported substantial improvements, such as achieving near-perfect accuracy in contract processing, slashing contract backlogs by overwhelming percentages, and reporting dramatic gains in stakeholder satisfaction. Such success stories offer a glimpse of what is possible when traditional paradigms are discarded in favor of an integrated, customer-aligned strategy.

Ultimately, the objective is to provoke a reassessment of what contracts mean to an organization. Moving away from a perception of contracts as isolated legal documents and toward an understanding of them as engines that drive business performance stands as a strategic imperative. A renewed model of contract management encapsulates core business objectives while simultaneously mitigating risk—an approach that serves dual purposes by enhancing efficiency and propelling growth.

In facing the challenges of today's competitive business environment, organizations that reengineer their contract processes are better equipped to navigate uncertainty, capture emerging opportunities, and cultivate robust, long-lasting customer relationships. This comprehensive rethinking of contract management represents not only an operational upgrade but also a strategic commitment to sustainable excellence.

The discussion ahead outlines clear steps and frameworks designed for leaders seeking to transform their contract management practices. Focusing on practical methodologies and measurable outcomes, the examination presents an integrated approach that bridges the traditional divide between legal administration and business strategy. By refining internal processes and embracing new technologies, companies can reorient their contract management functions to deliver real value, enhance customer experience, and secure their position in increasingly competitive markets.

This reimagined concept of contract lifecycle management challenges conventional wisdom. It invites leaders to critically assess internal practices and reconfigure systems in ways that align with broader business objectives - a task that, while demanding, promises a substantial return on investment. The transformation described throughout these pages highlights the tangible benefits of a contract management system that is as dynamic as it is efficient, as customer-centric as it is risk-averse, and as strategically integrated as it is operationally sound.

When organizations commit to this transformative approach, they reduce the direct costs associated with inefficient contract management and create a foundation for sustainable improvement that radiates through every facet of the enterprise. The ability to detect, monitor, and act on key contractual metrics in real time creates a reliable basis for decision-making, ensuring that the organization remains agile and well-prepared for future challenges.

In closing, rethinking the traditional contract management model is more than a corrective measure, it is a strategic imperative that can redefine an entire organization's approach to business. By treating contracts as dynamic, customer-focused instruments rather than static documents, companies can protect themselves against operational pitfalls and position themselves for robust, long-term growth. This conversation aims to equip executive leaders with the perspectives, practices, and tools necessary to make this shift a reality, transforming a chronic weakness into a strategic asset that drives performance and builds a lasting competitive advantage.

⁜

- THE BROKEN STATE OF CLM AND ITS IMPACT ON GROWTH -

Contract management in many organizations has become a burden rather than a benefit—a critical weakness that undermines profitability, stifles innovation, and places companies at a distinct disadvantage against more agile competitors. When separated into isolated functions with little clarity on end-to-end accountability, the process of handling contracts creates confusion, inefficiency, and missed opportunities. This section examines the pervasive state of current contract management practices, explores this broken system's financial and operational impacts, and clarifies why addressing these shortcomings is a strategic urgency.

Organizations across industries rely on contracts to secure everything from vendor relationships and supplier agreements to partnerships and revenue-generating deals. Despite the importance of these documents, many companies continue to manage contracts with procedures that are archaic or poorly integrated into broader strategic operations. The fragmented nature of these systems creates significant gaps in visibility, leading decision-makers to underestimate potential risks and overlook opportunities for improvement. The results are striking - lost revenue, operational injuries, and a growing disconnect between business objectives and contract administration.

Consider the dynamics of resource allocation in companies that have yet to modernize their contract practices. Time and energy are consumed by efforts to locate critical documents, verify compliance, and ensure timely renewals. Instead of being invested in strategic projects that drive growth, staff members are burdened with manual reviews, unpredictable delays, and endless administrative follow-ups. The cost of this inefficiency is not simply measured in labor hours; it translates into a systemic drain on financial resources. When organizations see figures in the millions related to lost revenue or the cost of compliance failures, it becomes clear that the impact of outdated contract management is far-reaching.

The financial metrics alone are sobering. My experience has quantified the hidden expenses tied to poor contract management—losses that are directly tied to inefficient process execution and misaligned priorities. Many client companies sometimes lose an estimated $1.7 million annually per 100 employees because of the time wasted on manual contract processing and related inefficiencies. Beyond these direct costs lie more subtle forms of revenue leakage: opportunities where renegotiated terms could have realized better margins, or instances where non-compliance results in penalties that tarnish both the balance sheet and the company's reputation. This economic bite reaches into every corner of an organization, reinforcing the need for a more thoughtful, comprehensive approach.

The operational challenges compound these financial considerations. Inefficient contract processes often result in backlogs that strain administrative teams and delay decision-making. When contract approval processes become bottlenecks, they slow down the pace at which companies can react to market demands. In today's highly competitive climate, speed matters. Organizations that are mired in manual, disjointed procedures find it increasingly difficult to seize timely opportunities or adjust quickly to changes in customer expectations. This latency not only impacts revenue but also affects the overall customer experience, an aspect that modern businesses cannot afford to ignore.

A further complication arises from a lack of clear communication and systematic oversight in handling contractual obligations. When contracts are spread across disparate systems or managed by different departments with limited interaction, the result is a failure to track essential milestones, such as renewal dates or performance benchmarks. This dispersed structure is especially damaging when precise timing is critical, for example, when a delay in contract renewal translates directly into lost revenue opportunities. Without a cohesive system that provides timely alerts and a clear overview of contract performance, companies risk both short- and long-term setbacks in their operational efficiency.

The broken state of contract management extends deeply into customer relationships, a critical area for any organization aiming to maintain a competitive edge. Customers view contract terms as signals of an organization's reliability and commitment. When contract processes are cumbersome or prone to error, they undermine customer confidence. Managing contract interactions poorly in today's market, where consumers expect speed, clarity, and responsiveness, can leave lasting negative impressions that reduce loyalty and limit market competitiveness. Companies that continue to treat contract management as a mere administrative necessity do so at the expense of cultivating robust, enduring business relationships.

While some improvement initiatives are often attempted, many efforts fail because they address only the symptoms, not the underlying cause. Incremental adjustments—such as digitizing some processes or implementing partial automation—are steps in the right direction. However, these measures rarely achieve the transformative impact required to realign contracts as strategic business assets.

What is needed is a comprehensive reassessment of how contracts are conceived, executed, and utilized within the overall business model. This broad-based rethinking should challenge the traditional view of contracts as static documents and instead recognize them as dynamic instruments that can drive revenue, guide strategic decisions, and empower front-line teams.

In concrete terms, the issues arising from a broken contract management system can be traced back to several core challenges. The first of these is the sheer volume of contracts that organizations handle daily. When contract sprawl occurs without a unifying management approach, relying on memory or isolated recordkeeping to monitor compliance, manage risks, or seize renegotiation opportunities becomes dangerous. This leads to scenarios in which key contractual obligations are missed or overlooked entirely. In environments where every detail counts, such oversights create vulnerabilities that are difficult to repair once they manifest into larger operational problems.

Another challenge is the inherent risk of fragmentation. Contract management systems lack integration, and data becomes siloed in various business units. Each silo operates under its procedures and with varying levels of technological support, meaning that the organization as a whole struggles to maintain a unified perspective on contractual obligations. This fragmentation not only leads to duplicated efforts and wasted resources but also complicates the process of making data-driven strategic decisions. When management lacks clear, centralized oversight of contract performance, they are forced to make decisions with incomplete information - a predicament that can prove costly in fast-moving market conditions.

In addition to organizational and process challenges, a cultural element perpetuates the broken state of contract management. For many companies, contracts have long been relegated to the legal department and treated primarily as risk management tools. This narrow perspective limits the potential of contracts to serve as drivers of business growth—if the focus remains solely on avoiding pitfalls, opportunities for creating value are overlooked. A cultural reframe is required to move beyond this defensively oriented mindset and to begin viewing contracts as key components of a strategic framework that can enhance customer engagement and streamline operations.

Addressing this cultural challenge demands a deliberate shift in perspective among leadership. Executives must recognize that outdated contract management practices do not simply represent a minor administrative nuisance; they are symptomatic of larger systemic issues that can compromise the entire organization. The impact is multi-dimensional: Financial setbacks are compounded by operational inefficiencies, and the erosion of customer trust magnifies both. The investment required to redesign these systems is justified and essential for leaders who see the potential for contractual improvements to contribute directly to business growth.

This reinvention involves embracing new processes and technologies that can restore clarity, efficiency, and strategic focus to contract management. Modern technological solutions offer promise by automating repetitive tasks, streamlining workflows, and providing real-time data that informs decision-making. However, technology alone is insufficient. The success of any technological upgrade depends largely on organizational willingness to integrate these tools within a broader strategic vision—one that aligns with overall business objectives and prioritizes customer satisfaction as much as risk mitigation. An integrated approach that combines technology with a renewed focus on relationship-building can transform the current challenges into competitive advantages.

A practical illustration of this challenge can be seen in the case of companies that have struggled with contract overload. In these organizations, manual processes and disparate systems lead to significant delays in processing, often resulting in missed deadlines and surrendering of negotiation leverage when time is of the essence. The impact of these delays isn't isolated to administrative strain; they ripple outward into customer interactions, where speed and precision in contract handling become a direct factor in maintaining trust and securing repeat business. Conversely, companies that have implemented structured, process-driven systems report improvements in efficiency and significant gains in customer satisfaction and revenue realization.

Defining the objective behind these initiatives is critical. The overarching goal is to reframe contract management as a strategic resource tool that, when properly configured, can streamline operations, mitigate risk, and directly support the bottom line. This requires shifting from a reactive, fragmented approach to one that is proactive and integrated. The need is clear: organizations can no longer afford to view contract management as a peripheral function. Instead, it must be recognized as central to business strategy and operational success.

Central to this renewed focus is a commitment to transparency and accountability. By establishing clear performance measures and systematic controls across the entire contract lifecycle, businesses can eliminate discrepancies and reduce the risk of non-compliance. These measures also provide valuable insights to guide future negotiations and contract adjustments. When performance metrics are clearly aligned with strategic objectives, organizations consistently uncover areas where further improvements can drive incremental income gains and bolster overall operational health.

Furthermore, an effective contract management strategy also requires continuous improvement. Processes must evolve in response to changes in market dynamics, customer expectations, and internal operational shifts. Rather than being static, a dynamic approach to managing contracts presents an ongoing challenge to refine procedures, integrate new technological capabilities, and respond to an evolving business environment. This perspective demands that organizations establish a baseline of effective practices and mechanisms for ongoing review and adjustment. This dynamic feedback loop ensures the contract management system remains aligned with strategic goals over time.

This comprehensive rethinking of contractual processes forms the backbone of the approach advocated throughout this book. It is both a call to action and a framework for tangible change. The insights shared here are not abstract musings - they are rooted in observable shortcomings and informed by concrete data that outlines the real costs of maintaining the status quo. The transformation described is not an optional upgrade; it is a necessary response to challenges affecting every enterprise layer.

The analysis of current contract practices and the resulting direct and indirect costs articulates a clear rationale for change. Organizations that continue to operate with outdated, inefficient systems risk short-term financial losses and a long-term decline in competitive positioning. The broken state of contract management does more than create operational drag; it undermines confidence among stakeholders, limits the ability to innovate, and restricts the flexibility needed to adapt in an increasingly fast-paced business environment.

In practical terms, addressing these issues begins with a thorough review of existing processes, identifying the specific points where inefficiencies occur, and setting measurable targets for improvement. Leaders can prioritize interventions that provide the greatest return on investment by breaking down these systems into manageable components, ranging from document management and workflow automation to contract performance monitoring and renewal management. This methodical approach ensures that transformation is comprehensive and tailored to the organization's unique challenges and opportunities.

Ultimately, rethinking contract management aims to convert a chronic problem into an operational strength. The transformation is measured not solely in cost savings but also in enhanced customer trust, improved operational agility, and a robust framework that can adapt to the uncertainties of a shifting market landscape. It positions contracts as active participants in revenue generation, operational stability, and strategic growth—indispensable elements in today's competitive business arena.

The clear message emerging from this discussion is that

contract management must be repositioned from a burdensome compliance necessity to a purposeful strategy that supports overarching business goals. With a renewed focus on transparency, efficiency, and customer engagement, companies can transform their contractual processes into a meaningful asset. This transformation requires commitment, clarity, and a willingness to challenge long-held assumptions about the role of contracts in business operations.

For organizations prepared to take this path, the rewards are substantial. Improved process efficiency translates directly into cost savings and operational agility; a customer-focused contract approach builds stronger, more resilient relationships; and a data-driven strategy provides the insights needed to refine and enhance performance continuously. In addressing these core issues, companies mitigate existing risks and unlock potential for new opportunities that drive future growth.

As the narrative unfolds, the focus will continue to center on how organizations can methodically recalibrate their approach to contract management. The goal is clear: Transform contracts from static obligations into vital mechanisms that accelerate business performance, ensuring that every agreement contributes meaningfully to immediate fiscal results and long-term strategic objectives.

This systematic transformation calls for a strategic, integrated approach in which every facet of contract management is scrutinized, refined, and aligned with the company's broader goals. By methodically addressing the broken elements within the current system, leaders can begin to rebuild a functional infrastructure that cuts costs and creates a fertile environment for sustained innovation and growth. Such a recalibrated model is vital to overall organizational resilience, equipping companies with the agility and precision needed to navigate complex and unpredictable markets.

In summary, a broken contract management system is not an isolated issue confined to administrative logistics. It touches upon financial performance, operational efficiency, customer satisfaction, and strategic competitiveness. The evidence is substantial, and the directive is clear: Companies must examine, reassess, and reengineer their approach to managing contracts to thrive in today's competitive business environment. Through a comprehensive understanding of the current deficiencies and a robust transformation plan, organizations can secure a future where contracts serve not as burdens but as dynamic instruments of growth and opportunity.

::::

- INTRODUCTION TO CUSTOMER-CENTRIC CLM PHILOSOPHY -

The intricate challenges within contract management extend far beyond the visible inefficiencies of outdated systems. A closer examination reveals a complex interplay between operational weaknesses, financial losses, and a stagnation of strategic potential that hampers rather than supports growth. Throughout many organizations, contract chaos has become an accepted cost of doing business, even as it undermines long-term objectives and weakens the overall competitive position. When contracts are managed reactively and in silos, the organization not only loses out on potential revenue but also risks damaging valuable relationships both internally and with external partners.

A significant contributor to this pervasive state is the absence of centralized oversight and unified processes. When different departments adopt disparate systems, a cohesive picture of contractual obligations is lost. This fragmented environment creates blind spots that allow key milestones and renewal dates to slip through the cracks. The lack of comprehensive oversight means that business leaders often must work with incomplete data, making it difficult to predict future risks or capitalize on upcoming opportunities. The resulting uncertainty stifles informed decision-making and restricts the organization's ability to respond swiftly to evolving market dynamics.

In addition to centralization issues, the manual nature of many contract management processes contributes heavily to inefficiency. A reliance on physical files, spreadsheets, or outdated software increases the likelihood of human error while also slowing down execution. The absence of automated workflows forces teams to spend countless hours on routine administrative tasks, diverting critical resources away from strategic initiatives. These repetitive processes drain valuable time and create opportunities for mistakes that can have far-reaching consequences. From misinterpreting contract terms to missing critical deadlines, the fallout from such errors can directly impact revenue and customer satisfaction.

Financial repercussions resulting from inefficient contract management are quantifiable and alarming. Firms that invest in manual processes incur hidden costs that affect both short-term performance and long-term strategic capability. Every delayed renewal or missed renegotiation represents lost income and a potential breach in trust with customers and suppliers. When pricing models fail to adjust to market fluctuations because of rigid contract terms, the organization risks leaving substantial value on the table—value that could otherwise bolster profitability. Additionally, compliance failures often lead to regulatory penalties or legal disputes that further strain financial resources. The cost of maintaining antiquated systems becomes unsustainable when every minute is calculated in lost opportunity.

Beyond the cold statistics, there is an equally significant impact on customer relationships. In many cases, the experience of interacting with a company is marred by clunky, slow, or inconsistent contract processes. When customers encounter delays or errors in contract management, it plants seeds of doubt regarding the company's overall competence and reliability. This erosion of trust can have cascading effects that extend well beyond a single transaction, influencing future business and long-term loyalty. Companies that ignore these signals risk being perceived as indifferent to client needs, ultimately compromising their brand reputation and market standing.

Furthermore, inefficiencies in contract management contribute to a culture of risk aversion within organizations. When every contract is handled reactively, there is little room for proactive innovation or strategic experimentation. Decision-makers become so entangled in resolving immediate operational challenges that they struggle to set aside time for forward-thinking initiatives. This short-sighted focus curtails creativity and limits opportunities for improvement. Instead of refining and optimizing the business model, organizations remain mired in the daily struggle to manage chaos—a predicament that is a barrier to sustainable growth.

The interplay between risk and inefficiency in contract management also creates a breeding ground for compliance issues. As contracts continue to pile up without proper oversight, the risk of regulatory non-compliance escalates. Many organizations underestimate the impact of failing to adhere to contractual obligations until penalties and fines emerge as tangible consequences. Apart from the immediate financial burden, non-compliance can lead to a loss of credibility in the eyes of regulators, investors, and customers alike. For organizations striving to build a reputation as reliable market players, such missteps can have long-lasting repercussions that extend well beyond the immediate fiscal quarter.

Another critical factor in the persistence of contract chaos is the reluctance to invest in comprehensive process re-engineering. Even when leaders acknowledge the deficiencies in current systems, many feel overwhelmed by the scale of the challenge, or the costs associated with a complete overhaul. As a result, piecemeal improvements, though beneficial, often fail to address the root causes of inefficiency. Without a willingness to question entrenched practices, organizations remain trapped in a cycle of short-term fixes that postpone meaningful change. This incremental approach may provide temporary relief, but ultimately allows deep-seated issues to endure, continuously undermining performance and growth potential.

It is essential to recognize that contract management challenges are not isolated to large enterprises alone. Mid-sized companies, in particular, find themselves caught in a precarious balance between managing growth and coping with legacy processes. For these organizations, the consequences of inefficient contract management are magnified, as limited resources and tighter margins leave little room for error. In such settings, every misstep translates into a more pronounced financial impact and a greater risk of operational paralysis. Therefore, the ability to transform contract management into a strategic advantage becomes a competitive differentiator and a critical factor in survival.

When taken together, the cumulative effect of these operational and financial shortcomings creates an environment where strategic potential is stifled. Business leaders are forced to operate within a reactive rather than predictive framework. Instead of using contracts for future planning and growth, they are burdened by the immediate need to manage disjointed and error-prone processes. This reactive stance leaves little capacity for innovation or strategic recalibration, elements that are essential in today's rapidly evolving business landscape. The net result is an organization perpetually one step behind, unable to fully harness the advantages that efficient, integrated contract management could provide.

Considering these challenges, it becomes evident that transforming contract management is not merely an operational improvement but a strategic necessity. By reimagining the contract management function as a cohesive, integrated process, companies can begin to convert a chronic problem into a competitive strength. This transformation requires a fundamental shift in mindset, moving away from the perception of contracts as static legal documents and embracing them as dynamic, revenue-generating assets. Organizations can unlock hidden value, streamline operations, and build stronger, trust-based relationships with customers and partners.

A strategic overhaul begins with a comprehensive audit of existing processes. By mapping out each step of the contract management lifecycle, leaders can identify the exact points where inefficiencies, delays, or errors occur. This detailed analysis serves as a baseline from which targeted improvements can be made. Through this systematic assessment, organizations can begin to understand the true scope of their challenges and prioritize investments that will yield the highest returns. Rather than addressing issues in isolation, a holistic approach ensures that all interconnected elements are refined to work together, thereby reducing the overall risk and maximizing operational efficiency.

Advanced technological tools play a pivotal role in this transformative journey. Modern contract management platforms offer functionalities that automate and streamline many labor-intensive tasks traditionally associated with this function. From automated alerts for renewal dates and compliance requirements to real-time tracking of contractual performance, these systems provide the transparency and accountability vital for effective management. However, technology should be seen as an enabler rather than a cure-all. Its successful implementation depends on a broader strategic framework that redefines how contracts are perceived and utilized within the organization. Combined with a clear strategic vision, automation and data analytics can fundamentally change how contracts contribute to business performance.

Another layer of complexity arises from the need to integrate contract management with broader business systems. In many organizations, contracts exist in a vacuum, disconnected from other critical functions such as finance, procurement, and customer relationship management. This siloed existence creates barriers to seamless data flow and collaboration across different units. Organizations can achieve a unified perspective on contractual data by integrating contract management systems with enterprise resource planning (ERP) software, customer relationship management (CRM) tools, and other relevant platforms. This integration enhances operational efficiency and equips business leaders with comprehensive insights for informed decision-making.

The benefits of addressing these foundational issues extend beyond immediate improvement in contract processing speeds. When contract management becomes a strategic function, it has the potential to enhance the overall customer experience significantly. Accurate, timely, and responsive contract management sends customers a strong message about the organization's commitment to excellence. It reassures them that the company can manage risks and is proactive in ensuring that contracts are a basis for effective and mutually beneficial relationships. This improved customer perception can lead to higher satisfaction levels, increased loyalty, and enhanced financial performance.

Practically, the path toward operational transformation

involves setting clear performance metrics and regularly reviewing outcomes against these benchmarks. Organizations can continuously monitor their progress by establishing key performance indicators (KPIs) reflecting process efficiency and strategic value. These metrics might include the average time taken to finalize a contract, the rate of contract renewals, the frequency of compliance breaches, and customer satisfaction levels. Regular tracking of such metrics helps create a culture of accountability and continuous improvement, ensuring that the contract management function evolves in line with business needs and market realities.

The shift toward a more integrated, transparent, and customer-oriented approach to contract management requires unwavering commitment from leadership. Change cannot be imposed solely through technological upgrades; it must be driven by a clear strategic vision that aligns with overall business objectives. Leaders must champion the idea of reconfiguring contracts into strategic assets and encourage all stakeholders to adopt new methodologies. Such a cultural shift, while challenging to implement, is essential for ensuring that the benefits of improved contract management permeate throughout the organization, from boardroom strategy discussions to day-to-day operational practices.

As the organization progresses from diagnosing the problem to implementing solutions, it becomes critical to stress the importance of communication and collaboration across all enterprise levels. Breaking down silos and establishing cross-functional teams dedicated to contract optimization can accelerate the pace of transformation. These teams provide the expertise needed to design and implement new processes and act as internal advocates for change, ensuring that improvements are consistently applied and refined over time.

The cumulative impact of these measures goes beyond immediate operational gains. Organizations can unlock previously hidden sources of value by turning contract chaos into a well-structured, dynamic process. Stream-lined operations translate into faster processing times, reduced error rates, and more agile responses to market changes. Over time, these improvements create a virtuous cycle: the enhanced efficiency of contract management provides the resources and insights necessary to pursue new business opportunities and expand market share.

Ultimately, the transformation of contract management from a reactive administrative task to a proactive strate-gic function represents a pivotal shift. It demands not only the adoption of advanced technologies but also a rethink-ing of long-held assumptions about the role of contracts in the modern enterprise. The potential benefits include far-reaching improvements across financial performance, operational efficiency, risk management, and customer satisfaction. The resulting strategic advantage can be transformative for organizations willing to tackle the chal-lenges head-on.

In essence, the journey toward an integrated and dynamic contract management system is not simply about patch-ing up broken processes. It is about reimagining the very framework through which agreements are conceived, exe-cuted, and reviewed—a framework where contracts serve as living instruments of business strategy rather than stat-ic documents stuck in a cycle of routine compliance. With a renewed focus on transparency, proactive oversight, and cross-functional integration, companies can reposition themselves to take full advantage of the opportunities that lie within their contractual relationships.

Considering the scope of these challenges and opportunities, it is clear that the path forward requires a bold reconfiguration of current practices. *Organizations must be prepared to invest the necessary time, resources, and leadership attention to dismantle outdated systems and construct a new model that is agile enough to meet the complexities of modern business and robust enough to protect against future risks.* The rewards of such a transformation extend beyond simple cost reduction; they include a renewed capacity for strategic decision-making, improved customer engagement, and the creation of a sustainable competitive advantage that forms the backbone of long-term growth.

In conclusion, the deeper exploration of the costs and risks associated with contract chaos reveals an urgent need for transformation. The interconnected challenges stemming from fragmented oversight, manual inefficiencies, and siloed data flow combine to create an operational environment that is both unsustainable and strategically limiting. By addressing these issues through a comprehensive, integrated approach, organizations can move from a state of reactive management to one where contract processes actively contribute to business success. This reconfiguration minimizes financial and operational risks and opens the door to opportunities for strategic innovation and improved customer relationships, ultimately positioning the organization for continued success in an increasingly competitive marketplace.

⁂

- WHY THIS BOOK MATTERS: A STRATEGIC OVERVIEW -

The challenges and opportunities presented by contract management are best understood when seen as part of a broader narrative that connects operational efficiency, strategic foresight, and customer engagement. A careful reflection reveals that at the heart of this discussion lies a common truth: contracts, when appropriately managed, have the potential to be a powerful driver of business performance. Every misstep in the process, every overlooked deadline, and every disjointed system serve as a reminder of the vast gap that exists between the current state of contract management and its latent capability as a strategic asset.

It has become clear that fragmented systems and manual processes slow down operational performance and sap an organization's ability to make proactive decisions. The earlier sections have outlined how inefficiencies translate into missed opportunities—a delay in a contract renewal can mean lost revenue, and a missed performance metric can disrupt customer trust. When these factors come together, they create an environment where operational risk overshadows potential growth. In many ways, these challenges are symptomatic of a deeper issue: a misalignment between how contracts are managed today and how they should be managed to support a modern, dynamic business.

A key takeaway is that the fragmentation of processes and data results in an incomplete view of contractual obligations. Without a centralized system or integrated oversight, the organization is forced to rely on disparate pieces of information, often leading to reactive management. The absence of a unified framework means that opportunities for synergistic improvements, such as improved pricing models or better vendor negotiations, are lost. Instead, contract management remains at the mercy of isolated actions rather than being part of a cohesive strategy that aligns with overarching business goals.

To address these shortcomings, it is essential to recognize that the true power of contract management lies in its ability to serve as an enabler of strategic operations. An integrated system streamlines processes and provides valuable insights into performance—insights that can drive more informed decision-making. When organizations invest in modern technologies that automate manual tasks, the result is a transformation from ad hoc operations into a clear, predictable process. Automated workflows, real-time data updates, and proactive alerts all contribute to a robust system that reduces errors and enhances visibility. This level of operational clarity is critical when every minute and every decision can impact competitive positioning in fast-paced markets.

Another aspect that emerges from this discussion is the cultural dimension of contract management. Too often, contracts are seen merely as legal documents intended for risk avoidance. This narrow view can prevent organizations from capitalizing on the broader potential of well-managed contractual processes. A shift in perspective is required—one that embraces contracts as integral components of customer and vendor relationships. When contracts are perceived as living documents that evolve with business needs, they can be powerful tools for building trust and enhancing customer satisfaction. In this view, every contractual interaction represents an opportunity to reinforce a commitment to operational excellence and customer service.

Furthermore, the role of leadership in transforming contract management cannot be understated. Senior decision-makers must move beyond the comfort of established routines and champion a new, innovative, and pragmatic approach. The willingness to undergo significant operational changes indicates strategic vision. Leaders who recognize the hidden costs of poor contract management—such as revenue leakage, regulatory non-compliance, and diminished customer trust—also understand that a proactive, technology-enabled approach is essential. They must be prepared to foster an environment where new ideas, reinvigorated processes, and cross-departmental collaboration flourish. The business can only move past the reactive mindset and embrace a future where contracts are seen as strategic enablers rather than burdensome obligations.

As the evidence shows, the path toward a strategic overhaul of contract management is not solely about adopting new technology or fine-tuning existing processes but also about creating a continuous culture of improvement. Dynamic feedback loops, where performance metrics are constantly monitored and reviewed, are indispensable. By setting clear, actionable key performance indicators (KPIs), organizations can track the impact of process improvements and take corrective measures as needed. Metrics such as turnaround times, compliance adherence, renewal rates, and customer satisfaction all serve as critical barometers of success. When these metrics are regularly scrutinized, gaps between target outcomes and actual performance become apparent - and with that awareness comes the opportunity for systematic change.

Considering the broader strategic implications of a recon-figured contract management process is also important. A streamlined, well-integrated system can extend far be-yond cost savings. It lays the foundation for agility and adaptability—indispensable traits in today's fast-changing business environment. When reliable data and clear com-munication channels underpin processes, organizations are better poised to react to market fluctuations, negotiate favorable terms during periods of uncertainty, and seize opportunities that competitors might overlook. This agili-ty is not merely beneficial from an operational standpoint; it translates directly into financial performance and long-term competitiveness.

The transition from a reactive to a proactive contract management system brings opportunities for enhanced risk management. Proactively identifying and monitoring contractual obligations significantly prevent compliance issues and other risks that could derail major business initiatives. As organizations adopt more sophisticated systems that track contract performance in real time, the margin for error is reduced substantially. This risk-averse posture, however, must be balanced with the pursuit of opportunities. In other words, while it is critical to avoid pitfalls, organizations should also design their processes to capture incremental improvements that add up over time. The right balance creates an environment where risk is managed effectively, and at the same time, the door re-mains open to embracing value-generating strategies.

Customer engagement, too, benefits from a transformed

approach to contract management. As organizations deliver more accurate, responsive, and customer-focused contractual processes, the overall brand experience is strengthened. Customers—be they vendors, partners, or end users—begin to see the tangible benefits of a streamlined process. They experience fewer delays, more transparent negotiations, and a greater sense of confidence in the commitments made. Improved customer satisfaction, in turn, bolsters loyalty and can lead to a virtuous cycle of repeat business, referrals, and improved market positioning. In essence, transparent and efficient contract management is a foundation for building lasting, trust-based relationships that contribute directly to the bottom line.

However, one of the more significant obstacles to achieving this transformation is the challenge of overhauling deeply entrenched systems and habits. Resistance to change, while understandable, can create considerable inertia. Employees, accustomed to long-standing procedures, often view new technologies and processes with skepticism. This cultural resistance must be countered with comprehensive training, transparent communication, and a systematic change management strategy. Leaders must articulate a clear vision, linking the benefits of improved contract management to tangible business outcomes. Through consistent reinforcement and demonstration of early successes, they can overcome resistance and foster a receptive climate to change.

When considering the broader implications for competitive advantage, it is evident that the ability to manage contracts with precision is no longer a luxury - it is a strategic necessity. In environments where every contractual detail can influence the bottom line, organizations that maintain outdated processes put themselves at a severe disadvantage. Competitors who have reengineered their contract management systems reap significant benefits: faster cycle times, more effective cost controls, and stronger, more enduring customer relationships. These advantages eventually lead to improved market share and sustainable growth. Organizations that ignore the transformative potential of a modernized contract management approach risk being left behind in competitive markets that reward agility and foresight.

As the focus shifts from problem identification to solution implementation, the benefits of a reengineered contract management process become increasingly tangible. The transformation begins with a clear audit of existing practices, followed by a carefully planned reconfiguration that addresses both technological and operational gaps. With the integration of advanced automation, improved data sharing, and a commitment to cross-functional collaboration, organizations can create a system that is robust, agile, and aligned with strategic objectives. This holistic approach ultimately converts a chronic weakness into a formidable strength.

The comprehensive reimagining of contract management does more than streamline processes - it reshapes the organization's strategic framework. By placing contracts at the center of business decision-making, organizations open up pathways for innovation and growth. Every contract becomes a data point that informs future strategies; every renewal opportunity becomes a chance to negotiate better terms; and every customer interaction through contract management reinforces trust and builds reputation. This strategic realignment ensures that contract management is no longer a secondary concern but a primary driver of business performance.

With this transformation comes a renewed ability to manage operational risk, reduce financial leakage, and improve customer satisfaction concurrently. A modern, agile contract management system is an investment that pays dividends across multiple facets of the business. It supports a continuous improvement cycle where efficiency leads to savings, savings fuel further investment in process enhancement, and process enhancement drives better outcomes. In this cycle, every contract safeguards against risk and is a stepping stone to greater market potential and financial stability.

Ultimately, the comprehensive insights shared in these discussions form a compelling case for rethinking how contracts are managed. What starts as a focus on fixing fragmented processes evolves rapidly into a larger, strategic vision, where the contracts become building blocks for a more agile, responsive, and competitive organization. While the challenges of legacy systems, siloed data, and cultural resistance are considerable, they are far from insurmountable. Organizations can transform contract management from a liability into a significant asset with the right blend of technological innovation, process re-engineering, and leadership commitment.

As the narrative draws to a close, it is worth reiterating the central message: every contract, every clause, and every deadline holds the potential to advance business objectives if managed under a unified, strategic framework. By addressing fragmented oversight with a unified system, eliminating manual inefficiencies through automation, and integrating contract management with broader business processes, companies chart a clear course from operational chaos toward proactive, value-driven excellence. This repositioning mitigates risk and enhances revenue potential, cementing the role of contract management as an integral element of business strategy. This role can propel an organization ahead of its competition.

The path to this transformation is multifaceted, requiring a deep understanding of current shortcomings and a willingness to reconceptualize processes at every level. In doing so, leaders send a clear signal that contracts are not simply administrative burdens but key levers in driving customer relationships, operational efficiency, and sustainable growth. Embracing this perspective marks a decisive step toward turning challenges into opportunities, setting the stage for a future where every contract actively supports the organization's strategic imperatives.

In closing, the discussion reinforces that the issues inherent in contract management are critical for operational performance and long-term strategic viability. Organizations that can transform these challenges into measurable strengths stand to gain a significant competitive advantage. With proactive systems in place, the risks associated with fragmented processes and manual inefficiencies are minimized, freeing up resources that can be reinvested in growth-centric initiatives. The resulting transformation fosters an environment where contracts, far from being a necessary evil, function as dynamic instruments that continuously drive business success.

This comprehensive evaluation of the current landscape and its possibilities leaves us with a clear mandate: to rethink and redesign contract management in an integrated, proactive, and relentlessly focused on both customer success and operational excellence. As the end of this chapter approaches, the key messages remain unmistakable—fragmented, inefficient processes are not merely an administrative challenge; they are fundamental obstacles to achieving a competitive edge. Through strategic reconfiguration and a commitment to ongoing improvement, organizations can convert these obstacles into stepping stones for a brighter, more agile future, ensuring that every contract becomes a catalyst for enduring success.

CHAPTER 2:

UNDERSTANDING THE REAL COST OF CONTRACT CHAOS

The transition from fragmented, inefficient processes to a strategic, customer-centric contract management system reveals the operational challenges many organizations face and the profound financial implications that can undermine overall business performance. As we carry forward the insights from the previous discussion, it becomes clear that the cost of contract chaos extends far beyond the immediate administrative burdens—it infiltrates every facet of an enterprise, affecting revenue, risk, and long-term strategic positioning.

Organizations that cling to outdated contract management practices often pay an invisible price in lost opportunities. As we explore this theme further, it is critical to recognize that the financial strain imposed by disjointed systems is not a matter of isolated incidents but rather a systemic issue that disrupts performance at multiple levels. The cumulative impact can be staggering when inefficient processes lead to overlooked renewal dates, unrecognized contractual obligations, or missed negotiation opportunities. The resulting revenue leakage and heightened operational risk represent challenges that demand a rigorous, data-driven examination.

Drawing on extensive case studies and quantitative research, we see that the effects of contract inefficiencies manifest in several key areas. First, the financial ramifications are immediate and quantifiable. Cost overruns, compliance penalties, and stalled negotiations are the tip of the iceberg. For instance, organizations that rely on manual reviews and disjointed tracking methods often incur hidden costs running into millions of dollars annually—a stark reminder that every inefficiency directly undermines the bottom line. These inefficiencies erode profit margins, strain budgets, and ultimately compromise the organization's ability to invest in growth-oriented initiatives.

Beyond direct financial loss, the operational consequences of contract chaos are equally compelling. When contracts are dispersed across multiple departments without a unified management structure, critical data becomes trapped in silos. This fragmentation hampers the ability to monitor contract performance consistently and undermines the precision needed for effective risk management. When teams cannot rely on accurate, real-time data, every decision - from pricing adjustments to vendor negotiations - is made with less certainty. The knock-on effect is a reduction in the organization's overall agility, which, in today's rapidly evolving market, is a disadvantage that few companies can afford.

The hidden costs of inefficient contract management are unrelated to internal processes. They also significantly impact customer relations. Companies that struggle with contract compliance and timely renewals inadvertently send a message of unreliability to their customers. The resulting erosion of trust can have long-term consequences, affecting repeat business and tarnishing the brand's reputation. In an environment where every customer interaction counts, any lapse in contractual administration may translate into lost loyalty and a diminished competitive edge.

Furthermore, the systemic nature of contract management failures introduces risks that extend well beyond unforeseen financial consequences. Poorly managed contracts often conceal potential liabilities and expose the organization to compliance breaches that attract legal penalties and invite regulatory scrutiny. Such vulnerabilities cannot be underestimated in a marketplace where risk management is increasingly intertwined with corporate reputation. The discipline required to maintain rigorous contract oversight is essential to sustainable business practices, particularly for companies seeking to navigate global markets and complex regulatory environments.

It is also essential to address the broader strategic implications of these challenges. When the focus remains solely on mitigating immediate risks, organizations miss the opportunity to harness the full potential of their contractual relationships. The value embedded within contracts, as instruments of long-term customer engagement and as levers for operational efficiency, is largely ignored in a reactive approach. By contrast, a proactive, integrated system helps minimize the immediate costs of oversight and creates a foundation for strategic growth. When managed thoughtfully, contracts become valuable data sources for identifying market trends, negotiating better vendor terms, and even shaping future business development strategies.

The shift from a reactive posture to a proactive management hinges on adopting comprehensive, technology-enabled solutions. Automation and data analytics, for example, can transform contract management from a repetitive, error-prone process into an insightful and agile system. Advanced platforms can trigger timely alerts, highlight performance discrepancies, and even suggest adjustments based on historical data, contributing to a more predictable revenue stream and a more secure operational environment. By embracing technological innovation, companies can bridge the gap between cumbersome legacy systems and the lean, integrated processes that modern business demands.

Yet, while technology provides the necessary tools, the broader transformation requires a strategic framework that aligns contract management with overall business objectives. This alignment means embedding contractual oversight within the larger fabric of the organization's planning and decision-making processes. Leaders must view contracts not as isolated documents or routine administrative details, but as dynamic assets that reflect and support the company's growth trajectory. In doing so, they ensure that every contractual interaction, from initial drafting to final execution, contributes concretely to narrowing operational inefficiencies and celebrating tangible financial gains.

This discussion is reinforced by observable patterns in companies that have successfully overhauled their contract management frameworks. Organizations making the shift report dramatic improvements in several key areas: a reduction in processing times, enhanced compliance rates, and, most importantly, a marked decrease in instances of revenue leakage. Such examples underscore the fact that the high costs of contract chaos are not an inevitable burden; they are symptoms of a system that can be effectively reengineered to deliver stronger, more sustainable business performance.

Moreover, the cultural aspect of this transformation cannot be overlooked. Reevaluating contract management practices requires a change in organizational mindset. Internal stakeholders, from legal teams to finance and procurement departments, must work in tandem to support a paradigm that prioritizes strategic foresight and operational clarity over short-term fixes. The establishment of cross-functional teams dedicated to enhancing contract oversight and performance is one way to break down the silos that have long hampered effective management. Such collaboration not only accelerates the process of identifying inefficiencies but also creates a shared sense of purpose and accountability when it comes to streamlining contractual processes.

The journey to understanding the true cost of contract chaos is as much about quantifying financial losses as it is about recognizing the opportunity costs that abound. When organizations are mired in the complications of fragmented systems, they inadvertently miss out on the competitive benefits that refined processes could otherwise offer. The time and resources squandered in managing manual tasks and correcting avoidable mistakes could be redirected toward initiatives that foster innovation, enhance customer relationships, and ultimately drive market share. In this light, the shift toward proactive contract management is not merely a remedial measure—it is a strategic investment in the future resilience and competitiveness of the business.

As we dissect these multifaceted impacts, it becomes evident that reforming contract management practices represents one of modern organizations' most critical challenges. Contract chaos's financial and operational costs are powerful motivators for change. The evidence is clear: inefficiencies, redundancies, and misaligned processes contribute to a firing line of lost opportunities, increased risk exposure, and diminished customer trust. Addressing these issues head-on through technological innovation, integrated systems, and strategic leadership lays the groundwork for a robust, resilient contract management approach.

Beyond immediate cost reductions, the strategic transformation of contract management elevates the entire business model. It creates an environment where contractual data drives proactive decision-making and underpins the execution of long-term strategic initiatives. With accurate, real-time insights into contractual performance, business leaders can make informed decisions that avert potential risks and seize emerging opportunities. This capability is indispensable in markets characterized by rapid change and intense competition, where the ability to pivot quickly can mark the difference between leadership and obsolescence.

The insights gathered at this stage of our analysis catalyze a deeper exploration of both the underlying causes and the expansive possibilities inherent in transforming contract management. They compel us to scrutinize the financial metrics associated with inefficient practices and the broader strategic implications of a fragmented approach. I aim to provide a thorough understanding of these dual dimensions, setting the stage for pragmatic, evidence-based strategies to bridge the gap between current deficiencies and future aspirations.

In the following sections, we will walk through data-driven case studies, expert analyses, and practical frameworks designed to illuminate the path forward. By breaking down complex concepts into actionable insights, this discussion will serve as an indispensable guide for leaders intent on stopping revenue leakage and harnessing their contractual relationships' full potential. The questions we face are clear: How can we systematically identify the weaknesses embedded in our current practices? What resources and changes are necessary to build an efficient and strategically aligned system with growth objectives? How do we measure success in a transformation affecting every organizational layer?

The answers to these questions lie in a comprehensive reassessment of the contract lifecycle—from initiation to execution, and ultimately, to renewal and termination. Each stage of this journey offers opportunities to introduce safeguards, optimize performance, and enhance strategic value. The pathway to a revolutionary overhaul of contract management becomes discernible through meticulous data gathering and rigorous process analysis. It is not a question of replacing one form of inefficiency with another, but instead of reimagining the entire contractual framework so that each element contributes harmoniously to the overall business strategy.

As we embark on this detailed exploration, the narrative remains anchored in the realities of modern business. The cost of contract chaos is tangible, its impacts measurable, and its potential for improvement vast. The goal is to empower decision-makers with the knowledge and tools to redirect resources from managing deficits to driving growth. The methodologies discussed will provide a blueprint for identifying, quantifying, and eliminating wasteful practices while unlocking new avenues for operational excellence.

The gravity of the situation demands that we approach this challenge rigorously and creatively. While the deficits of current systems are well documented, the potential for transformation is equally significant. With a carefully planned strategy and sustained commitment from leadership, organizations can transition toward a model that mitigates risks and actively contributes to enhanced performance and profitability. This transformation is not just about cost-cutting—it represents a fundamental shift in how contracts are perceived, managed, and leveraged as distinguishing assets in a competitive market.

In conclusion, exploring the real cost of contract chaos reveals a dual narrative: one of tangible financial loss and one of untapped strategic potential. The lessons drawn from inefficient practices set the stage for an imperative need to transform contract management from an operational liability into a strategic asset. As we delve deeper into this analysis, we remain committed to providing a clear, actionable pathway for making these essential changes. This path promises improved efficiency, heightened customer trust, and a foundation for future growth. The journey ahead offers both a challenge and an opportunity; by understanding the full scope of what is at stake, leaders are better equipped to make the critical decisions that will shape the organization's competitive future.

:#:

- ANALYZING REVENUE LEAKAGE AND RISK -

The current discussion raises a pivotal question: What is the tangible cost of being mired in outdated contract management practices? From the fragmented systems that breed inefficiency to the revenue leakage and risk exposure that follow, organizations face challenges that extend far beyond the administrative realm. In this section, we set out to quantify and illuminate the actual cost of contract chaos that affects not only the bottom line but also the enterprise's operational integrity, customer trust, and strategic foresight.

At first glance, the deficits introduced by inefficient contract management may appear as isolated inconveniences: delays in contract processing, missed renewals, and a reliance on manual methods that invite human error. However, a closer examination reveals that the impact runs much deeper, overlapping multiple dimensions of business performance. The direct loss in revenue is but one facet of a broader challenge. Whenever a renewal window is missed or a contract term is overlooked, an opportunity for better pricing, improved vendor conditions, or enhanced customer value is lost. While less visible than straightforward delays, this opportunity cost culminates in significant financial leakage over time.

The lack of transparency across departments compounds the issue when organizations rely on outdated systems. Many enterprises still manage contracts in isolated silos—a situation that not only obscures data but also weakens the collective insight required for strategic negotiations. In such cases, vital information about terms, compliance dates, and performance benchmarks is scattered and disconnected, making it challenging to harness data effectively. The absence of a unified system means that decision-makers are often forced to make estimates or rely on incomplete records. This state of affairs exacerbates risks considerably: Companies run the risk of non-compliance and legal penalties, and become vulnerable when opportunities to optimize and renegotiate contracts are missed entirely.

The financial repercussions of this inefficiency are stark.

Numerous case studies during my practice reveal that organizations hampered by manual, fragmented contract processing incur hidden costs that can cost millions annually. Consider a medium-sized enterprise where every delayed renewal or mismanaged contract results in a missed chance to secure improved terms. In the aggregate, these individual lapses add up to a substantial drain on resources—resources that could otherwise be allocated toward growth and innovation. When distributed over an entire organization, the cost per employee often reaches unsustainable figures over the long term. Moreover, the penalties incurred through non-compliance, whether in the form of regulatory fines or lost market opportunities because of weak contractual safeguards, further compound the financial strain.

Beyond the numeric consequences lies an even more significant aspect of the cost: Customer trust and market reputation erosion. In an era where every interaction counts, customers are not merely passive recipients of products and services—they are active partners in business success. When contract processes are cumbersome and error-prone, the resulting delays and miscommunications send a clear signal to customers: the organization struggles with basic operational competence. This perception may lead customers to question the reliability and agility of the business, undermining long-term relationships and tarnishing the brand reputation. The loss in customer trust is difficult, if not impossible, to quantify precisely. Yet its impact is palpable, manifesting as reduced customer retention rates, declining repeat business, and weakening competitive position in the market.

It is instructive to examine specific scenarios where inefficient contract management has led to measurable losses. One common scenario involves supplier agreements. When a company cannot track contract renewal dates accurately, it may inadvertently continue with unfavorable terms simply because the opportunity to renegotiate has passed unnoticed. In such a case, the immediate effect is an overpayment for goods or services that leak into the revenue stream, which, while seemingly minor on a case-by-case basis, aggregates to significant financial loss across the organization. Moreover, supplier dissatisfaction with unresolved contractual issues can lead to strained relationships, potentially affecting the quality and timeliness of future deliveries. In industries where supply chains are critical, such disruptions ripple outward into broader operational inefficiencies, further endangering the company's market position.

Similarly, consider sales contracts. When a firm struggles to handle these contracts promptly, it risks delaying the deployment of new products or services - a delay can be hugely detrimental in competitive markets where speed-to-market is a crucial determinant of success. The delay affects revenue generation by postponing sales and allows competitors to secure customer loyalty by demonstrating superior efficiency. Moreover, mismanagement of sales contracts may expose firms to revenue leakage: flexible pricing opportunities or incentive structures that, optimally captured, could significantly boost profitability are left untapped. Each missed opportunity in this context directly blows the company's growth engine.

The risk element tied to inefficient contract management is not confined solely to internal operations. Companies are increasingly exposed to regulatory environments that de-

mand rigorous oversight and strict adherence to contractual obligations. When processes are hindered by manual
oversight, the margin for error widens, significantly increasing the probability of breaches. Regulatory non-compliance issues are fraught with severe consequences: fines,
litigation, and even damage to the organization's public
standing. These risks, when aggregated, create an uncertain operational landscape in which even well-intentioned
strategies may falter due to the underlying vulnerabilities
in contract management.

Addressing the full spectrum of these costs requires more
than just patchwork solutions. It calls for fundamentally
rethinking of how contracts are managed throughout their
lifecycle. By taking an integrated approach that aligns operational processes with strategic objectives, companies
can develop systems that are efficient, agile, and responsive to emerging business needs. This transformation begins with a thorough audit of existing practices—mapping
the lifecycle of each contract from initiation to renewal.
By understanding every stage of the process and identifying key bottlenecks, organizations can begin to target
improvements that yield quantifiable benefits.

Advanced technological solutions provide a critical tool in
this transformation. Automation, for example, can replace
many of the manual tasks that currently bog down contract processing. With automated systems, routine tasks
such as monitoring renewal dates or flagging compliance
anomalies are handled in real time, reducing the inherent
latency in manual systems. These systems also allow for
better data integration; contracts that were once isolated
in disparate silos can now be centralized, ensuring that all
stakeholders have access to accurate, up-to-date informa-

tion to inform their decisions. Such visibility is paramount when negotiating better terms or assessing the actual cost of existing agreements.

Moreover, integrating robust data analytics can shift the focus from reactive corrections to proactive management. With comprehensive dashboards that display key performance indicators, such as the average turnaround time for contract processing, the frequency of missed renewal dates, and patterns in revenue leakage, executives can precisely gauge the performance of their contract management systems. This visibility supports better decision-making and creates a culture of continuous improvement. Employees understand that each process improvement has a direct and measurable impact on the organization's performance and, ultimately, on the bottom line.

Significantly, transforming contract management is not just a matter of enhancing internal efficiency but also about reinforcing customer relationships. A transparent and responsive contract process enhances overall customer engagement, ensuring that clients view the organization as both reliable and customer-focused. For instance, when a contract renewal is processed seamlessly without disruption, it reinforces the customer's perception of the company as attentive and efficient. Such improvements are particularly effective in building long-term loyalty, a critical component in today's competitive market landscape. Reinforcing customer trust through efficient processes has cascading benefits, leading to higher customer retention, more repeat business, and increasingly favorable word-of-mouth referrals.

In parallel, the strategic insights gained from revamped contract management practices can serve as a valuable resource for revenue generation. Detailed analytics enable the identification of trends that might otherwise go un- noticed—trends that can inform strategic decisions such as renegotiating contract terms or restructuring vendor agreements. For example, if analytics reveal that specif- ic contract clauses consistently lead to inefficiencies or elevated costs, these insights can drive targeted negoti- ations to mitigate those issues. Over time, incremental improvements of this nature accumulate into significant financial gains, proving that the investment in upgrading contract management systems is not merely remedial but also strategically advantageous.

The cumulative understanding of these various facets, the direct financial costs, the operational risks, and the indi- rect damage to customer relationships, forms a compel- ling case for a more sophisticated approach to contract management. It calls on organizations to view contract inefficiency not as an unavoidable by-product of doing business, but as a critical vulnerability that can be ad- dressed through process reengineering and technology substantiation. This multi-pronged strategy sets the stage for a transformation that plugs the financial leakages and reinforces the organization's competitive standing in an in- creasingly dynamic market.

Considering the broader implications, it is essential to note that the cost of contract chaos extends well beyond the immediate ledger entries. Every inefficiency, every missed opportunity, and every delay contributes indirectly to the organization's diminished ability to innovate and scale. Organizational agility—the capacity to pivot swiftly in response to market shifts—is undermined when resources are tied up in managing basic administrative tasks. Instead of focusing on strategic initiatives that drive growth, teams are locked in a perpetual cycle of correction and catch-up. This misalignment diverts energy away from proactive pursuits that could enhance market share and spur innovation. Consequently, the opportunity cost of inefficient contract management becomes even more pronounced, as it drains financial resources and stymies organizational evolution.

The road forward is clear: organizations must measure, manage, and ultimately minimize the actual cost of contract chaos. Establishing a clear correlation between process inefficiencies and their financial repercussions is the first step in building a compelling case for change. Once the link is established, the next logical step is overhauling the systems and practices contributing to these defects. This transformation is best achieved through a combination of advanced technology solutions, precision data analytics, and a recommitment to operational discipline across all departments involved in contract management. With a clear strategy in place, even companies entrenched in legacy practices can begin to reshape their contractual processes into dynamic engines for revenue generation and risk mitigation.

In conclusion, as we begin this examination of contract chaos, it is essential to recognize that the "cost" is multifaceted—embedded not only in the immediate financial outgoings but also in the missed strategic opportunities and weakened customer relationships that result from inefficient practices. The following dialogue will reveal these dimensions in detail, presenting a comprehensive view informing actionable steps. By quantifying both the tangible and intangible costs associated with current practices, executives can be better equipped to make informed decisions to reverse these trends. The ultimate objective is to transform contract management from a costly liability into a robust, integrated system that drives sustainable competitive advantage.

This comprehensive exploration sets the foundation for understanding that every inefficiency in contract management represents an untapped opportunity to optimize processes and the essence of how a business interacts with its partners, vendors, and customers. With careful analysis and deliberate strategy, it becomes possible to reengineer the current landscape into one where contracts are seamlessly integrated into the business model, delivering compliance, operational stability, and strategic growth. As we advance through the subsequent sections, we will build upon these insights, introducing practical frameworks and data-driven methodologies designed to bridge the gap between existing deficiencies and a future defined by efficiency, profitability, and agility.

∷

- IDENTIFYING INEFFICIENCIES AND THEIR CONSEQUENCES -

Inefficiencies in contract management reveal themselves in many dimensions beyond immediate financial loss. Expanding our understanding of the cost of contract chaos requires examining how process fragmentation and outdated oversight systems limit an organization's capability to operate at full potential. Every disjointed process and manual step that remains entrenched in legacy systems translates into missed revenue and a reduction in the organization's ability to innovate and respond effectively to market shifts.

One of the key issues lies in the absence of comprehensive data capture and analysis. When contract information is scattered across different departments and systems, decision-makers are deprived of a consolidated view of contractual performance. This creates an environment where strategic decisions are made based on partial or outdated data. The difficulties in tracking key performance indicators, such as contract renewals, compliance measures, or renegotiation opportunities, further exacerbate the situation. Without a single repository for all contract-related data, executives are forced to rely on estimates and audits that take additional time and resources, increasing the risk of error and amplifying hidden financial losses.

Detailed cost analyses have shown that organizations suffering from fragmented contract management may lose substantial sums in revenue leakage and face increased costs due to inefficiencies in operational processes. For example, the prolonged duration required to locate necessary documents, verify compliance, and execute timely contract renewals can result in delays that affect product launches, vendor relationships, and overall market responsiveness. While not always immediately quantifiable, these delays accumulate over time as missed opportunities and suboptimal contract terms accumulate. In many cases, the revenue lost on a missed renewal or delayed negotiation could have supported initiatives in research and development, marketing, or customer service—areas critical to long-term growth and competitiveness.

Moreover, when organizations allocate significant resources to manage contract processes manually, the resulting opportunity cost can be substantial. Employees spend hours on administrative tasks, such as data entry, document review, and follow-up communications, rather than engaging in strategic activities that could foster innovation or drive customer engagement. In cost-conscious environments, this misallocation of talent becomes particularly problematic. Ideally, the expertise of legal, financial, and operational teams should be directed toward value-adding initiatives rather than routine tasks. By not automating and integrating these processes, companies unnecessarily burden their workforce, limiting the potential for skill development and improved customer interactions.

Risk management, too, suffers from a lack of integrated contract oversight. The scattered nature of data can leave gaps where obligations, such as renewal dates or critical compliance clauses, are overlooked. This oversight carries the risk of regulatory penalties and increases the likelihood of performance breaches that may damage vendor relationships. In highly regulated industries, the cost of non-compliance can be severe - extending beyond fines to include reputational damage and diminished customer trust. Businesses that have experienced such consequences often find remediation costs, litigation expenses, and additional compliance audits draining their financial and managerial resources. Therefore, the risks associated with fragmented contract management are tightly interwoven with the inefficiencies that hinder organizational agility and responsiveness.

Beyond internal implications, the external impact on customer relationships and vendor negotiations is equally noteworthy. When contracts are mishandled or subject to delays, customers interpret these lapses as indicators of broader disorganization. In a competitive market, where customer experience is a strong differentiator, any perceived inefficiency can be detrimental to long-term relationships. For vendors and partners, unreliable contract management can create uncertainty about future terms, leading to less favorable negotiation positions or even losing key partnerships. Such outcomes emphasize that the cost of contract chaos extends far beyond immediately measurable financial losses—it permeates the entire ecosystem of business relationships, affecting reputation, loyalty, and future revenue potential.

Modern methodologies in contract management advocate for an integrated, systematic approach that reduces manual overhead and provides actionable insights. Implementing technological solutions such as cloud-based repositories, automated workflow systems, and advanced analytics platforms can fundamentally shift how organizations manage contracts. Automation plays a critical role by handling repetitive tasks, improving turnaround times, and reducing human error. For instance, automated review processes can ensure that every contract is consistently checked against compliance criteria. At the same time, integrated dashboards can provide real-time alerts on upcoming renewals or deviations from agreed terms. These platforms enhance operational efficiency and empower decision-makers with timely and accurate data.

The role of data analytics in transforming contract management cannot be understated. With rich, integrated data sets, organizations can identify trends that may indicate recurring issues in vendor agreements or internal process bottlenecks. For example, if analytics reveal that certain types of contracts consistently lead to revenue leakage due to unfavorable terms, these insights provide a basis for renegotiation strategies that can recapture lost value. Similarly, analytics can illuminate inefficiencies in internal workflows, showing where additional automation or process redesign can yield measurable improvements. This continuous feedback loop reinforces a culture of operational excellence, enabling companies to harness even marginal gains across the contract lifecycle.

Furthermore, integrating contract management with other enterprise systems, such as enterprise resource planning (ERP), customer relationship management (CRM), and financial systems, unlocks a wealth of possibilities for businesses. For example, when contracts are linked with real-time financial data, discrepancies between expected revenue and actual performance can be swiftly identified and addressed. This integration minimizes the gap between strategic planning and operational execution, ensuring that every contractual decision supports broader business objectives. For organizations looking to create a resilient and adaptable business model, connecting these critical systems is essential to aligning administrative processes with strategic goals.

While technology provides the backbone for improved contract management, its successful implementation requires a change in organizational culture. Companies entrenched in routine, manual processes may resist the shift toward automation and integrated systems. Overcoming this inertia is a challenge that requires both leadership and clear communication. Change management strategies should demonstrate the tangible benefits of a modernized contract management system—not just in terms of cost savings, but also increased agility, improved compliance, and enhanced competitiveness. Training programs and cross-departmental collaboration initiatives can facilitate this transition, ensuring that every stakeholder understands the value of the transformation and is equipped to contribute to its success.

Several of my case studies illustrate the multifaceted benefits of an integrated contract management system. In one example, a mid-sized enterprise facing significant revenue leakage due to overlooked contract renewals implemented an automated alert system tied directly to its centralized contract repository. Within months, the company reported a dramatic reduction in missed renewal opportunities and a corresponding improvement in vendor negotiations that saved the organization substantial sums annually. Similarly, a large organization integrated its contract management with ERP and CRM systems, enabling a seamless view of customer interactions and contract performance. This integration reduced processing times and allowed the company to forecast revenue better and allocate resources, aligning operational efficiency with strategic planning.

These "real-life" examples, in my 25+ years of experience, underscore that effective contract management is not an isolated initiative. It has profound implications for an organization's overall performance and strategic positioning. Companies can recast contracts as dynamic tools that drive revenue, reduce risk, and strengthen customer relationships by investing in technologies that automate routine processes and integrate disparate data sources. This reorientation marks a departure from the view of contracts as static legal documents, instead positioning them as vital components of the business strategy. The long-term benefits are clear: improved operational efficiency, enhanced financial performance, and robust risk management.

Perhaps one of the most compelling arguments for upgrading contract management systems is the cumulative impact of numerous minor improvements. When every department involved in contract processing works with a unified system, even minor reductions in turnaround time or error rates increase significantly over time. For instance, reducing the average contract processing time by a small percentage can result in substantial annual savings, freeing up resources to focus on strategic initiatives such as market expansion or product development. These incremental benefits help create a self-reinforcing cycle of improvement, where higher efficiency leads to better data, supporting further process optimization.

The interplay between this operational overhaul and broader business objectives is critical in today's dynamic market. Agile and responsive companies are better positioned to capitalize on emerging opportunities, adapt to changing customer demands, and withstand competitive pressures. By streamlining contract management, organizations address immediate financial loss and lay the groundwork for a more resilient business model. Every investment in enhanced processes, every effort to automate and integrate systems, is an investment in the future stability and growth of the enterprise.

Moreover, a modern, streamlined contract management system cultivates a culture of accountability and transparency. When processes are automated and data is centralized, assigning responsibility for every stage of the contract lifecycle becomes easier. This clarity prevents ambiguities that can lead to mistakes or delays. It also promotes internal discipline, with employees and departments holding themselves and each other accountable for meeting performance targets. This culture of continuous improvement contributes directly to the organization's overall health, as each success builds a stronger foundation for tackling future challenges.

In addition to fortifying internal operations, enhanced contract management directly impacts customer and partner relationships. When contract processes are efficient, mutually beneficial agreements are reached with greater reliability. Customers and vendors alike appreciate the transparency and predictability of a well-organized system. A seamless contract experience reinforces customers' confidence in the organization's commitment to service and quality. For vendors, it encourages a collaborative negotiation environment where equitable terms are established based on timely and accurate data. These relationships, built on trust and efficiency, are vital for maintaining a competitive edge in markets characterized by rapid change and increasing complexity.

The financial ramifications of these improvements extend to every corner of the organization. Streamlined contract management reduces direct expenditures associated with inefficiencies and errors and enhances the capacity for strategic investment. Savings accumulated from more efficient processes can be redirected toward projects that drive innovation, expand market reach, or improve custom-er service. In this way, upgrading contract management systems serves as both a defensive measure, by reducing risks and costs, and as an offensive strategy that unlocks additional value. The result is a more agile, responsive, and profitable organization better equipped to navigate the challenges of a competitive market.

As organizations quantify the actual cost of contract chaos, it becomes evident that the solution lies in a well-integrated, technology-enabled approach. The jour-ney from fragmented practices to a streamlined, strategic contract management model is not merely about elimi-nating inefficiencies. It is about reshaping the entire op-erational framework to support long-term success. Every contract is processed efficiently, every renewal is captured on time, and every missed opportunity reclaimed through data-driven insights, contributing to a cumulative compet-itive advantage that is difficult to quantify in isolation but unmistakable when viewed holistically.

In summary, the expansion of contract management inef-ficiencies and the resulting cost leakage is a multi-layered challenge affecting operational performance, financial health, and customer relationships. These challenges are compounded by the reliance on manual, isolated, and out-dated systems that prevent coherent oversight and rapid decision-making. By integrating advanced technologies—ranging from automation to robust data analytics—and repositioning contracts as dynamic business instruments, organizations can reclaim lost revenue and build a founda-tion for ongoing strategic growth. This comprehensive ap-proach, linking every element of the contract lifecycle into a unified system, represents the next evolution in transforming contractual obligations from burdens into drivers of sustainable success.

Through targeted investments in process reengineering, data integration, and technology adoption, companies can transition from reactive management to one where contracts fully align with and support overall business strategy. The benefits of this transformation are clear: reduced operational risk, enhanced customer and vendor relationships, and the ability to capture incremental opportunities that collectively drive significant financial gain. As the analysis reveals, addressing the inefficiencies and hidden costs of contract chaos is not merely a remedial exercise, it is a strategic imperative for any organization seeking to thrive in a competitive marketplace.

⁜

- THE HIDDEN COSTS OF MISSED OPPORTUNITIES -

Having explored in detail the tangible financial drain, operational bottlenecks, and the erosion of customer and partner trust caused by inefficient contract management, it now becomes apparent that what has been described is not merely a series of isolated challenges, but a systemic vulnerability that hobbles an organization's ability to grow and respond to changing market conditions. The discussion so far has offered a deep and measured analysis of how fragmented systems hamper data-driven decision-making, create gaps in compliance and oversight, and ultimately lead to real and recurring revenue losses.

This narrative has demonstrated that outdated, manual processes and the resulting disconnect among business functions are costly and undermine the strategic potential that a streamlined, integrated contract management system could offer.

The detailed examples and case studies presented in earlier sections have brought us face to face with stark realities: missed renewals, substandard vendor agreements, and delays in sales negotiations all contribute to a cumulative financial burden that cannot be ignored. Each missed opportunity represents a lost dollar amount and a setback in an organization's path to capturing market share and cultivating strong customer relationships. When contract details become scattered across disjointed platforms, the result is a picture that is both incomplete and prone to error—a picture that, in practice, forces leaders to make decisions based on partial knowledge and outdated information.

It is evident that the cost of contract chaos is multidimensional. On the surface, there is the apparent impact on the bottom line: excessive time and resources devoted to administrative tasks directly subtract from the energy that could be directed toward innovation and strategic customer engagements. Beneath the surface, the same inefficiencies sow the seeds of longer-term issues. Compliance becomes an afterthought instead of an explicit design feature of daily operations, and the delicate balance required to maintain trustworthy partnerships and favorable vendor relations is disturbed. The compounded effects of these challenges lead to a decline in overall market competitiveness, making it increasingly difficult for organizations to attract new business and retain existing clients in a climate where operational agility is paramount.

Throughout this examination, a recurring theme has been the transformative potential of advancing contract management from its current reactive state into a dynamic, integrated function that contributes actively to an organization's strategic ambitions. Organizations that have successfully modernized their contract management systems report measurable improvement in efficiency and cost control, demonstrating enhanced predictive capabilities and a more solid competitive footing. In those instances, investments in technology and process reengineering have paid off by reducing the cycle time for contract processing, providing clearer visibility into key business metrics, and ultimately supporting better decision-making at all enterprise levels.

The strategic implications of investing in modern contract management systems extend beyond the immediate relief of operational inefficiencies. When contracts are handled centrally and methodically, the resulting cohesion provides insights that ripple across the entire organization. Decision-makers benefit from a holistic view of contractual obligations, renewal dates, and performance indicators—all of which contribute to a cleaner, more predictable revenue stream. Moreover, the enhanced ability to pinpoint and address inefficiencies leads to a more cost-effective allocation of resources, enabling companies to reinvest savings into areas that further spur growth and market innovation.

Integrating technological solutions such as automated repositories, real-time data analytics, and centralized dashboards has emerged as an essential part of the remedy for the challenges described. These tools help ensure critical tasks—from tracking renewal dates to enforcing compliance measures—are executed automatically, reducing human error and increasing operational throughput. Doing so frees up valuable human capital, enabling teams to focus on strategic negotiations and customer engagement rather than being mired in administrative routine. Such a shift has been evidenced repeatedly in the case studies discussed earlier, where automation reduced processing times, captured missed renewal opportunities, and ultimately contributed to a steady improvement in the organization's financial performance.

Nevertheless, achieving a modern, integrated contract management system is not simply purchasing and installing new software. It calls for a fundamental cultural shift within the organization. Leaders must be willing to reexamine longstanding practices and embrace the idea that contracts are far more than static documents to be archived. Instead, they are active tools that can shape business strategy. This change in mindset is critical, as it alerts all stakeholders—from legal, finance, and operations teams—to the consequences of inefficient contract management. Only by aligning the organization's culture with the vision of a streamlined, dynamic, and integrated process can the transformation be entirely effective, ensuring that every contract contributes purposefully to organizational success.

As the discussions have illustrated, the overall cost of contract chaos is not confined to quantifiable fiscal losses. There is an equally significant impact on the erosion of trust - trust within internal teams, trust from external partners, and ultimately trust from customers. Professional relationships built on inconsistent, unreliable contractual practices can quickly disintegrate, leading to a broader deterioration of an organization's reputation. In competitive markets, reputation is an invaluable asset, and any factor that undermines it must be addressed with urgency and precision. The insights presented here make it clear that improving contract management processes is not simply an internal operational tweak but a critical factor reinforcing the organization's external standing and long-term viability.

Considering this multifaceted analysis, the imperative for transformation becomes undeniable. Organizations must view the cost of inefficiencies not merely as an administrative inconvenience but as a strategic liability that affects every level of corporate performance. The pathway to remediation is clear: a deliberate reassessment of legacy practices, a robust integration of automation and data analytics, and a collective commitment to aligning contract management with broader business objectives. This comprehensive approach not only plugs the gaps that allow revenue leakage and operational risk but also sets the stage for sustained competitive advantage in a rapidly evolving market.

The transformation journey involves several critical steps. Firstly, a complete audit of existing contract management processes is required to identify where delays, errors, and lapses most frequently occur. This initial assessment provides a baseline from which the benefits of modernization can be measured and tracked. From there, organizations can implement targeted improvements, such as centralized data repositories, automated workflow systems, and integrated analytics platforms, that address the identified deficiencies. Incremental improvements, when aggregated over time, lead to a significant reduction in manual workload and an increase in process accuracy. This improves the bottom line and reinforces the organization's capacity to operate nimbly and effectively in a competitive landscape.

Secondly, investing in the training and development of personnel responsible for managing contracts is critical. Building a workforce adept at utilizing modern contract management tools and understanding the strategic importance of each contractual element ensures that technology investments are reflected in real-world performance gains. Change management programs that reinforce a culture of continuous improvement help overcome resistance to new practices, ensuring that each stakeholder is prepared for and committed to the new operating paradigm.

Thirdly, integrating contract management with other key business systems, such as customer relationship management, enterprise resource planning, and financial reporting, contributes to a more cohesive approach to organizational management. When these systems are connected, data flows seamlessly between functions, enabling more accurate forecasting, faster response times, and improved strategic decision-making. The insights from integrated data provide an empirical foundation for refining contract terms and negotiating more favorable conditions with vendors and partners. This interconnected ecosystem supports internal efficiency and enhances the overall customer experience, offering a level of service that distinguishes the organization in a crowded marketplace.

In addition to these operational steps, measuring the success of any implemented changes is essential. Key performance indicators such as reduced processing times, improved compliance rates, captured renewal opportunities, and increased customer satisfaction should be tracked regularly. By establishing clear metrics, organizations can gauge the effectiveness of their transformation efforts and make necessary adjustments in real time. Establishing performance dashboards creates accountability at every level, ensuring that improvements in contract management are directly linked to strategic business outcomes and long-term profitability.

This final stage of our discussion underscores the costs associated with inefficient contract management are far more than mere numbers on a balance sheet. They represent a significant strategic disadvantage in markets where every operational lag can lead to lost opportunities, deteriorating partnerships, and a weakened competitive position. The evidence is clear: organizations that continue to operate with fragmented and outdated systems do so at their peril. The challenge, then, is to shift from a modus operandi defined by reactive management and administrative burdens to a proactive, integrated oversight that positions contract management as a central pillar of business strategy.

The lessons drawn from this chapter are both sobering and instructive. They compel leaders to look beyond the surface of administrative inconvenience and recognize the hidden toll these inefficiencies exact on every aspect of the enterprise. Whether it is the missed chance to negotiate better terms, the increased risk of non-compliance, or the erosion of stakeholder trust, each failure to manage contracts effectively undermines the organization's broader strategic goals. The cumulative impact of these inefficiencies highlights an urgent need for transformation that is best met by adopting a comprehensive, technology-based approach to contract management that realigns processes with the business's overall objectives.

As we conclude this chapter, the overarching message is about caution and opportunity. The hidden costs of contract chaos are deep and varied, affecting financial performance, operational efficiency, and strategic positioning. Yet within these challenges lies a compelling opportunity: by reengineering contract management practices, organizations can reclaim lost revenue, enhance operational reliability, and reaffirm stakeholder confidence. A methodical transition to an integrated, proactive system is not just a way to mitigate risks but to capture new sources of competitive advantage that drive long-term growth.

This conclusion serves as a bridge to the next phase of our discussion. Having established a clear understanding of the many costs associated with inefficient contract management, we are now poised to explore how reimagining contracts as strategic assets can transform these challenges into opportunities. The forthcoming discussions will shift the focus toward practical frameworks and methodologies designed to reconfigure contract management from a liability to a valuable resource—one that actively contributes to organizational growth and resilience.

The insights provided in this chapter confirm that addressing the multifaceted issues of contract management is a strategic imperative. Rather than accepting inefficiencies as an inevitable part of doing business, organizations must commit to comprehensively reevaluating their processes. Embracing technology, cultivating a culture open to change, and integrating contract management with broader business operations are essential steps toward creating a robust system that delivers real, measurable value. As we prepare to move forward, the lessons learned here will inform a new chapter that positions contracts at the heart of business strategy—a chapter focused on transforming administrative functions into strategic drivers that enhance every aspect of organizational performance.

In closing, the analysis laid out in this chapter underscores the necessity of viewing contract management not merely as an operational detail but as a cornerstone of business sustainability. With the evidence of financial leakage, operational delays, and the erosion of trust documented, the call to action is urgent and well justified. The journey toward a more integrated, data-driven, and proactive approach is the key to overcoming the challenges posed by outdated methodologies. By turning this critical function into a seamless, strategic process, organizations secure their immediate financial interests and build the foundations for future market leadership.

As we transition to the next chapter, the focus will shift to redefining traditional perceptions of contracts, demonstrating how their proactive management can unlock new avenues for growth. With a clear understanding of the costs and risks associated with fragmented practices, we can now examine practical strategies, real-world examples, and the step-by-step methodologies required to transform contracts into dynamic assets. This marks the beginning of a new perspective that recognizes contracts as powerful tools for strategic advancement rather than mere administrative formalities.

CHAPTER 3:

SHIFTING THE MINDSET: FROM LEGAL ADMIN TO STRATEGIC ASSET

Contracts have long been viewed as static legal documents, a necessary but purely administrative burden that guards against risk rather than driving growth. However, recent shifts in business dynamics have revealed that contracts, when managed strategically, become powerful instruments for achieving competitive differentiation. The notion of contracts solely as legal safeguards rapidly gives way to a more expansive perspective, one in which every clause and every renewal reinforces an organization's overall strategy. In this section, we explore how reorienting the mindset behind contract management can shift the function from a routine administrative chore to a strategic asset that actively contributes to business success.

Consider the example of a mid-sized enterprise that, over several years, struggled with a cumbersome contract backlog. This company was well-regarded in its market for excellent product quality, yet its contract processing was internally mired in delays and inconsistencies. Legal teams and operational managers treated contracts simply as files to review and archive. The result was a reactive process, where missed deadlines and data inaccuracies were commonplace. Yet when leadership reexamined their approach, triggered by mounting financial leakage and operational risk, they decided to invest in a comprehensive contract lifecycle management system. The transformation was dramatic: the organization saw its contract processing accuracy soar to nearly 99.9%, backlog volumes reduced by over 95%, and user satisfaction ratings climbed from 65% to 92%. This anecdote is far from unique; it exemplifies how shifting the organizational mindset can unlock significant value hidden within contracts.

The experience of that enterprise embodies the new philosophy we now advocate. Contracts are not enough to serve merely as reactive checklists aimed at sidestepping legal pitfalls. Instead, they must be reframed as dynamic engines that drive revenue growth, optimize resource allocation, and build long-term customer relationships. This chapter will examine the mindset shift required to make that transformation. It will explore practical examples and detailed frameworks, illustrating how properly managed contracts can become integral touchpoints across business operations rather than isolated legal artifacts.

A critical aspect of this evolution involves rethinking the responsibility for contract management. Traditionally, this responsibility has rested almost exclusively with legal departments, whose primary focus is risk mitigation. Consequently, contracts have been treated in isolation from operational strategy. Financial managers, procurement teams, and customer relationship experts are often sidelined during contract negotiations and renewals. In contrast, the emerging view is that every department has an inherent stake in the contract lifecycle. When contracts are carefully aligned with customer expectations, pricing strategies, and operational efficiencies, they create a foundation for the entire organization to build. Contracts are no longer a task to be outsourced legally; they have become a shared strategic asset, informing everything from vendor management to market positioning.

Several key drivers underpin this reorientation. First, technological advancements have enabled integration of contract management systems with broader operational platforms. Modern solutions include intelligent automation, real-time data analytics, and seamless connectivity with enterprise resource planning (ERP) and customer relationship management (CRM) systems. This integration streamlines process flows and empowers executives with unified insights. With dashboards that aggregate data from every stage of the contract lifecycle, leaders can anticipate issues before they arise and make informed decisions supporting risk management and growth. In effect, technology transforms what was once manual oversight into a continuous, data-driven strategic process.

Secondly, the customer's role in contract performance is increasingly recognized. Contracts should not be viewed solely from an internal compliance viewpoint, but also from the customer experience standpoint. Customers today value transparency, responsiveness, and tailored solutions that reflect their needs. When contracts are designed with customer-centricity in mind, every term and clause can signal commitment to quality and partnership. For instance, revising traditional blanket clauses to incorporate flexible, performance-based elements can foster a collaborative relationship rather than simply serving as a legal safeguard. This approach builds trust and positions the organization as a forward-thinking partner rather than a bureaucratic vendor.

Furthermore, the evolving competitive landscape has imparted a sense of urgency to transform contract management. In many industries, the speed at which agreements are negotiated and executed can make the difference between capturing market share and losing out to more agile competitors. Enterprises that treat contract administration as a strategic priority are better equipped to accelerate time-to-market, offer more competitive pricing, and respond nimbly to external challenges such as supply chain disruptions or regulatory changes. The experience documented by organizations that have reimagined their contract lifecycles confirms that when processes are aligned with strategic imperatives, efficiencies multiply and risk is minimized.

This chapter also explores the human element behind organizational change. Shifting the mindset around contract management is inherently a cultural challenge, requiring robust change management strategies and a commitment to continuous learning. Leaders play a crucial role in this transition; they must articulate a vision that emphasizes the strategic value of contracts and nurture an environment in which every team member recognizes their role. Cross-functional collaboration becomes essential, as departments that have historically worked in isolated silos must now coordinate to ensure that contractual strategies align with overall business objectives. Through targeted training sessions, realignment of incentives, and the establishment of accountable performance metrics, organizations can gradually build the cultural foundation necessary for this transformation.

One illustrative example comes from a large multinational that faced widespread frustration with its fragmented contract processes. Initially, the legal department, overwhelmed by a backlog, struggled to keep up with a high volume of contract renewals and negotiations. Recognizing the bottleneck, senior management initiated a cross-departmental review that involved legal, procurement, finance, and IT. By working together to map the entire contract lifecycle, the organization was able to identify redundancies, synchronize overlapping responsibilities, and better integrate technological solutions across departments. The resulting overhaul eliminated backlog inefficiencies and created a seamless interface with the company's financial and CRM systems. The outcome was a dramatic improvement in both contract processing speed and overall business performance metrics, a clear demonstration that reorienting contract management enhances operational agility and strategic effectiveness.

As we dive deeper into these themes, it becomes clear that the mindset shift from legal admin to strategic asset is not simply about streamlining processes; it is about fundamentally reconfiguring how organizations perceive and leverage a critical business function. In the traditional model, contracts were viewed as static artifacts—a means to an end for legal protection. Under the new paradigm, they evolve into dynamic tools that drive negotiation, facilitate revenue capture, and support long-term strategic planning. Every contract becomes an opportunity to illustrate the company's commitment to excellence, to build stronger alliances, and to create a more predictable and profitable future.

Another critical dimension relates to risk management. In the old model, risk was managed by externalizing contract oversight to highly specialized teams focused on avoiding pitfalls. Today, however, risk must be balanced with opportunity. A proactive approach to contract management involves anticipating potential issues early on and incorporating flexibility into agreements to manage risks without stifling creativity or speed. When contracts are designed to be living documents—adaptable to changing circumstances and reflective of ongoing business relationships—they allow for a more nuanced approach to risk. This flexibility mitigates the negative consequences of unforeseen events and creates opportunities for renegotiation or restructuring that can capture hidden value.

Technology, cross-functional collaboration, and a renewed focus on customer-centricity collectively pave the way for reimagining contracts as strategic assets. But beyond these operational and structural changes lies an even more profound shift in mindset. Leaders must begin to view every contract as a microcosm of the organization's strategic ambitions that, when executed correctly, underpins financial performance, safeguards reputation, and advances competitive differentiation. The process requires moving away from a purely defensive posture and instead embracing a proactive, data-driven, and customer-oriented approach.

The evidence supporting this transformation is plentiful. Organizations that have redefined their approach to contract management report not only cost savings but also increased revenue, improved stakeholder satisfaction, and enhanced agility in response to market fluctuations. One striking example involves a company that managed to integrate its contract management system with business intelligence platforms. This integration provided real-time insights that allowed the organization to pinpoint inefficiencies, optimize supplier relationships, and even forecast market trends. Over time, this strategic alignment translated into operational improvements that were measurable in terms of both productivity and profitability.

Ultimately, the goal is to create an environment where contracts are no longer seen as a necessary evil to be managed by legal teams but as dynamic components that underpin every facet of business strategy. By shifting perspectives, organizations can harness the full potential of contract management to secure revenues, drive operational efficiency, and support innovative growth. This transformation ensures that every contractual interaction is an opportunity to reinforce the organization's competitive advantage and build lasting, trust-based relationships with its partners and customers.

As we move forward in this chapter, the focus will shift from the theoretical underpinnings of the mindset change to a detailed exploration of practical strategies and frameworks that enable this transformation. We will examine case studies and best practices illustrating how companies have successfully transitioned to a model where contracts serve as strategic levers. Along the way, relevant anecdotes and data-driven insights will underscore the tangible benefits realized by organizations that have embraced this new approach.

In summary, reconfiguring contract management from a purely administrative function into a strategic asset is not only possible but essential for organizations aiming to thrive in today's competitive landscape. The transformation is driven by technology, cross-functional collaboration, cultural change, and a clear recognition that each contract is a component of a larger strategic puzzle. With this renewed perspective, organizations are better positioned to secure their competitive edge, drive sustainable growth, and build resilient business models that weather the uncertainties of a rapidly evolving market.

This chapter will serve as the foundation for understanding how to effect this critical change. Companies can unlock hidden value and drive long-term operational excellence by reimagining contract management as an integral part of business strategy, rather than a peripheral legal function. With a clear focus on actionable strategies and measurable outcomes, we now transition to a detailed discussion of the practical steps required to reshape this longstanding function into a dynamic engine for growth and innovation.

⁜

- RETHINKING CONTRACTS AS BUSINESS GROWTH TOOLS -

For many years, legal formalities and risk avoidance dominated the discussion around contracts. Contracts were seen, almost universally, as documents to be managed by legal departments with a singular focus on compliance and liability reduction. Today, however, change is not only inevitable but also essential. Transformation begins when an organization redefines its mindset, shifting from viewing contracts solely as legal artifacts to recognizing them as strategic assets that fuel business growth and operational excellence. In this new paradigm, every clause, every renewal, and every term is considered, considering how it can drive revenue, strengthen relationships, and support a more agile, data-informed organization.

The evolution starts with a fundamental yet profound change in perception. In the past, contracts were routinely handed off to legal teams for review and approval, largely isolated from the rest of the organization. Productivity suffered as teams complied with processes that, by design, were inherently static and bureaucratic. An anecdote from a well-known mid-market company illustrates this shift vividly. For years, the company struggled with a disjointed process that resulted in an ever-growing backlog of contracts. Renewals were missed, unfavorable terms continued unchecked, and key data remained buried in legal archives. When the leadership recognized that the system was not merely a cost but a missed opportunity, they initiated a comprehensive review. The outcome was striking—a transformation that streamlined processes and shifted the entire organization's approach to contracts. Departments outside of legal began collaborating on contract management, ensuring that every agreement aligned with the company's strategic goals. The result: improved efficiency, enhanced customer relationships, and a measurable boost in revenue. This example encapsulates the key insight of this chapter: that contract management, when reconceived as a strategic enterprise function, can unlock significant latent value.

The journey to this new approach requires rethinking roles, responsibilities, and even the nature of contracts. Contract management must become a collaborative endeavor rather than remaining confined to a siloed function. Finance, procurement, sales, and operations should all see contracts as integral to their work, promoting a cooperative culture where data and insights flow freely between departments. Bringing together diverse perspectives enriches the contract creation process and ensures that each agreement is purpose-built to support broader business objectives. For example, when procurement teams and sales managers collaborate on contract terms, pricing strategies can be optimized to reflect market conditions and customer expectations, rather than being driven solely by traditional risk mitigation.

At the heart of this transformation is technological innovation. Technology is more than a convenience in the modern business environment - it catalyzes change. Advanced contract lifecycle management systems now provide integrated platforms that allow all stakeholders to access real-time data related to contract performance. These systems offer dashboards that track key performance indicators, from renewal dates to compliance measures, within a single user interface. With this transparency, every contract becomes a living document, dynamically updated and easily modified to reflect market realities. Decision-making becomes faster and more informed when data flows seamlessly between legal, finance, and operational teams. Rather than reacting to missed deadlines or disputed terms after the fact, companies can proactively negotiate and adjust contractual provisions to better align with evolving business strategies.

The impact of such technological integration is far-reaching. Automated workflows replace manual data entry, reducing errors and freeing valuable human resources from rote administrative tasks. Furthermore, artificial intelligence and machine learning contribute to predictive analytics that forecast risks and identify opportunities. Consider using AI tools that evaluate historical contract data to predict which agreements will likely result in revenue leakage or which may need renegotiation to capture additional value. These insights transform contract management into a proactive function capable of safeguarding the organization against risks and promoting innovation and strategic growth.

The cultural shift accompanying this technological transformation cannot be understated. Tradition and habit often serve as formidable barriers, and many organizations find it challenging to break away from entrenched practices. It requires strong leadership to champion the idea that contracts are more than legal formalities—they are strategic instruments that warrant the attention of every department. The change starts at the top, with executives modeling cross-departmental collaboration and explicitly linking contract performance with overall business outcomes. Leaders can inspire a broader cultural change that permeates the entire organization by demonstrating how effective contract management can lead to enhanced operational efficiency, reduced costs, and stronger customer relationships.

Training and change management programs play essential roles in this cultural transformation. Employees at all levels must be educated about the strategic importance of contracts and how their work can collectively contribute to improved outcomes. Workshops, seminars, and targeted training sessions can equip stakeholders with the knowledge to use new technological tools effectively. As employees become proficient in these tools, they begin to see firsthand the benefits of a unified, data-driven approach to contract management. This process increases efficiency and fosters a sense of shared ownership, as every team member recognizes that success depends on their contributions.

Another critical element in redefining contract management involves reexamining the language and structure of contracts themselves. Traditional contracts, often characterized by dense and impenetrable legalese, can hinder understanding for non-legal professionals. By simplifying language and focusing on clear, actionable terms that reflect business objectives, organizations can create contracts that are not only legally sound but also readily understood by all stakeholders. For instance, contracts designed with performance metrics and clear benchmarks enable all parties to assess progress and hold one another accountable. This clarity builds trust and allows for more fluid negotiations as conditions change.

Real-world examples abound of the tangible benefits of this mindset shift. One multinational corporation encountered repeated issues with delayed contract renewals, leading to a cascade of missed opportunities. After thoroughly reviewing its processes, the company implemented a new contract management system that integrated data analytics with a simplified contract framework. The immediate results were that processing times decreased considerably, and the organization could renegotiate terms more effectively. Not only did this lead to cost savings and operational improvements, but it also enhanced the overall customer experience by reducing friction in service delivery. This success story demonstrates that when contracts are managed strategically, they protect the organization from risk and become a lever for competitive advantage and growth.

The intersection of customer-centricity and strategic contract management is particularly compelling. In today's marketplace, customers expect more than quality products or services—they demand proactive engagement and responsiveness. Contracts designed with customer needs in mind serve as an extension of the company's commitment to delivering value. For example, incorporating flexible terms that allow for periodic review and adjustment can create a more collaborative environment between the organization and its customers. Rather than locking parties into rigid arrangements, adaptable contracts help foster long-term partnerships, resulting in higher satisfaction, loyalty, and repeat business.

Moreover, embracing this strategic mindset addresses immediate operational challenges and positions an organization to navigate future market uncertainties better. In a rapidly changing environment, pivoting quickly and adjusting contractual terms is invaluable. Companies can prepare for unexpected market disruptions and capitalize on emerging opportunities by reimagining contracts as adjustable, proactive instruments. In effect, each contract becomes a strategic touchpoint—a chance to continuously recalibrate and improve business performance.

Considering the multifaceted benefits, transitioning from a traditional legal-admin model to a strategic contract management approach is an essential evolution for modern organizations. The evidence is clear: organizations that invest in transforming their contract management practices reap measurable improvements in efficiency, risk mitigation, and revenue generation. The shift is not merely an operational change, it is a strategic realignment that requires comprehensive change management, technological adoption, and collaborative culture-building across the enterprise.

The journey toward this new paradigm is a continuous one, marked by incremental improvements and the gradual dismantling of long-standing silos. It begins with a deep, critical examination of current processes—identifying bottlenecks, inefficiencies, and outdated practices that hinder progress. Once these issues are mapped out, organizations can develop targeted strategies to address them. Implementing integrated systems that facilitate seamless data sharing is a pivotal step, as is adopting performance dashboards that enable real-time monitoring of contract metrics. These tools lay the groundwork for a dynamic contract management environment that supports proactive decision-making and agile responses to changing market conditions.

As we embark on this exploration, it becomes evident that the strategic reconfiguration of contract management is not an isolated project but a catalyst for broader organizational transformation. The challenges of the past—misaligned responsibilities, manual inefficiencies, and siloed information—are not simply to be rectified; they must be reimagined as opportunities. Each adjustment and each incremental improvement builds toward a more robust, integrated system that empowers the entire organization. The cumulative benefits can be transformative when contracts are positioned not as isolated legal documents but as integral components of the strategic fabric.

In summary, this chapter examines the foundational mindset required to elevate contract management from a purely administrative task to a core strategic asset. It challenges the traditional view held by many organizations and introduces a new narrative—one where contracts are dynamic instruments that underpin growth, optimize operations, and build enduring relationships. The discussion has already highlighted compelling examples of organizations that achieved dramatic improvements by embracing this shift. The path forward involves harnessing advanced technological tools, redesigning processes to foster clarity and accountability, and cultivating an organizational culture that fully recognizes the strategic potential of every contract.

As you progress through this chapter, you will find detailed frameworks, real-world case studies, and actionable recommendations to guide this transformative journey. These insights are designed to inspire a shift in thinking and provide practical steps that can be implemented across various organizational contexts. By appreciating how every contract can contribute to operational excellence and long-term success, decision-makers are better equipped to drive initiatives that yield measurable improvements in performance and competitiveness.

Ultimately, the goal is to build an environment where contract management is not an afterthought but fully integrated into the business's strategic planning and execution. In this model, contracts serve as a linchpin in the organization's drive for efficiency and innovation, capturing immediate operational gains and long-term competitive advantage. With this clear direction and renewed perspective, we now use detailed strategies and methodologies to illustrate how organizations can make this vital transition.

⁜

- THE STRATEGIC ROLE OF CLM IN MODERN ORGANIZATIONS -

As organizations shift their focus from merely processing contracts to harnessing them as strategic tools, a deeper examination reveals that this transformation is as much about redefining operational processes as it is about altering mindsets. This section explores the advanced integration of technology, data analytics, and cross-functional collaboration to support a proactive approach that moves the contract management function beyond its traditional confines. These nuanced perspectives highlight how modern systems streamline administrative tasks and create opportunities for strategic innovation that, when properly executed, generate measurable business value.

One of the key facets in advancing this transformation is the effective use of integrated technology. Digital platforms are no longer simple repositories for documents; they have evolved into intelligent hubs where contract data flows seamlessly across business units. The integration of enterprise resource planning (ERP) systems, customer relationship management (CRM) solutions, and dedicated contract lifecycle management platforms creates an ecosystem in which contracts are managed holistically. In practice, this means that every stage of the contract – from negotiation to renewal – is visible in real time. Decision-makers access dashboards that aggregate data on contract performance, compliance status, renewal deadlines, and performance metrics to make more informed and agile decisions.

For example, consider how an organization might leverage

an integrated system to cull insights from historical data. By analyzing previous contract performance, companies can identify trends in renewal delays, pinpoint clauses that consistently trigger disputes, or even forecast potential revenue leakage. Data analytics allow managers to quantify risks and opportunities on a granular level. The predictive capabilities of such systems extend to anticipating when renegotiations might yield improved terms or when market volatility calls for adjustments to existing agreements. This level of foresight transforms contracts into dynamic instruments that guide strategic decision-making rather than static references tucked away in filing cabinets.

This intelligent integration is further empowered by automation. Routine tasks – such as monitoring compliance, sending a reminder for a renewal, or updating contractual terms in response to regulatory changes – can now be executed automatically. Automation minimizes the chances of human error and ensures consistency across the contract management process. For instance, automated workflows can trigger a series of actions when a key clause in a contract is nearing expiration, including alerting stakeholders, initiating internal reviews, and generating preliminary proposals for renegotiation. In environments where timing is critical, these automation features reduce delays and create a more seamless connection between operational activities and strategic planning.

In practical terms, this technological advancement leads to a significant reduction in administrative overhead. Employees who previously spent hours on manual data entry or document retrieval are now redeployed to tasks that require strategic insight and creative problem-solving. Shifting these responsibilities does not merely free up time; it reallocates intellectual capital to areas where it can drive growth. Legal, financial, and operational teams work in concert to analyze the impact of contract terms on broader business outcomes. In doing so, they foster a culture that recognizes each contract as an active component of the business strategy – one that must be continuously monitored, evaluated, and optimized.

Beyond technology and automation, the human element remains a critical driver of change. The transition from traditional, siloed contract management to an integrated, strategic approach is as much cultural as it is technological. Leaders must work diligently to break down long-held perceptions that consign contract management to the legal department alone. Instead, fostering cross-functional collaboration requires that stakeholders from finance, sales, procurement, and operations share responsibility for the contract process. When every department has access to consistent and accurate contract data, collaborative environments are created where joint decision-making becomes the norm.

A practical instance of this collaboration can be observed in organizations that have instituted cross-functional contract review committees. In such settings, representatives from various departments convene regularly to review contract performance, assess risk levels, and propose necessary modifications. This approach ensures that contractual terms are evaluated not just through the narrow lens of legal risk but also for their strategic alignment with business objectives. For example, finance teams might highlight how certain payment terms create unnecessary cash flow stress, while sales teams may advocate for more flexible clauses that improve customer responsiveness. The result is a more balanced and nuanced contract that serves multiple purposes simultaneously.

Moreover, leveraging cross-functional insights also improves vendor and customer relationships. When suppliers and customers notice that an organization's contract management processes are robust and dynamic, trust is built rapidly. Reliable, predictable contract behavior reduces friction and fosters long-term partnerships. Many organizations have noticed that when their contract processes are transparent and responsive, suppliers are more willing to negotiate better terms, and customers are more inclined to engage in long-term agreements. The direct consequence is a network of relationships that not only mitigate risk but also deliver incremental value over time.

The convergence of technology and human collaboration also raises the sophistication of risk management. Traditionally, risk was treated as something to be avoided at all costs—a domain exclusively managed by specialists in legal or compliance departments. The modern approach, however, advocates for balancing risk with opportunity. A proactive risk management framework encourages organizations to identify potential pitfalls early and design contracts with sufficient flexibility to adapt to unforeseen circumstances. For instance, incorporating clauses that allow periodic review of performance indicators or that include contingency plans for market downturns converts risk from a liability into a managed and often strategic element.

This strategic view to risk is intertwined with enhanced data analytics capabilities. With a centralized reservoir of contract data and powerful analytics tools, organizations can comprehensively map risk exposure. Sophisticated models may even pinpoint the likelihood of specific contractual deviations or enumerate hidden liabilities previously buried in the fine print. This advanced understanding enables proactive measures, such as renegotiating terms before they become problematic or reallocating resources to address emerging vulnerabilities. Ultimately, these advanced risk management techniques not only safeguard the organization but also create the environment for confident decision-making on both tactical and strategic levels.

Another aspect that deserves in-depth discussion is the transformation of contracts into tools for revenue generation. A significant benefit of revamping contract management is the ability to uncover, recapture, and enhance revenue losses. When contracts are routinely analyzed and their performance tracked over time, patterns emerge that may signal recurring inefficiencies or recurring underperformance. For instance, if a particular type of contract consistently results in lower-than-expected revenue, there may be underlying issues with pricing or service delivery that need addressing. With the insights provided through advanced analytics, organizations can directly negotiate improvements in terms, adjust pricing models, or even redesign contract structures to better fit market demands.

For many companies, the true monetary benefits materialize in these incremental revenue improvements. Consider a scenario where improved contract management reveals that a minor pricing adjustment across a large portfolio of agreements could generate millions in additional annual revenue. These improvements, while relatively small on an individual contract basis, accumulate into significant financial gains over time. Furthermore, by adopting a proactive negotiation framework enabled by real-time data, organizations can strategically time their contract renewals and renegotiations to maximize profit margins and secure advantageous terms that would otherwise be overlooked under a reactive framework.

In addition to strengthening revenue streams, a modernized approach to contract management often results in improved customer satisfaction. Contracts that are timely, clear, and adaptable contribute directly to a positive customer experience, which is increasingly important in today's competitive landscape. Customers who interact with an organization that demonstrates efficient, proactive contract management are more likely to view the company as reliable and customer-focused. This trust translates into long-term loyalty and, at times, even advocacy for the brand, all of which are invaluable in a market where differentiation is key.

The cumulative effect of these improvements—streamlined operations, enhanced risk mitigation, improved vendor and customer relationships, and incremental revenue gains—underpins the strategic advantage that modern contract management offers. When these elements work in harmony, they create a virtuous cycle: advanced technology and integrated processes lead to actionable insights, which in turn drive better decision-making. These decisions then inform subsequent iterations in process improvement, leading to a continuously evolving and strengthening organizational capability. This continuous improvement loop is a critical factor in maintaining a competitive edge, particularly in industries characterized by rapid change and heightened customer expectations.

One must also consider the importance of performance metrics and feedback loops. Establishing clear key performance indicators (KPIs) is essential for tracking the success of the transition to a modern contract management system. Metrics such as turnaround time for contract processing, the frequency and severity of compliance issues, revenue realized from renegotiated terms, and customer feedback scores provide a comprehensive picture of improvement. Regularly reviewing these metrics not only validates the effectiveness of the new system but also highlights areas that require further refinement. It is through these iterative cycles of measurement and adjustment that the transformative vision of contract management is fully realized.

Furthermore, the success of these initiatives is predicated on ongoing commitment and leadership support. Transformative change does not occur overnight; it demands sustained focus, internal advocacy, and an unwavering belief in the long-term benefits of a strategic approach to contract management. Executives must lead by example, demonstrating a willingness to invest in new technologies, to restructure traditional roles, and to encourage a culture of innovation. They must also communicate the strategic rationale behind these changes clearly and consistently throughout the organization. Only then can the shift in mindset required for long-term success be fully adopted at every level.

In conclusion, the advanced integration of technology, data analytics, and cross-functional collaboration is redefining what effective contract management looks like. This nuanced approach enables organizations to move beyond merely managing risk or fulfilling compliance requirements; it transforms contracts into versatile, strategic tools that drive revenue, optimize operations, and enhance stakeholder trust. By automating routine tasks and centralizing data, organizations create an environment where every contract is continuously monitored, analyzed, and improved upon. The benefits of such systems extend throughout the enterprise, producing tangible financial gains, strengthening relationships with vendors and customers, and enabling quicker, more informed decision-making.

The conversation around modern contract management now extends into a realm where proactive risk management, revenue optimization, and strategic agility become core components of business strategy. In this environment, every department—be it legal, finance, sales, or operations—plays a vital role in harnessing the full potential of contracts. The transition from a compartmentalized, reactive approach to a cohesive, data-driven strategy requires thoughtful investment in technology, robust change management, and above all, a clear vision that redefines contracts as critical assets rather than mere legal safeguards.

As organizations continue to refine their systems, the iterative feedback provided by integrated analytics and performance metrics will be indispensable. These improvements are not one-time fixes but part of an ongoing evolutionary process that aligns operational performance with strategic objectives. The benefits, while sometimes incremental in isolation, compound over time, creating a robust foundation for sustained competitive advantage.

By embracing these technologies and fostering a culture of collaboration, organizations position themselves not only to minimize risks and recover lost revenue but also to drive growth through smarter, more agile contract management practices. This dynamic and forward-looking approach transforms what was once a cumbersome administrative process into a strategic asset that supports long-term business success.

In summary, the nuanced exploration of integrated technology, collaborative processes, and proactive risk management in contract management reveals how these elements work together to create a sophisticated and strategic function. This evolved approach is essential for organizations that wish to secure their competitive edge, optimize operational efficiency, and build lasting partnerships. The insights discussed in this section lay the foundation for a robust framework that moves contract management from a reactive necessity into a transformative driver of enterprise-wide excellence.

✣

- OVERCOMING TRADITIONAL MISCONCEPTIONS -

Throughout this chapter, we have traced the evolution of contract management from a rigid, legal-administered function into a dynamic, data-driven, and collaborative strategic asset. The transformation described here moves beyond traditional notions of contract administration and redefines every contractual interaction as a potential driver of competitive advantage. By integrating advanced technologies, automating routine processes, and fostering cross-functional collaboration, organizations are now poised to turn contracts into living instruments of growth.

One of the central themes we explored is the integration of technology. Modern contract management systems are no longer mere repositories for agreements; they have evolved into comprehensive platforms that interconnect with ERP, CRM, and other critical business systems. This integration creates an ecosystem in which contract data flows seamlessly across departments, offering real-time insights into renewal dates, compliance statuses, risk exposures, and performance metrics. With dashboards that aggregate data from every stage of the lifecycle, decision-makers are empowered to make informed, timely decisions. This availability of integrated data transforms contracts into proactive resources rather than passive obligations. In this new paradigm, every contract becomes a dynamic tool that supports efficient operations, reduces administrative overhead, and even reveals opportunities for revenue optimization—elements that any forward-thinking enterprise cannot afford to ignore.

Automation also plays a pivotal role within this evolved framework. The ability to automate repetitive tasks—such as sending renewal alerts, monitoring compliance, and updating contractual terms—creates significant time savings and minimizes the potential for human error. For instance, automated workflows streamline the entire process, ensuring that every critical milestone is addressed promptly and accurately. Consider the case of a multinational corporation that recently implemented an automated contract lifecycle management system. Prior to the implementation, the legal team found themselves overwhelmed by manual processes that resulted in frequent delays and inaccuracies. As automated workflows took over routine tasks, not only did processing times shrink dramatically, but deeper insights were uncovered through the integration of advanced analytics. This example vividly illustrates the transformative impact of automation in reducing risk and bolstering efficiency.

Equally important is the cultural and organizational shift that accompanies these technological advancements. Transitioning to a modern contract management system is not solely about implementing new software; it is about rethinking roles and responsibilities throughout the organization. Traditionally, contracts have been confined to the legal department, and as a result, they were often disconnected from the strategic priorities of finance, sales, procurement, and operations. We have seen through examples in this chapter that effective contract management requires true cross-functional collaboration. When all departments share responsibility for the success of each agreement, contracts can be aligned more closely with overall business strategies. Cross-functional review committees, where representatives from various units come together to analyze contract performance, ensure that every contractual term is scrutinized for its impact on broader objectives. This collaborative approach not only improves contract quality but also nurtures a culture of shared ownership and collective accountability.

The modern approach to contract management also redefines risk management. Rather than treating risk as an external threat to be avoided at all costs, organizations are now adopting a proactive stance that balances risk with opportunity. Advanced analytics enable managers to identify potential issues, such as unfavorable contract terms or submission delays, long before they evolve into costly problems. Companies can create agreements that adapt to changing market conditions and emerging business realities by incorporating flexible clauses and performance-based elements into contracts. Such proactive risk management reduces the likelihood of compliance breaches and legal disputes while simultaneously positioning organizations to identify opportunities for renegotiation or improvement. This balanced approach to risk, supported by data insights and real-time monitoring, is essential in a business environment where uncertainty is the norm.

Throughout the chapter, we have also highlighted the importance of transforming contracts into tools for revenue enhancement. By continuously monitoring and analyzing contract performance, organizations can uncover patterns that signal opportunities for improved profitability. For instance, the use of predictive analytics can reveal that minor adjustments in pricing terms across a large portfolio of contracts could cumulatively generate significant additional revenue. These insights are invaluable in a competitive market, where the ability to negotiate more favorable terms or capture overlooked opportunities can have a dramatic impact on the bottom line. Such incremental improvements are not isolated wins—they contribute to an overall increase in revenue and offer a compelling argument for investing resources into the modernization of contract management.

A key aspect that ties these elements together is the use of comprehensive performance metrics and continuous feedback loops. Establishing clear key performance indicators (KPIs), such as average turnaround times, compliance rates, and revenue capture from renegotiations, provides a measurable way to assess the success of contract management initiatives. Regular review of these metrics ensures that the benefits of the new systems are not only sustained but also improved upon over time. In organizations that have embraced these practices, incremental successes compound into substantial gains in operational efficiency and strategic agility. This continuous improvement cycle reinforces a culture of excellence, where every contract is constantly refined to better meet the evolving needs of the business.

Several real-world anecdotes underscore the transformative power of these integrated approaches. One notable example involved a mid-market company plagued by chronic delays and burdensome manual processes. Faced with mounting customer dissatisfaction and observable revenue leakage, the leadership undertook a comprehensive overhaul of its contract management framework. By seamlessly integrating automated workflows and identifying cross-departmental synergies, the company not only reduced its backlog by over 90% but also boosted its customer satisfaction metrics dramatically. The organization's proactive handling of contracts resulted in renegotiated terms that delivered unexpected financial savings, setting a clear demonstration of how technology and cultural change can jointly drive improvements. Such examples abound, highlighting that strategic contract management is not an abstract ideal but a practical necessity with tangible benefits.

Another compelling case comes from a large enterprise that reimagined its risk management approach by embracing adaptive, flexible contractual clauses. Faced with an unpredictable market environment, the organization had traditionally been hyper-focused on shielding itself from risk, often to the detriment of opportunity. However, after a cultural shift driven by leadership and supported by integrated analytics, the company began to view risk in a more balanced light. Ingredients such as predictive models and real-time data insights allowed the business to anticipate market shifts and renegotiate terms in advance, rather than reacting after adverse events occurred. As a result, the organization not only minimized legal and compliance-related issues but also unlocked value by incorporating performance-based adjustments that directly influenced revenue outcomes.

Taken together, the integration of fluid technology, cross-functional collaboration, and proactive risk and revenue management establishes a robust framework for modern contract management. The chapter has laid out a clear roadmap, demonstrating that every contract is not merely a legal safeguard but a dynamic asset that, when managed correctly, drives operational and strategic enhancements across the organization. The evidence is compelling: improved turnaround times, enhanced compliance, clear cost savings, and the unlocking of hidden revenue streams are all within reach. Enterprises that commit to this strategic reorientation can expect a substantial return on investment—both in financial terms and in the sustainable competitive advantage that emerges from a well-managed contract lifecycle.

As we conclude this chapter, it is important to reiterate the transformative potential that modern contract management offers. Advanced technology has redefined how contracts are managed, turning static legal documents into live assets that actively support business performance. Cross-functional practices break down the silos of the past, allowing all stakeholders—from legal to sales, from finance to procurement—to contribute to and benefit from a more integrated approach. Meanwhile, a balanced view of risk not only protects the organization but also opens the door to opportunities for improvement and growth. These elements, when combined, create a dynamic system that continuously evolves and delivers measurable value.

The insights shared in this chapter serve as a foundation for the next phase in our journey. Having understood the tactical and strategic advantages of transforming contract management into a comprehensive, integrated function, we are now ready to transition to the next overarching theme. The upcoming chapter will focus on shifting the organizational mindset further—from seeing contracts as purely administrative tasks to recognizing them as engines of customer-centric excellence. It will delve into how a customer-oriented approach to contracting can enhance loyalty, optimize value delivery, and ultimately contribute to business growth. By linking the internal efficiencies of contract management with the external benefits of improved customer engagement, the narrative will continue to build on the pillars we have established here.

In summary, this chapter has advanced our understanding of how modern technology, intelligent data analytics, and collaborative organizational practices can redefine contract management. The resulting system is not simply about compliance and risk avoidance; it is a strategic enabler that affects every layer of business performance. The benefits are far-reaching—from operational efficiencies that save time and money to risk management techniques that safeguard the organization, and even to revenue enhancements that secure a more profitable future. The lessons learned here, illustrated by numerous real-world examples and case studies, firmly establish that the evolution of contract management is an essential component of driving sustainable growth and competitive differentiation.

As we now move into the final phase of this discussion, the focus will shift towards the customer. The next chapter will explore how a customer-centric approach to contracting not only streamlines internal processes but also directly influences the external experiences that build trust and drive loyalty. By connecting the dots between internal efficiency, customer satisfaction, and overall growth, we will uncover strategies that harness the full power of contracts as strategic business tools. In doing so, organizations can ensure that every contractual interaction becomes an opportunity to reinforce their position in the market and achieve long-term success.

This transition marks the end of our comprehensive exploration of modern contract management strategies. With the understanding that contracts represent far more than administrative necessities, the stage is set to redefine them as critical assets that drive strategic and customer-centric value. The journey through this chapter demonstrates that by leveraging integrated technology, fostering collaborative cultures, and balancing risk with opportunity, organizations can transform what was once a burdensome process into a dynamic engine for business excellence. The path forward is clear, and the opportunity to capitalize on these insights promises a new era of efficiency, innovation, and growth.

CHAPTER 4:

CUSTOMER-CENTRIC CONTRACTING

In today's highly competitive business environment, where every aspect of operations is scrutinized for efficiency and strategic value, organizations increasingly recognize that an effective contract management system is critical to mitigate risk and drive growth. As we transition into this new phase, we must shift our focus from transforming existing processes to building a comprehensive blueprint—a CLM playbook—that operationalizes best practices into a repeatable, scalable framework. This chapter, dedicated to establishing your CLM playbook, is designed to serve as a practical guide for executives and operational leaders, providing actionable frameworks and step-by-step methodologies to embed contract management seamlessly into every facet of the business.

The previous chapters have laid a substantial foundation by dissecting the hidden costs of fragmented contract management, illustrating the transformative impact of integrated technology, and redefining contracts as dynamic, strategic assets. We have learned that inefficiencies—ranging from missed renewals to revenue leakage—compound over time if left unchecked, and that bridging cross-departmental collaboration, leveraging automation, and deploying data analytics are not optional but essential actions for today's enterprise. Now, the challenge is to consolidate these insights into a coherent playbook. This systematic, practical approach not only addresses current inefficiencies but also prepares the organization for future growth in an increasingly agile and data-driven market.

Building your CLM playbook begins with an honest assessment of existing practices. It is crucial to map out the entire contract management lifecycle, from initiation and negotiation to execution and renewal. This diagnostic phase identifies bottlenecks and highlights opportunities for process enhancement. For instance, consider a mid-sized organization that once struggled with a labyrinth of uncoordinated processes, resulting in significant revenue loss and compliance risks. By conducting a thorough process audit, they pinpointed redundancies in data entry and inconsistencies in contract review procedures. The insights from that audit paved the way for a tailored playbook that redefined workflows, introduced automated alerts, and centralized contract repositories. This foundational step is not merely an exercise in detecting problems; it is the launching pad for creating a strategic framework that transforms fragmented inputs into coherent, streamlined processes.

The next critical component of the CLM playbook is designing a robust governance framework. A clearly defined governance structure establishes roles, responsibilities, and accountability across the organization. It is no longer sufficient for contract management to reside solely within the legal department. Instead, as we have discussed previously, a cross-functional approach is necessary—one that engages finance teams, procurement specialists, sales managers, and even customer service units. By outlining explicit governance protocols, companies can ensure that contract-related decisions are aligned with broader business objectives. For example, a multinational corporation restructured its contract review process by creating a cross-departmental committee that oversaw every stage of contract execution. This improved transparency in contract negotiations and created a culture of shared ownership, where each department's input was recognized as critical to reducing risk and capturing value. Establishing a governance framework in your playbook should be a top priority, as it lays the groundwork for sustained collaboration and continuous improvement.

Equally important is the need to design and implement standardized processes. Standardization is the key to consistency and efficiency, providing every stakeholder with clear guidelines on managing contracts at each stage of their lifecycle. A standard operating procedure (SOP) can codify best practices such as checklist-driven contract reviews, automated migration of data between systems, and clearly defined escalation procedures for contract disputes. Standard processes minimize the risk of oversight, reduce errors associated with manual processing, and ensure that every contract is evaluated uniformly. Consider the anecdote of a company that significantly improved its renewal rate by deploying an SOP that required automated alerts well before expiration dates. Such standard procedures not only streamlined operations but also instilled confidence in both internal teams and external partners, demonstrating a commitment to honor contractual obligations and seize opportunities for renegotiation when needed.

Integration of technology forms the backbone of the modern CLM playbook. Advanced systems now allow organizations to consolidate contract data, automate routine tasks, and generate real-time analytics that inform strategic decisions. In your playbook, technology is not an end but a tool that reinforces the standardized processes and governance models you establish. For example, an integrated system might automatically flag contracts with less-than-optimal terms, prompting a review and renegotiation process that could recapture nearly lost revenue. Cloud-based platforms facilitate easy access to contract documents by authorized personnel across different geographies, fostering transparency and faster response times. Moreover, when these systems are integrated with enterprise resource planning (ERP) and customer relationship management (CRM) solutions, the resulting synergy provides a holistic view of every contractual relationship. This unified approach helps identify trends, measure performance against key benchmarks, and ultimately recalibrate strategies for improved operational and financial outcomes.

Another key element to incorporate in your CLM playbook is an emphasis on continuous improvement. The market, technology, and business models are in constant flux; thus, your contract management framework must be designed with flexibility and agility in mind. This means establishing performance metrics and feedback loops that allow for periodic review and adjustment of the processes. Key performance indicators (KPIs) such as contract cycle time, renewal rate compliance, and revenue captured through renegotiated terms provide measurable benchmarks that can guide iterative enhancements. For example, a leading enterprise in the technology sector implemented a quarterly review process that leveraged analytics data to adjust workflow parameters and improve contract turnaround times. Over a series of successive periods, their average processing time was cut by nearly 30%, translating into significant cost savings and improved customer satisfaction. Embedding a culture of continuous improvement into your playbook ensures that your contract management system remains responsive and aligned with evolving organizational needs.

Change management is another critical consideration when building your CLM playbook. Transforming contract management practices is not solely about process redesign and technological upgrades—it also necessitates a shift in organizational mindset. Employees at all levels must be brought on board with the new vision and provided with adequate training to adapt to new systems and processes. The successful implementation of a CLM playbook often hinges on effective communication strategies that underscore the strategic benefits of the transformation. Case studies abound of organizations that have successfully implemented new CLM systems only after implementing comprehensive training programs and change management workshops. These initiatives help to overcome resistance, boost user adoption, and ensure that the technological tools are utilized to their full potential. Your playbook should include a detailed change management plan, outlining steps for communication, training, and feedback collection, ensuring that every stakeholder understands their role in the new system and the benefits it brings to their work and the organization's overall performance.

Additionally, aligning your CLM playbook with broader business strategy and objectives is essential. Contracts do not exist in isolation - they are integral to the functioning of the entire organization. As such, the playbook should be designed to improve the efficiency of contract management and support strategic initiatives such as growth expansion, enhanced customer engagement, and risk management. For example, aligning contract terms with pricing strategies and customer service commitments can create a competitive edge that translates into higher customer loyalty and increased revenue. The playbook should clearly articulate how contract management supports overall business goals, linking specific processes and performance metrics with strategic outcomes. Doing so reinforces the idea that effective contract management is a key component of competitive differentiation and long-term business sustainability.

Another indispensable component of the playbook is documenting lessons learned and best practices. Over time, as you refine your process and respond to evolving challenges, a repository of insights and improvements will become an invaluable resource. This documentation serves as both a historical record and a training tool for new team members, ensuring that valuable institutional knowledge is not lost during transitions or leadership changes. Capturing best practices and maintaining an updated playbook allows for faster onboarding, consistent application of standards, and readiness for audits or performance reviews. The iterative nature of this documentation reflects a commitment to excellence—a living guide that evolves alongside the organization's needs.

In developing your CLM playbook, attention must also be paid to compliance and regulatory requirements. Maintaining compliance through standardized processes is paramount with an increasingly complex web of local, national, and international regulations. The playbook should detail how compliance is monitored, governed, and reported, ensuring that the organization is consistently prepared for regulatory audits and potential legal challenges. Embedding compliance checkpoints and clearly defined escalation procedures into the playbook safeguards the organization from legal pitfalls while reinforcing the reliability and trustworthiness of its contract management system. High compliance standards protect the organization and bolster its reputation with partners, customers, and regulators alike.

Including case studies and examples within your playbook that highlight successful adaptations and improvements is also beneficial. Anecdotes from organizations that have overcome similar challenges add credibility and provide practical insights into how theoretical frameworks can be implemented in the real world. For instance, an enterprise that reduced its contract backlog by 90% through a combination of technological integration and standardized processes offers a compelling model for replication. Such case studies serve as benchmarks, motivating teams to strive for similar results while also providing a roadmap of proven strategies and tools. Integrating these real-world examples into your playbook enables a more relatable and instructive guide for all stakeholders.

As we reflect on the multifaceted elements required for constructing a robust CLM playbook, it becomes evident that the process is as much about strategic vision and organizational culture as it is about process engineering. The playbook is not just a manual for administrative procedures—it is a strategic roadmap designed to align contract management with the organization's long-term business objectives. It encapsulates a vision where every contract is treated as an asset, every process is optimized for efficiency, and every employee from legal to finance plays a part in driving strategic outcomes.

In summary, this chapter guides you through building your own CLM playbook. This comprehensive, strategic framework integrates technological innovations, standardized processes, governance structures, and continuous improvement mechanisms into one cohesive system. The playbook serves as a blueprint for not only managing contracts more efficiently but also turning them into dynamic tools that support growth, mitigate risk, and enhance customer and stakeholder relationships. Drawing on real-world examples, data-driven methodologies, and best practices, we will outline the essential components, processes, and cultural shifts necessary to create a playbook that is both practical and transformative.

The next sections of this chapter will delve into each of these components in more detail. We will explore the steps required to map out your current contract processes, design a centralized governance and standardization plan, and implement technological solutions that integrate seamlessly with your existing systems. We will also address how to embed a culture of continuous improvement and change management into the playbook, ensuring that it evolves alongside your organization. By the end of this chapter, you will have a clear, actionable guide that not only outlines best practices but also provides the tools necessary to convert contract management from an administrative necessity into a strategic asset—a playbook that will drive efficiency, enhance compliance, and ultimately support the organization's long-term growth agenda.

The journey to building an effective CLM playbook is both challenging and rewarding. It requires a thorough understanding of the current state of your contract management processes, a commitment to change, and a willingness to invest in the necessary technology and training. However, the results speak for themselves: improved efficiencies, reduced operational risks, more favorable contract terms, and enhanced stakeholder trust all contribute to a stronger, more competitive business. With a well-crafted playbook, every contract becomes an opportunity to reinforce your organization's strategic vision and drive measurable business outcomes.

As we transition into the practical components of building your playbook, remember that this framework is not static. It should be viewed as a living document that evolves and adapts as your business grows and market conditions change. The insights and methodologies provided here are designed to empower you to take control of your contract management operations, transforming them into a key lever for operational excellence and strategic growth. This is the essence of building your CLM playbook: a commitment to continuous improvement, cross-functional collaboration, and a strategic reorientation that leverages every contract as a steppingstone to greater success.

With this foundation established, we now move forward into the detailed exploration of each element of the playbook. The subsequent sections will offer step-by-step guidance, real-world examples, and performance metrics that you can tailor to your organization's unique needs. Together, these insights will help you construct a comprehensive, actionable CLM playbook that not only streamlines operations but also fuels innovation, mitigates risk, and delivers a lasting competitive advantage.

In conclusion, building your CLM playbook is fundamental to transforming contract management into a strategic asset. Your organization can lay the groundwork for a system that drives efficiency and fosters growth through careful assessment, standardized processes, integrated technology, and ongoing cultural change. The road ahead is clear: by institutionalizing best practices and leveraging continuous improvement, you can ensure every contract is an opportunity to reinforce your strategic objectives and propel your organization forward.

⁜

- ALIGNING CONTRACT PROCESSES WITH CUSTOMER NEEDS -

Today's dynamic business landscape demands that building a comprehensive CLM playbook is emerging as a strategic necessity rather than a mere operational upgrade. As organizations recognize that well-managed contracts can fuel growth, enhance compliance, and drive revenue, the need to codify best practices, establish standardized processes, and integrate technology into every phase of the contract lifecycle becomes paramount. This subchapter lays the groundwork for such an initiative by introducing the core elements forming a CLM playbook's foundation. It presents a clear vision, anchored in practical frameworks and real-world insights, to help leaders transform fragmented contract practices into a disciplined, repeatable process that delivers measurable business results.

The first step in crafting a CLM playbook is to confront your organization's current state of contract management. A candid, thorough assessment of existing practices reveals the inefficiencies and hidden opportunities beneath daily operations. In many companies, contracts have been managed as isolated legal obligations—files scattered across diverse systems, maintained by different departments, and lacking cohesive oversight. This fragmented approach often leads to outdated terms, missed renewal dates, and uneven performance tracking. For example, consider a mid-market firm that once struggled with multiple contract versions stored in disparate folders. A lack of centralized oversight meant that strategic negotiations and timely renewals were frequently overlooked, resulting in revenue leakage and escalating compliance risks. The awakening for such companies comes when leadership recognizes these inefficiencies are not acceptable in a competitive marketplace, and that a formalized playbook can serve as the blueprint for much-needed transformation.

The diagnostic phase of your CLM playbook should involve mapping out every step of the contract lifecycle—from initiation and negotiation through execution and renewal - and identifying process bottlenecks and gaps in data governance. This baseline exercise is not solely about cataloging problems; it is about uncovering opportunities that, when addressed, can significantly enhance operational performance. For instance, when an organization audits its contract processes, it may discover that manual data entry is time-consuming and a source of repeated errors that complicate contract renewal schedules. Recognizing such issues provides the impetus to streamline workflows and integrate automated solutions. Therefore, the playbook's initial phase serves as a diagnostic tool that highlights both areas of concern and opportunities for transformation.

Once the baseline has been established, the next critical element is to design a robust governance framework. Governance in contract management extends beyond mere oversight—it's the establishment of clear roles, responsibilities, and accountability measures for every stakeholder involved. Historically, the legal department has shouldered the primary responsibility for contract management, often in isolation from other critical functions such as finance, procurement, and customer service. However, a modern, strategic approach requires that these functions work collaboratively. By developing a formal governance structure, organizations ensure that every contract decision is aligned with broader business objectives. For example, a large multinational restructured its contract management process by forming a cross-functional committee that included legal, finance, and sales representatives. This committee met periodically to review contract performance metrics, recalibrate negotiation tactics, and update compliance protocols based on market trends. The outcome was a markedly improved transparency and accountability, reducing manual oversight failures and financial risk.

Central to the governance framework is the creation of standardized processes. Establishing standard operating procedures (SOPs) for contract management helps create consistency and efficiency across the board. These SOPs dictate every step, from how contracts should be drafted and reviewed to the criteria that trigger escalations or automated alerts for renewals. For instance, implementing a checklist-driven review process can ensure that essential components such as compliance reviews, risk assessments, and pricing benchmarks are consistently completed. One organization introduced a digital checklist that automatically flagged missing clauses or inconsistent terms during the review process; as a result, their contract approval time decreased significantly, and overall contract quality improved. Standardized processes eliminate variability and redundant efforts, ensuring that every contract meets a defined quality standard and supports the organization's strategic goals.

Integrating advanced technology is indispensable to moving from a documented process to a dynamic one. Modern contract lifecycle management systems offer more than digital storage solutions—they provide automated workflows, real-time analytics, and seamless integration with other enterprise systems like ERP and CRM. These technologies transform the contract from a static document into a living, adaptive instrument. With automated systems, tasks such as sending renewal reminders, tracking key performance indicators (KPIs), and generating preliminary drafts of contract amendments can occur with minimal human intervention. For example, one company integrated its CLM system with its financial software, enabling real-time tracking of obligations and revenues related to contract performance. This kind of integration allowed them to negotiate more favorable terms by identifying areas where existing agreements were underperforming and adjusting accordingly. Therefore, the technology improves efficiency and serves as a strategic tool, empowering decision-makers with actionable insights.

In parallel with integrating technology, a rigorous focus on continuous improvement must be built into the playbook. The market, technology, and internal business dynamics are constantly evolving, so a static process will quickly become outdated. The system achieves Continuous improvement by embedding feedback loops and performance metrics. Establishing KPIs—such as contract cycle times, compliance metrics, renewal ratios, and revenue captured through renegotiations—provides a way to measure success and adjust processes in real time. For instance, by monitoring the average time to execute contracts, an organization can identify and eliminate bottlenecks, further reducing delays and enhancing productivity. Regular reviews of these metrics create a culture of excellence, where every stakeholder is motivated to optimize their contributions continuously. This feedback-driven approach ensures that your CLM playbook remains relevant, nimble, and aligned with evolving business priorities.

Change management is an essential, yet often underestimated, component of building your playbook. The most meticulously designed processes and technologies can be ineffective if the organization does not buy into the change. The transition from ad hoc, fragmented contract practices to a unified, strategic process requires a shift in mindset. Every employee involved, from legal teams to sales representatives, must understand the strategic rationale and see the tangible benefits of an integrated approach. Effective change management includes comprehensive training programs, clear communication of the playbook's benefits, and establishing cross-functional working groups to facilitate adoption. For example, companies that have invested in change management initiatives report higher user adoption rates of new CLM tools and a more enthusiastic embrace of standardized practices. When employees are engaged and understand that these changes enhance their productivity, the overall organizational culture shifts, making the playbook a living document that evolves with the company.

The CLM playbook must also address the regulatory and compliance dimensions inherent in contract management. Maintaining compliance is not optional in an increasingly complex regulatory environment. It is a critical business imperative. The playbook should outline detailed procedures for compliance monitoring, risk assessments, and the documentation of audit trails. Incorporating automated compliance checks within the CLM system can reduce non-compliance risk and protect the organization from legal pitfalls. For instance, an automated system can flag contracts that deviate from standard clauses known to be in line with regulatory requirements, prompting immediate review. Not only does this proactive approach prevent costly penalties, but it also reinforces the organization's reputation for reliability and diligence in managing its contractual obligations.

Beyond internal processes and compliance, your playbook should foster a customer-centric orientation. As we have discussed in previous chapters, contracts that are managed effectively not only mitigate risk but also enhance customer satisfaction. A customer-centric playbook considers the customer's end-to-end experience and seeks to align contract terms with customer needs and expectations. This could involve setting flexible performance benchmarks or including service-level commitments that build trust and drive long-term loyalty. For example, a company might adjust contract terms periodically based on customer feedback and performance data, ensuring the agreements remain relevant and mutually beneficial. By embedding customer-centric elements into your playbook, you position contracts as strategic tools that support internal efficiency and external competitive differentiation.

Documenting lessons learned and best practices as part of your CLM playbook is also valuable. As your organization implements new processes and technologies, building a repository of insights gained from real-world applications will prove invaluable. This repository serves multiple purposes: it functions as a training tool for new team members, it provides a historical record of process evolution, and it lays the foundation for future improvements. For instance, documenting a successful negotiation strategy that led to more favorable terms or identifying recurring challenges that necessitated a process tweak can ensure that such knowledge is not lost and can be leveraged moving forward. This continuous capture of best practices fosters a culture where excellence is expected and rewarded.

In addition to strategic process design and technical integration, a successful CLM playbook must reinforce the need for proactive vendor and partner management. Contracts often serve as the primary interface between your organization and external stakeholders. Therefore, ensuring that these agreements meet internal standards and promote robust external relationships is crucial. Your playbook should include protocols for regular vendor reviews, performance evaluations, and renegotiation strategies aligned with shifting market conditions. By establishing these protocols, the playbook becomes a comprehensive guide that streamlines internal processes and contributes to building lasting and mutually beneficial relationships. This dual focus—internal efficiency and external partnership—creates a competitive advantage that is hard to replicate.

The journey to building a comprehensive CLM playbook is undoubtedly complex, but the rewards are substantial. Each element—from the initial process audit and governance framework to technology integration, continuous improvement, and change management—contributes to transforming contract management from a reactive, fragmented task into a strategic engine for growth. The playbook is, in essence, the roadmap that guides an organization toward operational excellence and competitive differentiation. It encapsulates the best practices, and the cultural and strategic shifts needed to integrate contract management into the business's fabric.

As you embark on this transformation, remember that the playbook is a living document. The business environment is ever changing, and the playbook must evolve to incorporate new insights, technologies, and market conditions. Regular reviews, updates, and training sessions ensure the playbook aligns with organizational goals. Continuous refinement will help establish a resilient and adaptive contract management system that supports short-term operational gains and long-term strategic objectives.

In conclusion, the first subchapter of this chapter sets the stage for building your CLM playbook by emphasizing the critical foundations required for success. It begins with an honest assessment of current practices, moves through the design of a robust governance framework and standardized processes, highlights the central role of technological integration, and underscores the importance of continuous improvement and change management. Organizations can construct a clear, structured, and dynamic playbook that transforms contract management into a strategic asset by setting these fundamental elements in place. This plays a pivotal role in mitigating risk, capturing hidden revenue, fostering cross-functional collaboration, and enhancing customer satisfaction.

The insights and examples provided here illustrate that a well-crafted CLM playbook is a tool for operational efficiency and a strategic framework that can propel your organization forward in an increasingly competitive and agile market. With a solid foundation in this initial phase, you can delve deeper into the practical steps and detailed methodologies that will eventually form the complete playbook. The journey ahead is both challenging and rewarding, but it promises substantial returns in improved efficiency, risk management, and overall business performance.

As we transition to the subsequent sections of this chapter, we will explore each component of the playbook in greater detail—mapping out current processes, designing governance and operational standards, and integrating cutting-edge technologies. With a clear and actionable roadmap laid out before you, the path to transforming your contract management function becomes apparent and achievable. This is the beginning of a transformative process that will convert every contract from a mere administrative document into a vibrant, strategic asset—one that drives growth, fuels innovation, and sustains competitive advantage in an ever-evolving business landscape.

※

- BUILDING CUSTOMER RELATIONSHIPS THROUGH EFFECTIVE CLM -

As organizations set out to transform their contract management function through a comprehensive CLM playbook, a detailed analysis of each component becomes essential to unlocking tangible benefits. In this section, we delve into the deeper layers of the playbook's design, exploring how standardized processes, robust governance, technological integration, and continuous improvement coalesce to create a dynamic and strategic system. Each element is a standalone improvement and interlocks with the others to form an ecosystem that drives efficiency, mitigates risk, and supports growth.

One of the cornerstones of a solid CLM playbook is the establishment of standardized processes. In many organizations, contract management has historically been *ad hoc*, with each department following its own procedures. This variability leads to inconsistent practices, duplicated efforts, and gaps in oversight. By developing standard operating procedures (SOPs), companies set a uniform framework everyone adheres to, reducing the risk of errors and enhancing overall quality. For instance, a common practice involves using digital checklists for contract review. These checklists ensure that every contract is evaluated according to pre-determined criteria - whether compliance with regulatory standards, verification of key clauses, or confirmation that negotiation benchmarks have been met. The consistency of such standardization means that, regardless of who reviews the contract, the result always aligns with the organization's quality standards.

Standardization extends beyond checklists. It encompasses mapping the entire contract lifecycle—from initiation and drafting to negotiation, execution, and eventual renewal or termination. Documenting every step in this cycle allows organizations to identify bottlenecks and redundancies. For many companies, the diagnostic phase reveals that manual data entry, repetitive reviews, and fragmented approvals are common culprits behind delays and inefficiencies. Once these pain points are identified and documented, they can form the basis for designing streamlined workflows. A detailed process map clarifies roles and responsibilities and establishes clear timelines for each stage. When every stakeholder knows precisely what is expected and by when, delays become the exception rather than the norm.

Complementing standardized processes is the need for a robust governance framework. In this context, governance is establishing clear roles, responsibilities, and accountability measures that span all relevant departments. Traditionally, contract management has been siloed within legal departments; however, modern best practices demand a cross-functional approach. By developing a governance structure—perhaps in the form of a cross-departmental committee or a dedicated CLM team—organizations ensure that every contract decision is made with input from key stakeholders such as finance, procurement, sales, and even customer service. A well-defined governance framework signals that contract management is not the sole domain of one team but instead is a shared responsibility. This collaborative approach improves transparency in contract negotiations and embeds the process within the broader strategic objectives of the organization.

For example, consider an organization that implemented a governance model whereby quarterly review meetings were held with representatives from legal, finance, and operational departments. In these meetings, the team reviewed performance metrics, discussed risk exposures, and evaluated contract terms in the context of market conditions. Not only did this approach result in more effective negotiations, but it also fostered a culture of shared ownership and engagement. Each department's voice was considered, creating more nuanced contract terms that balanced risk and opportunity. This collective responsibility is the cornerstone of sustainable contract performance.

Integrating technology is another decisive factor in building a practical CLM playbook. The evolution of contract lifecycle management systems has transformed them from digital repositories into powerful, integrated platforms that automate routine tasks and provide data-driven insights. These systems facilitate real-time tracking of contract milestones, automatic alerts for events such as upcoming renewals, and seamless integration with other enterprise systems like ERP and CRM. For instance, a company integrating its CLM software with financial systems can instantly reconcile contract performance data against revenue projections. This integration offers a holistic view of the organization's economic health and helps identify areas where contract terms might be renegotiated for better margins.

Automated workflows, one of the most practical aspects of technology integration, minimize the likelihood of human error and free up critical human resources. Instead of spending hours on manual reviews or data entry, employees can focus on strategic tasks such as analyzing contract performance or negotiating improved terms. Take the example of a multinational enterprise that reduced its contract processing time by implementing automated alerts for key renewal dates. The system flagged contracts approaching expiration and integrated historical performance data to suggest optimal renegotiation dates. Such proactive insights empower managers to take timely actions to recover revenue and reduce risk.

Data analytics, supported by these integrated systems, adds another layer of strategic value. Organizations can identify recurring trends that signal risk or missed opportunities by examining past contract performance. Analytics can uncover patterns, for instance, if particular types of contracts reliably result in revenue leakage or if specific clauses lead to frequent disputes. Armed with this information, companies can standardize better terms or adjust pricing models to capture value previously left on the table. Over time, the predictive capabilities of data analytics evolve, allowing the organization to shift from a reactive stance to a proactive strategy in contract management. This continuous loop of data, analysis, and adjustment creates an environment where every contract is viewed as both a current asset and a future opportunity.

While technology paves the way for these improvements, continuous improvement is indispensable for ensuring that the CLM playbook remains relevant. The volatile nature of business environments means today's best practices may need to be updated tomorrow. Organizations should embed performance metrics and feedback loops into their contract management processes to keep pace. KPIs such as contract cycle time, renewal rates, compliance adherence, and the revenue impact of renegotiated terms provide quantifiable benchmarks that can be reviewed regularly. For instance, a technology company might track its contract turnaround time monthly to spot any emerging inefficiencies. If metrics indicate that processing time is creeping upward, the team can investigate and refine the workflow before it becomes a significant issue.

Establishing a sustainable culture of continuous improvement also requires organizations to document lessons learned and best practices. Over time, the institution accrues valuable insights from both successes and setbacks. By capturing these experiences in internal documentation or a centralized knowledge base, the organization creates a living record that can serve as a reference for future training and process refinement. Not only does this practice enhance operational consistency, but it also contributes to a culture of innovation and adaptability. New employees gain access to tried-and-true methods, while veteran staff can build upon past experiences to drive further enhancements.

Equally important is the human element in this cycle of continuous improvement. Change management strategies must be employed to ensure that every organization member, whether legal, financial, or operational, is aligned with the new processes and committed to their continuous evolution. Comprehensive training programs and open lines of communication help to overcome resistance and ensure that the workforce fully embraces technological and process enhancements. Examples from organizations that have successfully adopted a continuous improvement mindset show that when employees understand that their daily tasks are being streamlined and that their input directly influences operational performance, overall job satisfaction and efficiency improve markedly.

Moreover, the role of compliance in the playbook cannot be overlooked. As regulatory requirements become increasingly complex, maintaining compliance through standardized processes is critical to mitigating legal risks. A well-designed CLM playbook outlines clear procedures for regulatory checks and audit trails, ensuring that every contract meets the necessary legal parameters. Automated compliance monitoring tools can be integrated into the system to flag any deviations from standard clauses known to meet regulatory standards. This proactive approach prevents costly fines and reinforces the organization's reputation for diligence and transparency. When embedded seamlessly into the CLM playbook, regulatory compliance protects the organization while supporting its strategic objectives.

Beyond internal efficiencies and compliance, the CLM playbook must be designed with a customer-centric focus. Modern contract management recognizes that contracts are about protecting the organization and enhancing the customer experience. A customer-centric playbook considers factors such as transparency, responsiveness, and flexibility. For example, contracts might be structured to allow periodic reviews and adjustments based on customer feedback and market dynamics. This approach ensures that contractual terms remain mutually beneficial and continue to align with the customer's evolving needs. In practice, companies that have incorporated customer-centric principles have seen improved customer retention rates and stronger, trust-based relationships with their partners. By positioning contracts to enhance customer satisfaction, the playbook transforms them from static documents into dynamic, value-creating assets.

Integration of vendor management protocols further enriches the playbook. Contracts often represent the primary touchpoint between an organization and its external partners. Standardizing methods for vendor reviews, establishing clear performance metrics, and scheduling regular renegotiations ensure that contracts continue to serve the dual purpose of minimizing risk and capturing value. A well-designed playbook might include structured protocols for evaluating vendor performance, enabling the organization to adjust contract terms in response to changing conditions. This strategic engagement with vendors streamlines internal processes and builds a foundation for robust, long-term partnerships.

To summarize this in-depth analysis, the second subchapter of this chapter emphasizes that constructing a CLM playbook is a multifaceted process that requires a balanced integration of standardization, governance, technology, continuous improvement, human collaboration, compliance adherence, and customer-centric practices. While powerful, each element forms an integral part of a comprehensive framework designed to transform contract management into a strategic asset. The process begins with an honest assessment of current practices and follows through with establishing standardized procedures and robust governance frameworks. It then leverages technological advancements and data analytics to automate processes and inform decision-making. Finally, it embeds a continuous improvement and cross-functional collaboration culture, ensuring that the playbook aligns with the organization's strategic goals.

Organizations implementing such a playbook successfully experience measurable benefits—reduced processing times, improved contract quality, decreased risk exposure, and enhanced revenue capture. Real-world examples demonstrate that with a well-constructed playbook, what once was a fragmented and reactive process becomes a proactive, integrated system. Over time, these cumulative improvements unlock significant competitive advantages, reinforcing the concept that contracts are not just administrative tasks but are, in fact, cornerstones of the enterprise's strategic framework.

The insights drawn from this analysis are not theoretical abstractions; they are grounded in the real-world experiences of organizations that have transformed their contract management practices. The ability to pivot quickly in response to market shifts, increase operational efficiency, and nurture stronger vendor and customer relationships are all outcomes that attest to the effectiveness of a well-executed CLM playbook. As industries evolve and business conditions become ever more challenging, the organizations that have embedded these practices into their operational fabric are the ones that not only survive but thrive.

In conclusion, building a comprehensive CLM playbook is a challenging yet gratifying process. It requires a deep commitment to reengineering processes, investing in advanced technologies, fostering a collaborative culture, and continuously monitoring performance against well-defined benchmarks. The analysis presented here illustrates that every element—from standardized procedures to integrated technological platforms—plays a critical role in creating a resilient, agile, and strategically aligned contract management system. This integrated approach mitigates risks and transforms contracts into tools for proactive revenue enhancement and customer satisfaction. As you reflect on these insights, it becomes clear that the transformation of contract management is integral to building a sustainable competitive advantage that drives operational excellence and supports long-term growth.

With these principles firmly established, the next phase of our discussion will move into the practical methodologies and step-by-step strategies for implementing this playbook within your organization. The goal is to provide actionable guidance that demonstrates how to standardize and optimize your contract processes and measure success through continuous improvement initiatives, ensuring that every contract contributes to your organization's strategic vision.

⁙

- CREATING VALUE WITH CUSTOMER-FOCUSED STRATEGIES -

Throughout this chapter, we have systematically built the foundation for establishing a robust CLM playbook that transforms contract management from a fragmented, ad hoc process into a strategic, integrated engine that drives efficiency, mitigates risk, and unlocks hidden revenue. As we conclude this fourth chapter, it is essential to reflect on the insights discussed and to clearly articulate how these elements converge to form a dynamic framework, a blueprint for organizations determined to extract maximum value from every contract.

The discussion began by confronting the challenges of legacy contract practices—isolated systems, inconsistent processes, and a lack of unified oversight, all contributing to missed renewal opportunities, compliance risks, and revenue leakage. Recognizing these inefficiencies was the first step that compelled organizations to reassess their internal practices. The diagnostic phase provided a clear picture of the current state, underscoring the opportunities for improvement hidden within everyday inefficiencies. This introspective analysis revealed recurring issues such as manual data entry errors, decentralized contract repositories, and ambiguous responsibilities that often lead to delays and suboptimal contract terms.

From there, the emphasis shifted to forming a robust governance framework. We saw how traditional siloed approaches were replaced by a collaborative, cross-functional model whereby every stakeholder, from legal and finance to procurement and customer service, shares responsibility in overseeing the entire contract lifecycle. In doing so, organizations achieved greater transparency and accountability and fostered a culture of shared ownership. For example, when a multinational engaged representatives across departments to form a regular review committee, it resulted in better-aligned strategic decisions and more responsive contract negotiations. This governance structure is not just an administrative mandate but a strategic tool ensuring every contractual decision moves the organization closer to its overarching business goals.

Standardized processes emerged as another critical pillar of the playbook. Establishing clear, documented standard operating procedures across each phase of the contract lifecycle—from drafting and negotiation through execution and renewal—ensures that every contract is processed consistently and efficiently. Standardization minimizes human error and eliminates redundant steps. One organization's experience implementing a digital review checklist demonstrated how this approach reduced approval times, improved contract quality, and reinforced internal accountability. With standardized protocols in place, organizations can benefit from enhanced predictability, strengthening internal planning and external stakeholder confidence.

The transformative power of technology was also deeply analyzed. Modern contract lifecycle management systems have evolved from simple document storage solutions into sophisticated, integrated platforms that automate routine tasks and provide actionable, real-time analytics. These systems offer functionalities, such as automated alerts for impending renewals, tracking key performance indicators, and seamless integration with ERP and CRM platforms, that convert static contracts into living tools. Such technological enhancements drastically reduce manual workload, allow for predictive risk management, and enable organizations to capture incremental revenue improvements that would otherwise be overlooked. One multinational enterprise's success in reducing contract processing time through automation, thereby recovering significant lost revenue, is a powerful testament to what integrated technology can achieve.

In parallel with technological integration, continuous improvement received considerable attention. The volatile nature of market dynamics, regulatory environments, and internal business priorities demands that contract management practices remain fluid and adaptable. Embedding feedback loops and establishing key performance indicators enable organizations to monitor their progress and swiftly adjust processes when needed. This cycle of measurement and refinement cultivates a culture where every stakeholder is invested in achieving operational excellence. Organizations that adopt such proactive measures see tangible improvements in contract turnaround times and overall revenue capture, risk mitigation, and customer satisfaction.

The cultural and change management aspects underpinning this transformation were characterized as equally important. Even the most meticulously designed processes and technological systems can fall short if the human element is neglected. The successful adoption of a new CLM playbook requires a shift in mindset across the entire organization. Employees must be brought on board through transparent communication, comprehensive training programs, and ongoing support. When staff at every level understand the strategic rationale behind a unified, cross-functional approach to contract management, they are better equipped to contribute to its evolution. Real-life examples highlighted in this chapter illustrate that companies investing in robust change management initiatives experience higher user adoption rates of CLM tools and build an enduring culture of continuous improvement and shared responsibility.

Compliance and regulatory adherence were also integrated into the playbook, emphasizing that a practical contract management framework must streamline internal operations and safeguard the organization against potential legal pitfalls. Automated compliance monitoring tools and clearly defined audit trails ensure that all contracts adhere to relevant statutes and industry-specific regulations, thus protecting the organization from costly penalties and reputational damage. By weaving compliance into every stage of the contract lifecycle, organizations solidify their reputation as diligent, trustworthy market players, significantly enhancing stakeholder confidence.

A customer-centric philosophy also played a vital role in shaping the CLM playbook. Recognizing that contracts are the primary touchpoints between an organization and its customers, the playbook must incorporate principles that enhance transparency, responsiveness, and flexibility. Structuring contracts for periodic reviews, adjustments based on customer feedback, and alignment with service levels transforms them from static documents into dynamic instruments that protect the organization's interests and promote enduring, mutually beneficial relationships. In practice, companies that have embedded such customer-centric elements into their contractual processes report improved customer retention and increased trust, which are crucial in sustaining long-term competitive advantage.

Furthermore, the playbook's design stresses capturing lessons learned and documenting best practices. Over time, organizations accumulate invaluable insights from successes and setbacks in their contract management journey. Creating a centralized repository of these lessons facilitates continuous learning and accelerates the adoption of new process refinements. Such documentation serves as a training resource for new employees and a strategic tool that ensures the organization remains agile and responsive to changes in both the internal environment and the broader market.

Vendor management protocols were also seamlessly integrated into the CLM playbook. Recognizing that contracts are the primary interfaces with external partners, the playbook should incorporate clear methods for ongoing vendor evaluations and structured renegotiations. Establishing these protocols ensures contracts align with current market conditions and internal performance standards. This dual focus—internal process optimization coupled with strengthening external partnerships—reinforces the idea that a well-crafted CLM playbook is a comprehensive guide, addressing every aspect of contract management to support the organization's strategic objectives.

In reflecting on the comprehensive analysis of these critical components—standardization, governance, technological integration, continuous improvement, change management, compliance, customer-centricity, and vendor management—it becomes evident that the CLM playbook is far more than a procedural manual. It represents a strategic roadmap aligning contract management with the organization's vision and long-term goals. The cumulative effect of implementing these interconnected elements is a profound transformation in how contracts are perceived and leveraged. Instead of being viewed as static, burdensome documents, contracts emerge as dynamic assets that propel growth, drive efficiency, and foster innovation.

This chapter discusses real-world examples and case studies that reinforce these insights. Organizations that have adopted comprehensive CLM playbooks report significant improvements in operational efficiency, with noticeable reductions in processing times and error rates. These organizations also report enhanced revenue capture attributed to more favorable contract terms. These examples provide concrete evidence that a strategically aligned contract management system is achievable and essential for maintaining a competitive edge in today's fast-paced business environment.

As we conclude this chapter, several key insights must be underscored. First, the importance of a thoroughly assessed baseline cannot be overstated—only by understanding the current state of contract management can organizations identify and capitalize on opportunities for improvement. Second, a governance framework fostering cross-functional collaboration is critical to ensuring contract management aligns with broader strategic objectives. Third, integrating cutting-edge technology and automating routine tasks transforms contract management from a reactive process into a proactive, data-driven function. Fourth, embedding a culture of continuous improvement and robust change management ensures that the playbook remains dynamic and responsive to evolving market conditions and internal shifts. And finally, a commitment to compliance, customer-centric practices, and proactive vendor management enhances operational performance and the organization's market reputation and strategic positioning.

These conclusions form the foundation for the next phase in our narrative journey. Having laid out a comprehensive blueprint for building a CLM playbook, we are poised to move into a new chapter focused on customer-centric contracting. In the upcoming discussions, we will explore how aligning contract management practices with customer needs streamlines internal operations and drives external competitive advantage. We will delve into the strategies, frameworks, and case studies that reveal how organizations can design contracts responsive to customer expectations and capable of driving long-term loyalty.

The journey through this chapter serves as a reminder that the transformation of contract management requires a holistic approach that integrates process improvements, technology, cultural change, and strategic alignment. As we transition to the next chapter, our focus will shift from internal process optimization to external value creation. We will examine how customer-centric contract strategies lead to improved satisfaction, enhanced service delivery, and sustainable growth.

In summary, the insights and methodologies presented in this chapter articulate a clear and compelling vision for transforming contract management into a strategic asset. A well-designed CLM playbook is not an end; it is a continuously evolving system that supports strategic decision-making, improves operational efficiency, and drives revenue growth. It is a living document that reflects the cumulative learnings, technological advancements, and process optimizations implemented over time. With this framework in place, organizations are better equipped to navigate an increasingly complex and competitive business landscape.

As we close this chapter, take with you the understanding that each element of the playbook—from initial diagnostics and governance to technology integration and continuous improvement—works to transform outdated practices into a coherent, strategic system. This transformation is not just about internal efficiency; it is about positioning the organization to capitalize on every opportunity, mitigate risk comprehensively, and create lasting competitive differentiation. The next phase of our discussion will build on this foundation, exploring how a shift toward a customer-centric approach in contracting enhances internal processes and drives external growth and market success.

With a comprehensive CLM playbook established, organizations can confidently turn every contract into a potent strategic asset—a lever for operational excellence and long-term value creation. As we move forward, these insights will continue to guide our exploration of customer-centric strategies and their role in sustaining growth. The road ahead is defined by continuous innovation, strategic alignment, and a relentless focus on transforming challenges into opportunities.

CHAPTER 5:

BUILDING YOUR CLM PLAYBOOK

As organizations evolve their contract management capabilities into strategic assets, a critical question arises: What technology and tools are essential to support this transformation, and which ones merely add unnecessary complexity? In today's competitive landscape, the proper technological foundation streamlines contractual processes and empowers decision-makers with real-time data and actionable insights, contributing directly to growth and enhanced customer relationships. This chapter, focused on technology and tools, aims to demystify the options available, helping leaders discern what is needed and what should be set aside, and to provide a clear, data-driven roadmap for integrating these capabilities into a modern contract management strategy.

Over recent years, many organizations have experienced firsthand the pitfalls of relying on outdated systems that offered little more than digital storage. I recall the case of a mid-market company, long recognized for its operational excellence, which found its contract repository cluttered with disparate documents and lacking a cohesive structure. What began as a simple document management challenge soon escalated into missed renewal dates and a surge in compliance issues. With mounting revenue leakage and an increasing gap between contractual commitments and operational realities, the leadership eventually invested in a more integrated, automated contract management system. The result was transformative: not only did the new system streamline contract processing, it also provided real-time insights that empowered cross-departmental teams to negotiate better terms and proactively adjust strategies. This anecdote underscores a fundamental truth—when chosen and implemented with a clear strategy in mind, technology can convert static legal documents into dynamic instruments for business growth.

The purpose of this chapter is twofold. First, it comprehensively reviews the available technological solutions that can elevate the contract management function. We will examine various categories, from contract lifecycle management (CLM) platforms and automation tools to emerging technologies like artificial intelligence and machine learning applied in contract analytics. Each tool's capabilities, limitations, and compatibility with a broader enterprise ecosystem will be scrutinized. Second, the chapter offers practical guidance on integrating these tools within organizational processes. Rather than taking a one-size-fits-all approach, the discussion is geared toward helping decision-makers understand how to align technology investments with their specific strategic goals and operational requirements.

A key insight to consider is that technology should serve as an enabler, not as a substitute for a well-defined strategic vision. In previous chapters, we have explored how standardizing processes and establishing robust governance frameworks can lay the groundwork for improved contract management. However, even the best-designed systems may fall short without the appropriate tools to implement these processes. For example, automation in routine tasks such as data entry, scheduling of renewals, or compliance tracking is crucial, reducing human error and freeing up valuable time for strategic initiatives. Similarly, real-time dashboards and integrated analytics platforms allow organizations to monitor key performance indicators across the contract lifecycle, helping to ensure that decision-makers have immediate access to insights that can prevent missed opportunities.

Several case studies illustrate the profound impact of adopting the right technology. One multinational organization, for instance, integrated its CLM system with its enterprise resource planning (ERP) software. Before integration, the company often experienced delays in reconciling contract payments and documenting compliance metrics, issues that individually seemed minor but collectively contributed to a sluggish response to market changes. After integrating these systems, the organization benefited from automated alerts warning of upcoming critical dates, instant summaries of contract performance, and even predictive insights that indicated which contracts were on the verge of delivering additional revenue or risk. The integration improved operational efficiency and enhanced stakeholder confidence, proving that technology is instrumental in transforming the contract function into a living component of corporate strategy.

Yet, with an ever-expanding market of technological solutions, leaders encounter the challenge of discerning between what is truly needed and what may be superfluous. Not every shiny new tool delivers value in every context. The chapter will discuss common pitfalls, such as over-complicating systems with unnecessary features or investing in standalone tools that do not integrate well with existing systems. In doing so, the discussion will guide readers through a framework for evaluating technology based on scalability, ease of integration, user-friendliness, and return on investment. This framework ensures that technology enhances rather than complicates existing workflows.

Furthermore, as organizations adopt more sophisticated technologies, the interplay between human expertise and technological capability becomes increasingly important. Advanced tools, such as AI-driven contract analytics, can revolutionize how contracts are managed by revealing trends and anomalies that may not be apparent to even the most diligent teams. However, successfully adopting such tools requires that employees are adequately trained to interpret and leverage the data provided. Change management in this regard becomes a critical component of technological implementation. Leaders must ensure that training programs and support structures are in place so that technology complements human judgment rather than overwhelming it. In many cases, the benefits of these tools are fully realized only when they are harmoniously integrated into the daily routines of cross-functional teams.

The technology discussion also extends to the realm of compliance and risk management. In an era of evolving regulatory landscapes and increasing scrutiny, the need for tools that monitor contract adherence to legal and regulatory requirements has never been greater. Automated compliance checks and digital audit trails not only reduce the likelihood of costly breaches but also provide a robust framework for proactive risk management. For example, automated systems can flag contracts that deviate from established compliance standards, prompting immediate review and rectification before minor issues escalate into major liabilities. This proactive approach provides organizations with a safety net, reinforcing their reputation as diligent, well-managed enterprises—an essential factor in building both customer and partner trust.

It is instructive to note that many companies have experienced a dramatic turnaround after optimizing their technology landscape within contract management. After a lengthy period of grappling with manual processes and sporadic tool implementation, one large organization undertook a comprehensive technology evaluation. The company reduced its contract processing cycle by nearly 40% by carefully aligning new solutions with its process improvement initiatives. The benefits extended well beyond time savings; the improved system led to more accurate forecasts of revenue leakage and more strategic negotiations with suppliers and customers alike. These successes illustrate that when technology is effectively leveraged, it becomes a strategic asset, turning potential vulnerabilities into competitive advantages.

The chapter's exploration of technology and tools will review existing solutions and address how these technologies fit within the broader strategic narrative of contract management. It emphasizes that technology should be selected and implemented based on clear strategic imperatives rather than as an isolated, standalone project. Aircraft manufacturers, for example, have long relied on advanced analytics to manage complex supply chains and production timetables. Similarly, forward-thinking companies in our field use data integration and automation to bring precision and agility to every stage of the contract lifecycle. By drawing parallels between these sectors, we underscore the idea that harnessing technology is a key factor differentiating industry leaders from those mired in traditional practices.

The journey toward embracing enhanced technology in contract management also requires a central focus on interoperability. In today's interconnected business environment, contracts rarely exist in isolation. They form part of larger ecosystems, interfacing with supply chain management, customer relationship platforms, and financial systems. Therefore, a truly effective CLM solution must seamlessly integrate with these adjacent systems, ensuring that data flows freely and accurately throughout the organization. This integration paves the way for more informed decision-making and enables a holistic view of contract performance. Imagine a scenario where contract data seamlessly informs budgeting decisions, supplier negotiations, and customer service improvements—all in real time. Such integration is not merely an operational improvement; it represents a strategic leap forward that can redefine how an organization competes in the marketplace.

Another dimension covered in this chapter is the importance of scalability and flexibility in technology investments. As businesses grow, the number and complexity of contracts typically increase. Systems that work well for a small portfolio may struggle with a rapidly expanding contract base. Therefore, it is critical to choose scalable solutions that are capable of growing within the organization and flexible enough to adapt to new business models and regulatory requirements. Strategic technology investments should be future-proofed to the extent possible, ensuring they remain relevant even as market conditions evolve. This approach requires forward-thinking and a willingness to update or overhaul systems periodically—a process built into the continuous improvement cycle we have discussed extensively.

As our analysis continues, we will also explore emerging trends in contract management technology. Trends such as artificial intelligence, machine learning, and blockchain are beginning to reshape our approach to contractual data security, negotiation analytics, and the verification of contract authenticity. While these technologies may still be on the horizon for some organizations, understanding their potential benefits and limitations is essential for leaders aiming to craft a future-proof CLM strategy. Early adopters in various industries have demonstrated that even modest implementations of these advanced technologies can yield significant competitive advantages. Integrating these innovations within a thoughtful, strategically aligned playbook can further accelerate the transformation of contract management from a reactive process to a proactive, intelligent system.

In conclusion, this subchapter has provided a detailed examination of the key technological factors that underpin a successful CLM playbook. Standardized processes, robust governance frameworks, advanced integration of digital tools, and a commitment to continuous improvement all work together to create a dynamic, efficient, and responsive contract management system. The case examples and practical insights discussed here underscore that when the right technology is aligned with a clear strategic vision, it can transform contract management from a burden into a strategic asset. This digital transformation enhances operational efficiency and compliance and paves the way for better revenue capture and risk management.

By taking a holistic view of technology in contract management, organizations can move beyond sporadic, isolated improvements and develop a comprehensive system that supports their overall business strategy. The interplay between human expertise and automated tools has never been more critical, and this integration is the key to unlocking the full potential of contract management. As you continue to evaluate and implement technological solutions, remember that when appropriately selected and integrated, each tool contributes to a broader, more cohesive system that drives competitive advantage and sustainable growth.

The analysis presented here is a call to action and a roadmap for decision-makers. It invites leaders to critically assess their current technological infrastructure, identify gaps and inefficiencies, and invest in solutions that align with their strategic objectives. With the right tools in place, the contract management function can be transformed into a powerful engine for operational excellence—one that is agile, data-driven, and firmly embedded within the organization's broader operational framework.

As we transition into the next subchapter, where we will delve further into the practical methodologies for integrating these technologies and tools into your existing processes, remember that technology is only one element of the overall puzzle. Its true potential is realized when it is harmonized with standardized processes, robust governance, and a relentless focus on continuous improvement. Together, these elements form the backbone of a

CLM playbook that addresses today's challenges and anticipates tomorrow's opportunities.

The insights provided in this section should serve as a foundation for rethinking how technology can be leveraged to transform contract management from a static repository into a dynamic strategic asset. With detailed analysis, real-world examples, and an overview of emerging trends, we have set the stage for the next steps in building a comprehensive, effective CLM playbook. The journey toward digital transformation in contract management is complex, but the rewards—improved efficiency, enhanced compliance, stronger risk management, and greater revenue capture—are well worth the effort.

In summary, this subchapter underscores the critical role of technology in building a modern, efficient contract management system. It provides a thoughtful examination of the processes, tools, and strategic considerations that are essential for integrating technology into the CLM playbook, and it highlights how these elements together can drive remarkable improvements in organizational performance. As we continue our exploration, the next section will offer pragmatic guidance on implementing these technological solutions effectively, ensuring that every contract is managed with precision, speed, and strategic insight.

※

- DEVELOPING PRACTICAL FRAMEWORKS AND STEPS -

Advancing into the realm of contract management technology, it becomes clear that this chapter is not merely about introducing a suite of modern software tools but about fundamentally rethinking how technological innovation can drive strategic decision-making. This subchapter explores new concepts reshaping the contract management landscape, particularly the convergence of automation, data analytics, artificial intelligence, and integration. These innovations are no longer isolated features; they are core elements embedded in a unified system designed to transform how organizations approach and utilize contracts.

At its core, the digital transformation of contract management is about streamlining processes and removing inefficiencies that have long plagued traditional approaches. In many organizations, contracts are managed through outdated practices emphasizing manual data entry, siloed storage, and reactive oversight. By contrast, modern technological solutions are designed to create a proactive environment in which every contract, every clause, and every renewal date is monitored in real time. This shift is not simply about speed—it is about creating a framework in which technology works with human expertise to foster strategic insights and drive value.

One emerging concept that merits particular attention is automation. Automation replaces repetitive, manual tasks with computer-driven processes that execute predefined actions without human intervention. For instance, consider the process of contract renewals: through automation, a system can be configured to automatically send alerts to relevant team members when a contract is nearing its expiration date. Not only does this save countless hours otherwise spent on tracking deadlines, but it also minimizes the risk of oversight. I recall a case involving a regional corporation that previously encountered significant revenue leakage due to missed contract renewals. After implementing an automated alert system integrated with their contract lifecycle management (CLM) platform, they reported an immediate 30% improvement in timely renewals, accompanied by a measurable recovery in potential revenue. Such examples highlight how automation underpins both efficiency and revenue protection.

Yet, automation is only one facet of the broader technological ecosystem emerging in contract management. Equally transformative is the integration of robust data analytics. In today's data-driven economy, contracts are not merely static documents but treasure troves of actionable information. Advanced analytics platforms can process historical contract data, identify trends, and provide predictive insights regarding renewal probabilities, pricing anomalies, and compliance risks. For example, by analyzing patterns in past contracts, an organization might discover that contracts with specific clauses are consistently associated with delayed payments or lower-than-expected revenue. Such insights can prompt a strategic review of the contract templates, leading to renegotiations or revisions that improve overall performance. This analytical approach safeguards revenue and supports continuous process refinement by revealing antecedents to common pitfalls.

Building upon automation and analytics, the emerging field of artificial intelligence (AI) promises even deeper insights. AI-powered tools use machine learning algorithms to interpret complex patterns within large datasets. In contract management, these tools can help identify nuances that traditional manual review may miss. For instance, semantic analysis enabled by natural language processing (NLP) can detect subtle discrepancies between similar contracts—discrepancies that may signal either a risk or an opportunity for improvement. I recall an example from a multinational firm implementing an AI-based contract analytics solution. The system analyzed thousands of contract clauses and successfully flagged several instances where non-standard wording led to increased compliance risk. This allowed the company to revamp its template library and improve consistency across all agreements. The experience underscored that AI is not meant to replace human judgment but to augment it by providing decision-makers with high-fidelity insights that drive more precise negotiations.

Another technology that is beginning to influence contract management is blockchain. Although still in its early stages for many organizations, blockchain technology offers significant potential for enhancing security, traceability, and trust in contractual processes. Blockchain's inherently immutable ledger can be used to securely record contract revisions, track the signatures sequence, and ensure contract documents' authenticity. In industries where regulatory compliance and transparency are paramount, blockchain can be a robust mechanism for ensuring that all contractual data remains tamper-proof. While the adoption of blockchain in CLM is not yet ubiquitous, several forward-thinking organizations have begun piloting such systems to enhance auditability and reduce the potential for fraud. Over time, as the technology matures, it will likely become a fundamental component of an integrated contract management ecosystem.

A critical theme that emerges from these technological advances is the notion of interoperability. In the modern business environment, contracts are not isolated—they are part of a larger network that includes enterprise resource planning (ERP) systems, customer relationship management (CRM) platforms, and financial software. Interoperability refers to the ability of these disparate systems to communicate seamlessly, ensuring that contract data is shared accurately across the organization. For instance, when a CLM system is integrated with an ERP solution, the financial impact of a contract, such as revenue recognition or cost allocation, can be immediately reconciled and analyzed. Such integration ensures consistency in data and supports comprehensive performance tracking. An integrated approach transforms isolated data points into a continuous stream of information that informs strategic decision-making across departments.

Consolidating these technological concepts into a cohesive system leads us to another essential insight—user-centric design. The most advanced technologies will yield little benefit if the intended users find it challenging to navigate or if they disrupt established workflows. Therefore, an effective CLM platform must prioritize usability and intuitive design. In practice, this means that the interface should be designed to accommodate the needs of various stakeholders, from legal professionals and contract managers to finance teams and sales representatives. A user-friendly system facilitates broader adoption across the organization and ensures that the benefits of automation, data analytics, and AI are fully leveraged. A successful implementation at a leading healthcare organization demonstrated that when the CLM interface was redesigned with input from end users, complaint rates dropped significantly, and processing times decreased. Such outcomes reinforce that technology must be viewed not as a static tool but as a dynamic enabler that evolves based on user feedback and operational data.

Alongside usability, scalability remains a fundamental consideration when selecting technologies for contract management. As organizations grow, the volume and complexity of contracts typically increase proportionally. A system that serves well in a small enterprise may struggle to cope with the scaling requirements of a larger operation. Scalability ensures that the technology can handle increasing volumes of data and complex workflows without sacrificing performance or reliability. Decision-makers should evaluate potential CLM solutions based on their ability to scale alongside the business and adapt to changing market conditions. Future-proofing investments in technology is critical—a system that can easily integrate new modules or adapt to emerging trends, such as advanced AI capabilities, providing a significant competitive advantage over rigid and outdated solutions.

A further dimension in leveraging technology for contract management is the alignment with strategic business goals. The selection and integration of technological tools should be guided by clearly understanding the organization's long-term objectives. Technology should not be implemented in isolation; instead, it must serve as an enabler for executing strategic initiatives. For example, if a company focuses on improving customer satisfaction, its CLM system should integrate customer feedback mechanisms and track related performance metrics. In this way, technology becomes a bridge between operational efficiency and strategic execution. One notable example involves a retail conglomerate that integrated its CLM software with a customer insights platform. The company could pinpoint specific clauses that negatively impacted the customer experience by correlating contract performance data with customer satisfaction scores. Adjusting those terms led to improved retention rates and higher overall revenues, demonstrating that when technology and strategy align, the benefits extend far beyond efficiency gains.

Alongside these advancements, it is crucial that organizations also consider the human factor in technology adoption. The successful integration of advanced CLM tools requires thoughtful change management and comprehensive training programs. Introducing new technology can be disruptive if employees are not adequately prepared, leading to resistance undermining even the most promising systems. Therefore, building a supportive environment where employees are encouraged to embrace change is imperative. Training sessions, workshops, and ongoing support initiatives help bridge the gap between technological potential and practical application. In several organizations, initiatives that coupled new technology with robust change management strategies resulted in higher adoption rates and noticeable improvements in contract processing outcomes. This underscores the idea that for technology to deliver on its promise, it must be accompanied by an investment in people and processes that ensure smooth transition and continued usage.

In summary, as we delve into the technological dimension of the CLM playbook, several key concepts have emerged that are reshaping the field of contract management. Automation, data analytics, artificial intelligence, blockchain, and interoperability collectively transform a traditionally manual and fragmented process into a dynamic, integrated system that supports strategic decision-making. Usability and scalability ensure that these technologies are effective in the present and adaptable to the future. At the same time, alignment with strategic goals guarantees that technology investments generate meaningful business outcomes. Finally, through change management and training, the human element remains critical to successfully implementing these tools, ensuring that technology supplements rather than supplants the workforce's expertise.

Integrating these technological innovations offers a clear pathway for organizations aiming to convert contract management from a cumbersome, error-prone process into a strategic asset. The benefits are multifaceted: enhanced efficiency through automation, improved decision-making via data analytics, proactive risk management powered by AI, and a secure, traceable contract process supported by blockchain, technologically tied together by the interoperability of systems. These advancements collectively enable organizations to not just react to problems but anticipate challenges and identify opportunities before they impact the bottom line.

As you consider these emerging concepts and their implications for your organization, the key takeaway is that technology must be integral to your overall contract management strategy. It is not a set of isolated tools, but part of a broader ecosystem that, when designed and implemented thoughtfully, drives improved performance across the entire contract lifecycle. This subchapter encourages you to approach technology adoption not as a checkbox exercise but as a strategic initiative that requires careful evaluation, integration, and continuous refinement.

Looking ahead, the insights on automation, analytics, AI, blockchain, and system integration will serve as the foundation for the practical methodologies detailed in subsequent sections. These methodologies will guide you on implementing and optimizing your CLM playbook's technological components. The goal is to ensure that every contract is managed with the highest precision, speed, and strategic awareness possible.

As this discussion on technology and tools comes to a close, reflecting on the broader strategic implications is essential. These technological innovations do not exist in a vacuum; they are most effective when integrated into an overall contract management framework that aligns with the organization's strategic objectives. The future of contract management lies in systems that are agile, data-driven, and deeply interconnected with other enterprise functions. By embracing these new concepts, organizations can move from a state of reactive bedrock systems to an environment where contracts actively inform strategy, catalyze operational improvements, and support sustainable growth.

In conclusion, the fusion of automation, analytics, artificial intelligence, blockchain, and system interoperability forms a powerful nexus redefining technology's role in contract management. These developments enable organizations to optimize processes, mitigate risk, capture incremental revenue, and transform contracts into strategic assets. As you move forward with this knowledge, consider how each technological innovation can be integrated into your overall strategy to enhance the performance and accuracy of your contract lifecycle management. The insights shared here pave the way for more detailed, practical guidance in later sections that will help you implement these technologies in a manner that is both scalable and aligned with your long-term business objectives.

By leveraging these advanced technological tools, you will streamline contract operations and create a resilient, data-informed environment where every contract becomes a proactive element of your business strategy. With the foundation of robust technology, the following steps involve integrating these tools within your existing operations and harnessing their full potential to drive competitive advantage. The journey to transforming contract management through technology is challenging yet filled with promise, and the rewards, both in terms of cost efficiencies and strategic insight, are substantial.

This comprehensive examination of technology within the CLM playbook thus sets the stage for a transformative approach to contract management. As we transition into further sections, you will gain practical knowledge on effectively deploying these innovative tools and ensuring their seamless integration with your overall strategic vision. This next phase will ultimately empower your organization to harness the full benefits of advanced technology in managing contracts, positioning your enterprise for sustained excellence in a rapidly evolving market.

⁖⁙

- IMPLEMENTING EFFECTIVE CONTRACT MANAGEMENT PRACTICES -

Our previous discussion examined how technology can transform contract management through integration, automation, data analytics, and other emerging innovations. Now, we delve deeper into how these technologies streamline operations and create new opportunities for proactive decision-making and strategic alignment. This subchapter focuses on the detailed exploration of these ideas, weaving together riveting case studies, thoughtful analysis, and practical insights that illustrate how technology facilitates a shift from reactive contract administration to a robust, intelligence-driven process.

One of the most critical aspects of this transformation is the move toward a truly unified data ecosystem. In traditional environments, contract information is often trapped in isolated systems: documents stored in individual folders, separated by department, and updated manually in disparate spreadsheets. Such fragmentation leaves organizations with incomplete views of their contractual landscape, where vital details about renewals, compliance issues, and revenue obligations are either overlooked or delayed. Modern CLM systems, in contrast, create a unified repository that centralizes all contract-related data. This integration is key because it allows decision-makers to see the whole picture anytime.

For example, a well-known financial services firm struggled for years with inconsistent contract data—it maintained separate records in legal, finance, and procurement departments. As a consequence, audits frequently uncovered discrepancies: renewal dates were missed, and pricing terms were not updated across all systems, leading to revenue leakage. When the company adopted an integrated CLM solution, all contract data was consolidated into a single dashboard. Real-time analytics now provide alerts ahead of renewal dates and flag discrepancies before they become significant issues. The transformation improved compliance and enhanced strategic negotiations with vendors by ensuring that every decision was informed by the most accurate and current data available. This case vividly illustrates that a unified data ecosystem directly influences an organization's ability to mitigate risk and seize revenue opportunities.

Automation plays a pivotal role in this ecosystem by eliminating the arduous and error-prone aspects of manual data entry and process execution. In many organizations, routine tasks such as updating contract templates, monitoring compliance checkpoints, or sending renewal notices rely heavily on manual intervention. These processes are time-consuming and prone to human error, which can have cascading adverse effects on operations. In contrast, automated workflows ensure every process is executed reliably and on schedule. Consider a healthcare organization that historically faced significant delays in contract renewals because of manual follow-ups. Contract renewal rates improved dramatically once they implemented an automated alert system into their CLM platform. The system automatically notified the responsible parties well before each contract's expiration, and it even generated preliminary reports on contract performance to inform the renewal process. As a result, the time spent on routine tasks decreased by nearly 50%, freeing up resources for more strategic work. This example demonstrates that automation reduces risk and enhances operational efficiency and creates space for strategic initiatives that drive growth.

In addition to automation, advanced data analytics is a driving force behind this transformation. Modern analytics tools transform raw data into actionable insights, allowing organizations to examine historical trends and forecast future outcomes. When properly analyzed, contract data can reveal hidden patterns that signal potential risks or opportunities for renegotiation. For instance, analytics might identify that contracts containing specific clauses or language tend to result in higher revenue leakage or more frequent disputes. With this information, management can adjust contract templates and negotiation strategies to preclude these issues in new agreements. One notable example involves a multinational technology company that applied predictive analytics to its contract portfolio. The analysis uncovered that contracts with less flexible payment terms consistently led to delayed payments, adversely affecting cash flow. The company revised its standard payment clauses with these insights to incorporate more favorable terms. The change accelerated cash flows and improved supplier relationships by creating more predictable payment cycles. Such data-driven modifications exemplify how analytics can transform contract management from an administrative process into a strategic function that underpins financial and operational performance.

Artificial intelligence (AI) further augments the capabilities of automated analytics tools by providing deeper insights through machine learning and natural language processing. AI systems can "read" contract text, compare clauses with industry best practices, and flag unconventional language that might present hidden risks. In doing so, AI tools extend the reach of human oversight, allowing contract managers to focus on strategic decision-making rather than catching every minor error. For example, one large manufacturing company integrated an AI-powered contract analytics solution into its review process. The system automatically scanned thousands of contracts, identifying inconsistencies and problematic clauses that had been previously overlooked. By highlighting these issues, the organization was able to conduct targeted training sessions for its legal team and refine its contract drafting process. The result was a dramatic reduction in contractual disputes and an increased capacity for proactive risk management. This case underlines AI's potential to enhance accuracy and drive strategic improvements by learning from vast amounts of data.

Blockchain technology also emerges as a compelling tool, particularly for improving transparency and security in contract management. With its distributed ledger system, the blockchain provides an immutable record of every change made within a contract, ensuring that all stakeholders have access to a single, verified source of truth. In highly regulated industries, such as pharmaceuticals or finance, the traceability and security provided by blockchain can be invaluable. For instance, consider an international logistics firm that adopted blockchain to manage its contracts with suppliers. By recording every contract modification on a blockchain, the firm ensured that any attempt at unauthorized alterations was immediately evident. The increased transparency bolstered the firm's compliance posture and enhanced stakeholder trust, as partners could be confident that contractual terms remained consistent and unaltered throughout their lifecycle.

Interoperability is another concept that cannot be over-looked in the modern technological landscape. Contracts are rarely managed in isolation; they interact with other enterprise systems, such as ERP, CRM, and business intelligence platforms. When these systems are bridged effectively, the data captured from contracts can inform a range of business processes—from financial forecasting to supply chain management. For instance, a retail corporation integrated its CLM platform with its ERP system to link contract terms directly to inventory and financial data. This integration allowed the company to quickly adjust its purchasing strategies in response to shifts in market demand, thereby optimizing inventory levels and improving profit margins. Interoperability thus serves as the glue that binds isolated technologies into a cohesive, enterprise-wide solution, ensuring that the insights derived from contract management have a broad, strategic impact.

User-centric design stands out as a vital element in successfully deploying these technologies. Regardless of the sophistication of automation, analytics, or AI capabilities, these tools must be accessible and intuitive for all users. A well-designed CLM platform offers a dashboard that presents complex data in an easily digestible format, ensuring that users from various departments can interpret and act upon key insights. In one case, a multinational consumer goods company redesigned its CLM interface after gathering extensive feedback from its legal and procurement teams. The intuitive design increased adoption rates, reduced training time, and improved overall satisfaction, leading to more consistent use of the system across the organization. This experience reinforces the idea that technology should serve its users effectively, enabling them to focus on strategic priorities rather than grappling with technical complexities.

Scalability and flexibility are additional critical considerations as organizations assess their technology needs. A solution that meets the demands of a small, stable organization might not be adequate for a rapidly growing enterprise facing an expansion of its contract portfolio. The chosen tools must be scalable, capable of handling an increased volume of data and more complex contractual relationships without reducing performance. For instance, a global software firm required a CLM system that could support the rapid onboarding of new contracts as it expanded into new markets. The firm avoided performance bottlenecks by selecting a scalable, cloud-based platform that automatically adjusted to increased data loads and maintained a seamless contract management process. Scalability ensures that technology remains a long-term asset, able to evolve alongside the organization's strategic vision.

Beyond these functionalities, integrating advanced technology into contract management hinges upon robust change management practices. Introducing new systems and tools invariably disrupts established workflows, leading to potential employee resistance. Effective change management entails training and support and clear communication about the strategic benefits of the new technology. Many organizations have found that early involvement of key stakeholders in the selection and implementation process leads to higher buy-in and smoother transitions. One example involves a retail chain that introduced a new CLM system alongside comprehensive training sessions and feedback forums. By engaging employees from the outset and addressing concerns in real time, the company ensured a high adoption rate and achieved quicker returns on its investment. This holistic approach to change management is integral to realizing the full potential of technological enhancements.

Furthermore, aligning technological investments with long-term strategic goals is crucial. As companies operate in increasingly competitive environments, technology must not be seen as an isolated upgrade but as a vital instrument that supports overarching business objectives. For instance, if an organization's strategy centers on rapid market expansion, then its CLM system should be designed to facilitate swift contract negotiations and agile renewals. When strategic priorities are directly linked to the performance of contract management systems, the value of technology becomes evident in terms of market responsiveness and revenue optimization. In such circumstances, the technology is not a cost center but an investment that yields measurable strategic dividends.

Moreover, emerging trends such as machine learning and blockchain push the envelope further. Organizations that adopt these technologies early can gain a competitive edge by harnessing capabilities that are still relatively rare in the industry. Although early adoption may come with challenges, such as integration difficulties or the need for specialized expertise, the potential rewards are significant. Those who successfully implement these innovations gain operational efficiencies and a reputation as industry leaders in contract management. These pioneering efforts often set new benchmarks, encouraging other organizations to follow suit and driving industry-wide improvements.

This subchapter has explored how automation, advanced analytics, AI, blockchain, interoperability, and user-centric design converge to reshape the contract management landscape. Each technology contributes crucial elements that, when integrated into a unified system, transform contract management into a proactive, strategic function. These technologies unlock previously hidden value and drive continuous improvement by reducing manual processes, providing real-time insights, and ensuring data exchanges across various enterprise systems. The benefits of these innovations extend far beyond efficiency gains—they create a system that supports strategic decision-making, improves risk management, and contributes to revenue optimization.

As you consider integrating these technological tools into your CLM playbook, the key takeaway is that technology must be selected and implemented in alignment with your overall business strategy. It is not sufficient to opt for the latest software; each tool must serve to enhance your organization's capabilities and strategic objectives. With thoughtful planning, robust change management, and continuous refinement, these technologies transform contract management from a reactive process to a dynamic, intelligence-driven strategic asset.

As you reflect on these insights and explore the potential of these tools within your organization, remember that the journey toward a modern contract management system is iterative and ongoing. The technology landscape is continuously evolving, meaning that the systems you put in place today must be adaptable enough to incorporate future innovations. Establishing a strong foundation that prioritizes integration, usability, and strategic alignment sets your organization on a path toward sustained excellence in contract management.

In conclusion, the detailed exploration presented here emphasizes that advanced technology is not an end in itself but a means to create a more agile, proactive, and strategically aligned contract management process. The convergence of automation, analytics, AI, and blockchain into an integrated, user-friendly system lays the groundwork for exponential improvements in efficiency and risk management. These technological innovations drive transformative changes—increased accuracy, reduced processing times, and higher revenue capture—ensuring that contract management evolves from a mundane administrative function into a powerful strategic engine.

With the technological framework in place, your organization can shift from merely reacting to challenges to anticipating and capitalizing on opportunities. As we transition to the practical methodologies outlined in the following sections, this holistic integration of technology will serve as the cornerstone for building a resilient CLM playbook that supports your long-term business objectives. The insights and real-world examples discussed in this subchapter demonstrate that embracing advanced technology in contract management is not optional in today's competitive environment—it is a strategic imperative that can drive sustainable growth and lasting competitive advantage.

:::

- CASE STUDIES: SUCCESS STORIES AND LESSONS LEARNED -

This chapter has examined how technology transforms contract management from a cumbersome, manual process into an integrated, agile, and intelligence-driven function. We began by exploring various advanced technological tools – from automation and data analytics to artificial intelligence, blockchain, and interoperability – reshaping how organizations manage their contractual lifecycles. These tools are now essential as add-ons and core components of a modern contract management strategy that drives operational efficiency, risk mitigation, and revenue optimization.

The first subchapter introduced the central concepts behind the digital transformation of contract management. It highlighted how automation removes the repetitive, error-prone tasks that have long hindered efficiency, allowing teams to focus on strategic decision-making. A memorable case involving a regional corporation demonstrated that by implementing automated alerts for renewals, the organization recovered lost revenue and minimized compliance risks. We noted that automation sets the stage for real-time monitoring and proactive adjustments in contract performance, enabling firms better to manage deadlines, renewals, and term modifications.

The chapter then moved into a detailed examination of integration and advanced analytics. Modern CLM platforms allow decision-makers to access real-time dashboards and alerts by consolidating contract data into a unified repository. These systems comprehensively view the contract landscape across legal, finance, procurement, and customer-related processes. In one example, a financial services firm experienced significant discrepancies due to fragmented contract records; once integrated into a single system, their improved visibility immediately reduced compliance issues and enhanced strategic negotiations. Advanced analytics further empower organizations by turning raw data into actionable insights. By analyzing historical patterns and predicting potential risks, companies can adjust contract terms or pricing models ahead of possible disruptions, optimizing contract performance continuously.

In addition, the role of emerging technologies such as artificial intelligence and blockchain was examined. AI-powered tools expand the scope of traditional contract review, identifying subtle inconsistencies and flagging problematic language that might otherwise go unnoticed. For instance, a multinational manufacturer's deployment of an AI-based system resulted in the early detection of non-standard clause language, leading to immediate process refinements and reduced disputes. Meanwhile, blockchain technology brings a new level of trust and security to contract verification, offering immutable record-keeping that is especially valuable in regulated industries. Although still developing in widespread use within contract management, blockchain's promise for enhanced transparency and data integrity signals a future where the authenticity of every contractual modification is assured.

User-centric design was another critical theme. We discussed the importance of ensuring that these advanced tools are powerful and accessible to all stakeholders. A user-friendly CLM platform with a well-designed interface encourages broad adoption, reduces training time, and helps teams quickly adapt to new workflows. A multinational consumer goods company case illustrated the drastic improvement in employee satisfaction and reduced processing times when end-user feedback was incorporated into a redesigned system. This reinforces the necessity that advanced technologies must complement human expertise, not overwhelm it, and must be seamlessly integrated within existing business frameworks.

Equally essential is the consideration of scalability and flexibility in technology investments. As organizations grow and face increasingly complex contract portfolios, the need for systems that meet current requirements and scale to support future operations becomes paramount. A global software firm's experience with a scalable, cloud-based platform demonstrated that a well-chosen system could easily accommodate growth and adapt to evolving business models without suffering from performance bottlenecks. In this way, forward-thinking investments ensure that technology remains an enduring asset rather than a temporary fix.

The second subchapter provided an in-depth exploration of these technological concepts. By weaving together case studies, practical examples, and detailed analysis, we saw how integrated automation, sophisticated analytics, and cross-functionality converge to create a unified CLM ecosystem. This ecosystem reduces the administrative burden and actively enhances strategic decision-making. The discussion showcased how data integration eliminates gaps in visibility, allowing for more accurate financial forecasting, better risk management, and improved vendor and customer relationships. Advanced tools empower companies with predictive insights that inform negotiations and lead to incremental revenue improvements that, collectively, have a substantial financial impact.

The narrative further emphasized that technology must be implemented within a broader strategic framework that incorporates interoperability with enterprise systems such as ERP, CRM, and business intelligence platforms. Through interoperability, contract data becomes part of a continuous information stream that supports decision-making across the organization. A retail conglomerate's integration of its CLM system with its ERP solution was a prime example of how this interconnected ecosystem can optimize inventory management, adjust purchasing strategies, and ultimately enhance profit margins. Such strategic integration reinforces that each piece of technology does not operate in isolation but contributes to a holistic system to support overall organizational goals.

Additionally, the subchapter underscored that change management is the critical element behind every technological advance. A thoughtful approach to adoption of technology involves comprehensive training, early stakeholder engagement, and a robust framework for continuous improvement. When employees are supported through clear communication and hands-on training programs, the benefits of automation and data analytics become immediately apparent in their everyday work. This human-centered approach was evident in the experiences of organizations that combined new CLM tools with well-executed change management strategies, resulting in higher user adoption rates and significant process improvements.

As we draw this chapter to a close in the final subchapter, it is time to consolidate the key themes and insights regarding the role of technology in modern contract management. The advanced tools discussed throughout this chapter—from automation and advanced analytics to AI, blockchain, and interoperability—are not mere add-ons but essential components of a strategic contract management framework. They convert contracts from static documents into pivotal business assets that drive revenue, optimize operations, manage risks proactively, and support strategic decision-making. By creating a unified, real-time data ecosystem, reducing errors through automation, and enhancing insights through analytics and artificial intelligence, these technologies collectively form a powerful enabler for organizational transformation.

The insights provided have confirmed that when thoughtfully selected, effectively integrated, and supported by robust change management practices, technology can drive remarkable improvements in contract performance. Organizations that have embraced these technological innovations report not only reduced processing times and better compliance but also significant gains in revenue capture and operational agility. In turn, these enhancements lead to stronger partnerships with vendors, more satisfied customers, and ultimately, a more competitive standing in the marketplace.

Key takeaways include the following: First, automation streamlines processes that are traditionally manual and prone to error, thus freeing up human resources for more strategic efforts. Second, advanced analytics transform raw contract data into actionable insights, enabling proactive adjustments and more informed negotiations. Third, artificial intelligence extends the capabilities of contract review by identifying subtle risks that may otherwise go unnoticed. Fourth, blockchain technology, although still emerging, promises to enhance trust and transparency in contract management through an immutable record. Fifth, successfully implementing these technologies is inherently linked to interoperability, ensuring the benefits cascade across all relevant enterprise systems. And finally, user-centric design, scalability, and comprehensive change management ensure that these technological tools are practical and embraced by the employees who use them daily.

Each of these elements plays an integral role in shaping a contract management function that is agile, responsive, and strategically aligned with the organization's broader objectives. When these technological components are woven into a coherent system, they produce transformative outcomes. Converting contracts from burdensome administrative documents into strategic levers for growth and operational excellence is perhaps one of the most significant opportunities organizations face today.

This chapter has demonstrated that integrating technology into contract management is not a one-time project but a continuous journey. The pace of technological advancement means that organizations must remain committed to iterative improvement, continually refining systems, updating practices, and integrating new tools as they emerge. The benefits of such a proactive approach are cumulative; even incremental improvements in contract processing can collectively lead to substantial financial, operational, and strategic gains over time.

As we conclude this chapter on technology and tools in

contract management, it is clear that these innovations serve as a linchpin for modernizing the contract lifecycle. They enable organizations to move from a reactive position—where issues are addressed only after they arise—to a proactive stance that anticipates challenges and capitalizes on opportunities. This strategic shift is not merely about saving time or reducing errors; it fundamentally alters how contracts contribute to the organization's long-term success.

Looking forward, the insights from this chapter lay the groundwork for our subsequent discussion, where we will explore how to measure the success of these transformative efforts. The following chapter will focus on key performance indicators, executive dashboards, and reporting frameworks that translate the operational benefits of advanced contract management into clear, strategic metrics. By quantifying these improvements, leaders can validate the return on investment in new technologies and continuously optimize their processes for even greater impact.

Our exploration of technology and tools has shown that when integrated strategically, advancements such as automation, analytics, AI, and blockchain can transform contract management into a strategic asset. The journey from manual processes and fragmented systems to a dynamic, unified CLM solution marks a significant leap forward for organizations. The convergence of these technologies creates an environment in which contracts are managed more efficiently and aligned with broader business strategies, driving revenue, mitigating risk, and enhancing overall performance.

As you move forward with these insights, consider how

adopting these technologies can be tailored to fit your organization's specific needs. Achieving a fully integrated, agile contract management system is iterative and requires ongoing refinement. However, the rewards in improved efficiency, risk management, and revenue capture make this transformation an essential strategic priority. With technology as a cornerstone of your CLM playbook, you are well-positioned to meet the challenges of a rapidly evolving business landscape.

This chapter has thus provided a comprehensive overview of the technological enablers redefining contract management. It is the blueprint for an intelligence-driven CLM system that is both agile and responsive. As you transition to the next chapter on measuring success, remember that integrating sophisticated technology into contract management is not an end in itself - it is a means to a far greater strategic end. The next phase of our discussion will show how to quantify the impact of these innovations through robust performance metrics and reflective reporting frameworks.

In closing, integrating advanced technology into contract management represents a critical evolution in how organizations handle contracts. Combining automation, advanced analytics, AI, blockchain, and interoperability forms a comprehensive system that transforms contracts into actionable strategic assets. This evolution is essential for reducing risks, capturing hidden revenue, and driving continuous operational improvements. With this foundation in place, you are now equipped to move forward and measure the success of these transformative initiatives, ultimately turning every contract into a catalyst for sustained growth and competitive differentiation.

CHAPTER 6:

TECHNOLOGY & TOOLS — WHAT YOU NEED (AND DON'T)

As organizations that have transformed their contract management processes reap the benefits of reduced inefficiencies, enhanced compliance, and improved revenue capture, the next step is to measure these successes rigorously. In today's competitive landscape, it is not enough to implement new processes, integrate advanced technology, or restructure governance frameworks. Business leaders must quantify these improvements in clear, actionable terms to make informed adjustments and demonstrate tangible value. This chapter focuses on measuring success in contract lifecycle management, outlining the key metrics, reporting tools, and performance indicators that enable organizations to convert operational improvements into strategic, quantifiable gains.

The discussion opens by addressing a central challenge: accurately capturing the return on investment from CLM initiatives. The financial impact of streamlined processes and advanced analytics is often dispersed across various aspects of the organization, from shorter contract processing times and lower administrative costs to enhanced negotiation leverage and improved revenue recognition. Measuring success begins with establishing precise benchmarks reflecting each contract lifecycle stage. For instance, one multinational technology company, struggling with lengthy contract approval cycles, implemented new automated workflows and set baseline targets for turnaround time. Within months, the company reported a measurable decrease in cycle times—a reduction by nearly 30%, thereby contributing directly to improved cash flow and increased negotiation power with suppliers. Such case examples are instrumental in understanding that success is not an abstract concept, but one that manifests through specific, quantifiable improvements in operational performance.

Another critical dimension of measuring success involves using data analytics to track key performance indicators (KPIs) that matter most to stakeholders. Key metrics might include contract cycle time, the number of contracts processed per month, renewal rates, compliance adherence, and the overall financial impact of contract renegotiations. These metrics provide a snapshot of current performance and a predictive capacity that can inform future strategic actions. A robust dashboard, for example, can aggregate these figures in real time, enabling executive teams to continuously monitor performance against set targets. One case in point comes from a global financial institution that integrated its CLM system with business intelligence platforms. The resulting executive dashboard provided granular insights into contract performance, helping the company detect trends in attrition, identify bottlenecks, and take corrective measures before issues escalated into significant risks. This data-driven approach ensures that improvements are not merely anecdotal but are documented to substantiate ongoing investments in contract management systems.

In addition to quantitative measures, qualitative indicators are equally important in gauging success. These may involve customer and vendor satisfaction surveys, internal feedback from cross-functional teams, and thorough post-implementation reviews. When teams across legal, finance, and procurement report a renewed sense of ownership and reduced stress over contract administration, it signals that the transformation is yielding results. Consider the example of a mid-market company that observed a marked increase in internal satisfaction and trust from external partners after updating its CLM processes and integrating sophisticated analytics. The improved transparency and agility enhanced operational capabilities and boosted the organization's reputation, which often translates into long-term competitive advantage.

Central to this measurement process is the design and implementation of effective executive dashboards. These dashboards consolidate key data points into a single interface that executives can use to assess performance quickly and accurately. They should be customizable so stakeholders can view the precise data relevant to their decision-making process. For instance, while the finance team might focus on revenue capture and cost savings, the legal department will be more concerned with compliance rates and audit trail completeness. The dashboards are a focal point for continuous improvement initiatives by providing timely, accurate, and actionable insights. With such tools, organizations can track the progress of their CLM initiatives and make data-driven decisions that maximize strategic outcomes.

A robust methodology for measuring success also requires a culture of continuous improvement. Business environments are inherently dynamic—regulations change, market conditions fluctuate, and internal priorities evolve. Organizations mustn't regard their measurements as endpoints, but as ongoing benchmarks to be revisited and refined over time. Regular review cycles and feedback loops allow teams to update KPIs as needed and ensure that the contract management system remains agile. This continuous measurement and refinement culture transforms metrics into a strategic tool, enabling organizations to stay ahead of potential risks and seize new opportunities as they arise.

One practical way to embed continuous measurement into the organization is by instituting periodic review meetings that bring together all relevant stakeholders. At these meetings, teams analyze data trends from the executive dashboards, examine the effectiveness of current processes, and propose adjustments where necessary. Such cross-functional forums not only help uncover areas where performance could be further optimized but also foster a sense of shared purpose and collaboration. The lessons learned from these reviews feed into the training programs and process updates, creating a virtuous cycle of ongoing improvement. For example, a retail organization once conducted quarterly updates highlighting incremental gains in processing speed and qualitative improvements in vendor relationships. These meetings reinforced the benefits of the new CLM system and sparked innovative ideas for future enhancements, a clear indication that sustained measurement drives ongoing strategic initiatives.

Compliance and risk management are also integral components of measuring success. Beyond efficiency and revenue metrics, assessing how well the organization manages risk through its contractual processes is crucial.

Automated compliance checks, adherence to regulatory standards, and reducing contractual disputes are all quantifiable measures that indicate a healthier risk posture. In industries with high regulatory scrutiny, these measures can be the difference between averting costly fines and experiencing significant financial setbacks. For example, one healthcare organization utilized its CLM system's compliance tracking features to monitor key regulatory deadlines and quickly address deviations from standard practices. The outcome was fewer compliance issues and a strengthened reputation among regulators and partners, a scenario reinforcing the strategic value of well-measured contract management practices.

Furthermore, the strategic benefit of insightful measurement extends to financial planning. When organizations quantify the benefits of the transformed CLM system, they build a compelling case for further investment in their contract management strategies. Quantified improvements—such as faster contract processing times, reduced administrative costs, improved revenue through better-negotiated terms, and lower compliance penalties—collectively contribute to a tangible return on investment. Executives are better positioned to allocate resources and justify additional enhancements when they have clear, documented evidence of the savings and value generated by their CLM initiatives. This measurable benefit is compelling for internal stakeholders, external partners, and investors, who increasingly demand proof of operational excellence and strategic foresight.

Ultimately, measuring success in contract lifecycle management is about creating a comprehensive, data-driven picture of how strategic initiatives translate into better business outcomes. Key metrics, executive dashboards, and continuous feedback loops provide the tools to manage performance actively. Through the systematic assessment of these indicators, organizations can refine their contract management practices, address emerging challenges promptly, and capitalize on even incremental improvements that, over time, culminate in substantial competitive advantage.

To summarize the insights covered in this subchapter, several core themes emerge. First, a unified data ecosystem—enabled by integrated CLM systems—provides critical real-time visibility into every facet of the contract lifecycle. Second, automation reduces manual workload and ensures consistency, paving the way for increased efficiency and fewer errors. Third, advanced data analytics and AI transform raw contract data into actionable insights, facilitating proactive, strategic decision-making. Fourth, executive dashboards are the nerve center for monitoring key performance indicators across various functions, enabling leaders to gauge success quickly and accurately. Fifth, a culture of continuous improvement—bolstered by structured review meetings and robust feedback loops—ensures that the contract management process remains agile and responsive to change. Finally, measuring compliance, risk management, and the overall financial return on CLM initiatives completes the picture of what strategic contract management should achieve.

These interconnected themes underscore that measuring success is not a one-off exercise but rather an ongoing strategic activity tightly integrated with operational and financial planning. As organizations adopt these measurement practices, they gain the capacity to anticipate challenges, identify new opportunities, and maintain a competitive advantage through informed, proactive management.

Looking ahead, the insights and methodologies discussed in this chapter set a solid foundation for the next phase of our exploration. The following chapter will focus on designing executive dashboards and reporting frameworks that consolidate this data into actionable intelligence. We will examine how to establish a comprehensive system for monitoring performance that validates the value of CLM initiatives and drives continuous improvement across the organization. Transitioning to the next chapter will turn our focus from the metrics to the presentation and communication of these metrics, ensuring that strategic insights are accessible and aligned with broader business objectives.

In conclusion, this subchapter has provided a detailed examination of the strategic importance of measuring success within contract lifecycle management. Advanced metrics, integrated data systems, and continuous feedback mechanisms are essential tools that modern organizations must leverage to translate operational improvements into measurable competitive advantage. Organizations can better manage risk, optimize resources, and sustain long-term growth by quantifying the benefits of streamlined processes, improved negotiation outcomes, and enhanced compliance. The comprehensive measurement framework outlined here lays the groundwork for improved decision-making and positions contract management as an administrative function and a strategic enabler of business success.

As we prepare to transition into the next phase of our discussion, where we will explore the design of executive dashboards and reporting frameworks, remember that measuring success in contract management is a strategic imperative. With a robust set of performance metrics and a culture of continuous improvement, organizations can ensure that every contract contributes meaningfully to their overall objectives. The insights and case examples provided are a compelling reminder that when operational changes are captured in data and communicated effectively, the impact is quantifiable and enduring.

The journey toward quantifying success is continuous, requiring organizations to periodically reassess and refine their performance indicators, considering evolving market conditions and internal priorities. Ultimately, this rigorous measurement process will validate the initial investments in advanced CLM systems and inform future enhancements that drive extra value. As we step into the next chapter, where the design of executive reporting tools will take center stage, you are now equipped with a clear understanding of why measuring success is critical—and how it can be achieved in a methodical, data-driven manner.

※

- EVALUATING CLM TOOLS AND TECHNOLOGIES -

This subchapter delves into the core principles underpinning measuring success in contract lifecycle management (CLM). Our goal is to offer a comprehensive view of how key performance indicators, data integrity, and continuous feedback loops can be harnessed to ensure that every improvement in contract processes translates into tangible business benefits. By integrating a carefully designed measurement framework with your CLM strategy, organizations can track operational efficiency and drive strategic decision-making. This section presents the primary components of a success measurement system, illustrates their practical implementation through real-world examples, and explains why a rigorous measurement process is indispensable for sustained competitive advantage.

The first step in constructing a practical measurement framework is establishing a baseline of current performance. Without a clear understanding of how contracts are managed today, it is impossible to quantify improvements over time. This diagnostic phase involves gathering historical data on various metrics such as contract cycle times, renewal rates, compliance adherence, and revenue leakage from unfavorable terms. For example, consider an organization that once struggled with inconsistent processing times due to manual contract reviews. By auditing its existing processes, the company identified that its average contract cycle time was 45 days—a figure that delayed revenue recognition and increased the risk of missed renegotiation opportunities. Once this baseline was established, the organization set clear benchmarks against which future improvements could be measured. Determining these metrics is not arbitrary; it should be based on operational realities and previously recorded performance, ensuring that any subsequent performance enhancements are grounded in verifiable data.

Once the baseline is established, the next critical step is selecting and defining key performance indicators (KPIs) that align with strategic business objectives. KPIs serve as quantifiable metrics that reveal the health of the contract management process. They might include the number of contracts signed per period, the frequency of compliance breaches, average processing times, revenue captured through renegotiations, and even customer satisfaction scores concerning contract interactions. For instance, a multinational firm reduced its processing time substantially by targeting a decrease of 30 percent in its contract cycle time while simultaneously tracking compliance improvements. Each KPI must be clearly defined so that every stakeholder understands the measure, its calculation, and why it matters. Transparent definitions help eliminate discrepancies between departments and ensure all teams work toward a common goal, creating a shared language around performance.

A vital tool for managing these KPIs is the executive dashboard. A well-constructed dashboard provides real-time visibility into key metrics and lets leaders quickly grasp their CLM initiatives' operational and financial impacts. The dashboard may include dynamic charts, trend graphs, and drill-down capabilities that allow executives to investigate anomalies in specific data points. For example, a financial institution integrated its CLM system with a business intelligence platform to generate a dashboard that displayed average contract cycle time, renewal rates, and revenue leakage figures. When the dashboard revealed a sudden spike in processing times for a particular type of contract, the leadership was able to investigate and identify the underlying cause—a manual review bottleneck—and promptly implement corrective measures. The insights garnered from such dashboards facilitate rapid issue resolution and inform long-term strategic planning, demonstrating the indispensable role of real-time data in driving continuous improvements.

Data integrity is another cornerstone of a practical measurement framework. Decisions based on inaccurate or incomplete data can lead to misdirected efforts that fail to address the real challenges. To ensure high data quality, companies should implement robust data management practices, including regular contract data audits, standardized data entry protocols, and integrated systems that minimize manual input. For instance, when a large manufacturing company centralized its contract databases, it discovered that inconsistent data entry had previously led to unreliable reporting on renewal rates and compliance metrics. By standardizing the data collection process and automating parts of the input, the company not only improved the accuracy of its dashboards but also strengthened its ability to forecast and optimize contract performance. High data integrity gives the firm a dependable foundation for building strategic initiatives.

Monitoring compliance and risk management is crucial to the overall measurement strategy. Regulatory compliance is non-negotiable in many industries, and lapses in compliance can result in severe financial penalties, legal disputes, or reputational damage. To safeguard against such fallout, organizations must incorporate compliance metrics into their measurement frameworks. Automated compliance monitoring systems can track whether contracts adhere to internal standards and external regulatory requirements. For example, a healthcare organization implemented a system that automatically reviewed each contract for compliance with industry regulations and flagged deviations for immediate review. As a result, the organization saw a significant reduction in compliance breaches and was better positioned during audits. By embedding compliance as a key metric, companies reduce risk and reinforce their commitment to operational excellence.

It is also essential to appreciate the role of qualitative feedback in the measurement process. While quantitative metrics provide a solid foundation for performance tracking, qualitative data can offer context that numbers alone might obscure. Internal feedback from cross-functional teams, legal, finance, procurement, and even customer service provides insights into how improved contract processes affect day-to-day operations. Customer and vendor satisfaction surveys are equally valuable, showing how well the improved contract management processes meet external expectations. Consider a mid-market company that introduced post-contract review surveys. Employees reported higher satisfaction levels due to the streamlined processes, and customers noted a more transparent negotiation process. This qualitative feedback was an early indicator of the system's success, prompting further refinements that ultimately drove additional revenue improvements. Organizations achieve a more holistic view of performance by pairing qualitative insights with quantitative data.

An essential dimension of continuous measurement is the establishment of regular review cycles. The business environment is rarely static; market conditions, regulatory landscapes, and internal priorities change over time. Therefore, the measurement framework must be dynamic rather than fixed. Establishing periodic review meetings— monthly or quarterly—helps teams analyze current performance against set KPIs, identify emerging trends, and adjust strategies accordingly. These review cycles create a structured forum where cross-functional teams can discuss performance, share insights, and collaboratively determine corrective actions. For example, a global retail chain used quarterly review sessions to assess its contract performance metrics. Over successive cycles, they identified and addressed minor inefficiencies that reduced their contract processing times by a significant margin. These regular reviews ensure that the measurement system remains responsive and that performance improvements are sustained over the long term.

Integrating various enterprise systems is another essential element to enhance the measurement process. Contracts do not impact business operations in isolation. They are closely linked to supply chain operations, financial performance, customer relationship management, and more. Organizations can create a comprehensive view of their operational landscape by integrating the CLM system with ERP, CRM, and business intelligence platforms. This integration allows performance metrics from contracts to be correlated with financial outcomes, for instance, tracking how changes in contract turnaround times translate into improved cash flow or increased supplier discounts. A well-integrated system transforms disparate data sources into a coherent narrative that supports strategic decision-making across the organization.

The human factor cannot be underestimated when establishing a measurement framework. Successfully adopting performance metrics and dashboards depends on the engagement and motivation of the employees responsible for contract management. Change management practices are paramount during the transition to a data-driven culture. Comprehensive training programs help team members understand how to use the new tools and why these measurements matter. Employees who see clear links between their actions and tangible performance improvements are more likely to embrace changes enthusiastically. In one instance, a large professional services firm introduced interactive workshops to train its staff to interpret dashboard analytics and proactively address identified issues. This engagement led to faster adoption and a more substantial commitment to continuous improvement, demonstrating that effective measurement systems require technological implementation and human buy-in.

Furthermore, quantifying the benefits of improved contract management directly supports strategic planning and resource allocation. When organizations can measure the impact of their CLM initiatives—whether it's a measurable decrease in contract cycle time, a reduction in compliance breaches, or a quantifiable increase in revenue captured - leaders gain the confidence to invest in further enhancements. This well-documented performance fosters a virtuous cycle where improvements beget additional investment, leading to even greater operational efficiencies and competitive advantages. For example, a global consumer electronics company reported that its investment in an integrated CLM system reduced contract processing costs by 20 percent, translating into a substantial increase in operating margins. This clear return on investment justifies the technological upgrade and serves as a benchmark for continuous performance enhancement.

Risk assessment also forms a crucial part of the measurement framework. In every contract, there is an inherent risk from external factors such as market volatility or regulatory changes and internal challenges like processing delays and human errors. Quantifying risk through established metrics, such as the frequency and severity of contractual disputes or the incidence of non-compliance issues, contributes to a comprehensive understanding of the contract management landscape. Once these risks are measured, they can be managed proactively. In one scenario, an organization used predictive analytics to estimate the probability of a compliance breach based on historical data. By identifying high-risk contracts before issues arose, the organization implemented targeted interventions that protected against potential losses. Measuring risk is, therefore, not just about avoiding adverse outcomes; it also provides an opportunity to refine processes and optimize contractual terms.

In summarizing these components, it becomes clear that success in contract lifecycle management is achieved through a holistic, data-driven approach. Establishing a clear baseline, defining strategic KPIs, ensuring data integrity, and integrating across systems all contribute to a comprehensive measurement framework that delivers real strategic insights. Automation and advanced analytics work hand in hand to reduce manual errors and provide predictive insights, while qualitative feedback and regular review cycles ensure that metrics remain aligned with evolving business needs. The integration of these elements, coupled with robust change management practices, ensures that the measurement framework is not only effective in the short term but is also adaptable for future challenges.

By implementing these measurement strategies, organizations can transition from a reactive state—addressing issues only after they emerge—to a proactive, continuous improvement model. The insights gleaned from this comprehensive measurement approach empower decision-makers to identify bottlenecks, optimize operations, and capitalize on emerging opportunities quickly. This strategic shift is fundamental to transforming contract management from a cumbersome administrative function into a dynamic, value-generating asset.

Considering the components discussed in this subchapter, it is important to remember that the journey toward a robust measurement framework is iterative. The benefits of improved contract management are cumulative, and regular performance tracking validates initial investments in new systems and processes and provides direction for further enhancements. The lessons learned here underscore that success is measured not just in isolated data points but in a consistent, ongoing process of refinement that aligns operational performance with strategic business goals.

In the context of modern CLM, measurement is more than an operational necessity, it is a critical feedback mechanism that drives long-term business success. Each metric serves as a signal, highlighting areas where the organization is performing well and where improvement is needed. By continuously monitoring these signals, companies can stay agile, respond promptly to emerging challenges, and sustain competitive advantage over time.

This holistic and comprehensive measurement framework forms the foundation for managing contract-related risks, capitalizing on revenue opportunities, and achieving and exceeding strategic objectives. Ensuring that every stakeholder, across legal, finance, procurement, and operations, is aligned around these metrics creates a unified approach to performance management that benefits the entire organization.

In conclusion, this subchapter has provided an in-depth look at the essential components of a measurement framework for contract lifecycle management. We examined the importance of establishing a baseline, defining clear KPIs, ensuring data integrity, integrating cross-functional systems, and embedding a culture of continuous improvement. Real-world examples and case studies served to illustrate how these principles can be applied, resulting in tangible improvements in contract processing, compliance, risk management, and overall financial performance. The insights presented here not only demonstrate the strategic significance of measuring success but also provide practical guidance for implementing and refining these measurement systems within your own organization.

As we move forward, the insights from this discussion will serve as a foundation for the next chapter, where the focus will shift to designing executive dashboards and reporting frameworks. These tools will be critical in translating the operational metrics and qualitative feedback into actionable intelligence, enabling leaders to visualize performance and make data-driven decisions that further enhance the strategic value of contract management. With a robust measurement framework in place, organizations can confidently chart a course toward greater efficiency, reduced risk, and sustained competitive advantage.

⁘

- AVOIDING COMMON PITFALLS IN TECHNOLOGY SELECTION -

In this section, we further explore the deeper dimensions of measuring success in contract lifecycle management, delving into the intricacies of how precise metrics, robust analytics, and an ongoing commitment to data integrity converge to create an environment where every contract becomes a measurable, actionable asset. Building on our earlier discussion of baseline establishment, KPI selection, and the importance of executive dashboards, this subchapter focuses on strategically implementing these measurement practices. It highlights how organizations can transform raw data into a dynamic source of continuous improvement and competitive advantage.

A central element in this process is the refinement and segmentation of key performance indicators. While it is essential to establish overarching KPIs such as overall contract cycle time, renewal rates, and revenue impacts, a nuanced approach requires breaking these down into more granular, department-specific, and process-specific measures. For instance, several stages in a typical contract lifecycle contribute variably to the total cycle time. Organizations can pinpoint the precise areas that require intervention by measuring the duration of the drafting phase, negotiation phase, internal review, and final approval separately. One global enterprise, for example, segmented its contract process into detailed phases and discovered that the legal review stage was delaying overall cycle times by an average of 15 days compared to industry benchmarks. By implementing targeted process enhancements and specialized training for its legal team, the company was able to reduce this delay considerably. This outcome emphasizes that detailed segmentation of KPIs is not merely an academic exercise but a practical tool for uncovering hidden inefficiencies and optimizing each process component.

In parallel with granular metrics, the role of data visualization cannot be overstated. Effective executive dashboards do more than present aggregated figures. They tell a story. Dynamic dashboards that allow users to drill down from a high-level view to specific data points enable managers at different levels of the organization to investigate anomalies and trends in real time. A noteworthy example is a financial institution that integrated its entire CLM system with a modern business intelligence platform. The resulting dashboard, which was updated in real time, allowed executives to observe sudden changes in compliance metrics, identify a recurring delay in vendor contract renewals, and correlate these issues with external market shifts. Having this data at their fingertips meant that the institution could prioritize corrective actions swiftly, turning potential revenue loss into an opportunity for strategic renegotiation. Such visualizations not only enhance decision-making but also communicate performance improvements in a manner that is accessible and compelling to all stakeholders.

Data integrity remains a fundamental pillar in this measurement journey. Achieving high-quality, reliable data demands more than integrating systems; it requires constant verification, validation, and standardization. If not standardized, disparate data sources can lead to significant discrepancies that skew performance measurement. To prevent this, organizations must adopt robust data governance policies that enforce uniform data entry protocols and regular audits of the data stored in CLM systems. A multinational manufacturing company, for instance, undertook a comprehensive data cleansing initiative as part of its contract management overhaul. They discovered that different departments' inconsistent terminology and varied data input had previously distorted the actual impact of their contract cycle times. With standardized inputs and regular audits, the company improved the accuracy of its KPIs and restored confidence among its executive teams. This standardization, in effect, turned raw data into a reliable foundation from which strategic decisions could be derived.

Beyond the technical aspects of KPI measurement, another crucial facet involves amplifying the feedback loop—from quantitative performance data to the continuous improvement process. This cyclical approach ensures that each performance review is not merely a static assessment but a springboard for further enhancements. Organizations must establish recurrent review meetings—monthly, quarterly, or aligned with fiscal cycles—where cross-functional teams come together to assess the current performance against established benchmarks. During these sessions, teams analyze trends, discuss anomalies, and plan necessary adjustments. For instance, a retail corporation implemented quarterly performance reviews of its CLM system and discovered a subtle trend: contracts involving international suppliers consistently took longer to negotiate than domestic ones. Armed with this insight, the company initiated specific training in cross-border negotiation techniques and adjusted its standard contract templates to accommodate international legal and logistical complexities better. Over successive review cycles, these interventions led to noticeable improvements in processing times and supplier satisfaction. Here, the measurement framework does not merely assess performance; it actively influences strategic initiatives.

Risk management, often considered separately, is an integral component of the measurement strategy. Quantifying and monitoring risk in contract management involves tracking metrics such as the frequency of compliance breaches, the recurrence of contractual disputes, and the incidence of contractual non-performance. These metrics serve as early warning signals for potential issues that, if left unaddressed, could have severe financial implications. One compelling case comes from a healthcare organization that embedded compliance checkpoints into its CLM system. By automatically flagging contracts that deviated from regulatory guidelines, the system allowed timely interventions that prevented costly legal disputes and regulatory fines. Through extensive data analysis, they could even predict patterns that indicated higher risk in specific contract types. This proactive approach, enabled by continuous monitoring and risk measurement, transformed how the organization managed contractual risk, providing assurance and a competitive advantage over less vigilant peers.

Another dimension to consider in this sophisticated measurement framework is the financial justification of CLM initiatives. Consolidating the benefits of reducing contract cycle times, lowering administrative costs, and optimizing renewal terms provides a compelling case for continued investments in contract management technology. Organizations can articulate a clear return on investment (ROI) by assigning a monetary value to each improvement, such as calculating the revenue recovered through renegotiated terms or the cost savings from reduced processing times, organizations can articulate a clear return on investment (ROI). A global consumer electronics company quantified the benefits of its modernized CLM system by linking shorter contract processing times directly to increased market agility, contributing to faster product rollouts and improved revenue figures. When performance metrics can be directly tied to financial outcomes, it reinforces that CLM is not just an operational support function but a strategic engine driving profitability.

Alongside these quantitative measures, the qualitative aspects of performance measurement play a significant role. Employee feedback, customer satisfaction surveys, and vendor partnership reviews provide qualitative data that enrich the purely numerical KPIs. These insights help contextualize the quantitative results by revealing, for instance, that reducing contract cycle time has led to higher employee morale, or improved communication processes have increased vendor trust. In one example, a mid-market firm conducted regular post-contract execution surveys with both internal teams and external partners. The feedback indicated that the streamlined contract process cut costs and enhanced overall business relationships, leading to increased loyalty and repeat business. By integrating this qualitative data into the measurement framework, organizations obtain a comprehensive performance view encompassing complex numbers and human factors.

Moreover, the interplay between these measurements and strategic planning cannot be overlooked. Data collected from the CLM system is invaluable in scenario planning and forecasting future performance. As market conditions evolve, the ability to model different scenarios, such as the implications of a sudden regulatory change or a shift in supplier pricing, allows organizations to prepare better and adjust their strategies accordingly. In doing so, the measurement framework evolves from a reporting tool into a strategic decision-support system. For example, a financial services company used its performance data to conduct "what-if" analyses that simulated various market disruptions. The resulting insights enabled the management team to proactively adjust its contract negotiation strategies and pricing models, thereby mitigating potential risks before they materialized. This forward-looking application of measurement data underscores its strategic value beyond mere historical analysis.

Central to all these detailed insights is the idea that the measurement process is an evolving discipline. As organizations refine their CLM practices, they must continuously iterate on their measurement strategies to adapt to new challenges and capture emerging opportunities. The measurement framework should, therefore, be viewed as a living component of the CLM system—one that is regularly updated based on feedback from review cycles, technological advancements, and shifts in strategic priorities. This iterative process is crucial for sustaining performance improvements over the long term and ensuring that the contract management system remains aligned with the organization's evolving objectives.

Another key to a successful measurement framework is the importance of cross-functional alignment. While specific departments may focus on different metrics—legal teams on compliance, finance on revenue impact, and procurement on supplier performance—the overall insights must be synthesized into a single coherent narrative. This synthesis requires a coordinated effort to define and standardize organizational metrics. When stakeholders interpret performance data using the same criteria, the organization experiences a smoother, more integrated improvement process. Regular cross-departmental meetings, where these metrics are openly discussed and strategies harmonized, contribute significantly to a culture of accountability and shared success. The resulting alignment ensures that the entire organization works toward the same strategic objectives and that improvements in one area are recognized and reinforced across all functions.

As we progress, it is clear that the measurement framework serves to monitor performance and drive a cycle of continuous improvement. Each metric is a data point in a larger story—a narrative that ultimately informs strategic decision-making at the highest levels of the organization. Integrating advanced analytics, real-time reporting, and qualitative feedback forms a comprehensive picture of how every contract contributes to the organization's overall goals. Reviewing this detailed data regularly empowers leaders to recalibrate strategies swiftly, ensuring that the contract management process remains agile and resilient in the face of change.

In conclusion, the insights developed in this subchapter paint a detailed portrait of how a rigorous measurement framework is indispensable in modern contract lifecycle management. Organizations transform raw data into actionable intelligence by establishing clear baselines, refining KPIs, ensuring data integrity, and integrating quantitative and qualitative feedback. This, in turn, drives continuous improvement, underpins strategic planning, and ultimately ensures that every facet of contract management delivers measurable financial and operational benefits. The ability to track performance accurately and make data-informed decisions is the linchpin in transitioning from a reactive to a proactive contract management model.

The comprehensive measurement system described here mitigates risks by flagging issues in real time and uncovers opportunities for negotiation and revenue optimization that might otherwise go unnoticed. It provides decision-makers with the tools to correlate operational metrics with broader business outcomes, bridging day-to-day contract management activities and long-term strategic objectives.

Reflecting on these more profound insights, consider how integrating these measurement practices into your CLM system can transform your organization's approach. The process is inherently dynamic, with each improvement building on the last to create a continuous feedback and evolution culture. In effect, the measurement framework does more than quantify success—it becomes a strategic asset that informs every subsequent decision and improvement, ensuring that contract management is a core driver of organizational growth and competitive positioning.

By embracing a comprehensive and modular measurement framework, organizations can adapt flexibly to changes in the market, regulatory environment, or internal processes. The goal is to create an ecosystem where performance indicators are continuously monitored, challenges are identified and addressed promptly, and every contract is managed with the utmost strategic insight.

In summary, this subchapter has provided a detailed exploration into how advanced measurement techniques and a robust performance framework can transform contract lifecycle management from a routine task into a strategic function. Through rigorous baseline analysis, precise KPI definition, uninterrupted data integrity monitoring, and a commitment to continuous improvement, organizations lay the groundwork for sustained enhancements in operational efficiency, risk management, and revenue capture. Integrating cross-functional insights and real-time dashboards further refines this process, ensuring that every decision is data-driven and aligned with strategic business goals.

As we transition toward the final consolidation of measurement practices in the following subchapter, the insights discussed here will serve as a core foundation for understanding the tangible benefits of a carefully constructed measurement regimen. The journey of quantifying contract management success is ongoing, requiring never-ending evaluation and adaptation. With these detailed measurements in place, your organization is well-positioned to not only track its progress but also to leverage these insights in shaping future strategies, thereby creating a competitive advantage that is both sustainable and adaptable.

The themes and insights we have explored here are critical, as they demonstrate that the act of measuring success is far more than a set of routine administrative tasks. Instead, it is an essential strategic practice that turns every contract into a quantifiable asset, where each metric serves as both a benchmark and a guide for continuous improvement. In doing so, organizations can confidently manage their contracts with an eye toward future opportunities and emerging risks.

Building on these principles, the next step will involve using these measurements to develop predictive models and iterative improvement strategies that will be further elaborated as we move forward in this comprehensive discussion on measuring success. The following subchapter will focus on consolidating this framework into executive-level dashboards and reporting structures that ensure every relevant stakeholder can access these insights on demand, enabling real-time strategic adjustments and ongoing accountability.

Thus, as we conclude this deeper dive into the measurement framework, it is evident that a data-driven approach to contract management forms the backbone of a resilient and proactive operational strategy. With the insights garnered from these detailed analyses, organizations are now equipped to translate performance metrics into actionable improvements, continuously enhancing the value derived from each contract and reinforcing the overall strategic direction of the enterprise.

※

- INTEGRATING TOOLS WITH BUSINESS PROCESSES -

As we conclude this chapter on measuring success in contract lifecycle management, it is clear that a comprehensive, data-driven approach is indispensable for transforming contract processes into strategic assets. Throughout this discussion, we have explored the significance of establishing baselines, defining granular and strategic KPIs, ensuring data integrity through robust governance, and creating a feedback system that fuels continuous improvement. Each of these elements plays a critical role in enabling organizations to track the performance of their contract management practices and translate the insights from these metrics into meaningful, actionable business outcomes.

One of the fundamental takeaways is that without a clearly defined baseline, it is nearly impossible to measure progress. Our discussion highlighted how auditing existing practices—measuring contract cycle times, renewal rates, compliance incidences, or revenue leakage—establishes a starting point. This diagnostic phase, illustrated by examples from various organizations, allowed decision-makers to gain clarity on the inefficiencies that had persisted under manual processes. For instance, we noted how a company that previously averaged a 45-day contract cycle could set measurable targets after identifying bottlenecks. Establishing this baseline is crucial because it provides the reference against which all future improvements are measured, ensuring that the benefits of new implementations are not merely subjective assessments but objectively verifiable enhancements.

Building on this foundation, defining and segmenting key performance indicators emerged as an essential practice. By breaking down KPI measurements into granular stages—such as the drafting phase versus the negotiation phase—organizations are equipped to pinpoint precisely where delays and errors occur. This detailed measurement method facilitates targeted interventions and encourages cross-departmental collaboration, as each stakeholder understands their specific contribution to the overall contract performance. We discussed how a global enterprise segmented its contract lifecycle to isolate the legal review phase, leading to tailored retraining programs and process refinements that reduced delays by a measurable margin. These examples underscore that performance measurement is not a one-size-fits-all endeavor; it must be tailored to the unique operational nuances of each organization.

Integrating technology and advanced analytics is another critical theme in this chapter. Modern CLM systems provide a unified platform, consolidating contract data into a single repository accessible via real-time dashboards. This integration translates into decision-makers having immediate, actionable insights at their fingertips. For example, one financial institution's dashboard allowed executives to identify a spike in processing times and correlate it with operational bottlenecks. It prompted swift corrective actions that improved supplier negotiations and boosted revenue capture from favorable terms. Advanced analytics not only support the identification and segmentation of KPIs but also provide predictive insights that shift an organization from a reactive mode to a proactive, anticipatory posture when combined with automation and AI. One multinational manufacturer's experience with AI-driven contract analytics—flagging non-standard clauses before they led to compliance issues—demonstrates that predictive capabilities are increasingly central to effective risk management and strategic planning.

Data integrity is a recurring principle that underpins every aspect of the measurement framework. The discussion emphasized that reliable data is the foundation for building meaningful metrics. Our exploration showed how inconsistent data entry and fragmented system architecture can distort performance metrics, leading to misinformed decision-making. Initiatives such as regular audits, standardized data entry procedures, and integrated CLM platforms significantly enhance data quality. When a manufacturing company underwent a data cleansing initiative, it not only improved the accuracy of its KPIs but also restored confidence across the executive team. This example illustrates that maintaining rigorous data integrity practices is non-negotiable for any organization serious about measuring performance accurately and driving continuous improvements.

Another key insight relates to the interplay between quantitative metrics and qualitative feedback. While numerical KPIs provide a clear, objective measure of performance improvements, such as reduced cycle times or increased revenue from renegotiated contracts, the value of qualitative insights should not be underestimated. Feedback from cross-functional teams, customer satisfaction surveys, and vendor reviews adds context that enriches the raw numbers. In one instance, a mid-market firm's post-contract execution surveys revealed that streamlined processes reduced administrative burdens and increased overall satisfaction and loyalty among employees and clients. When combined with quantitative data, these qualitative insights yield a comprehensive picture of performance that drives holistic organizational improvements.

The importance of continuous improvement was a recurring theme in our analysis. Business environments are inherently dynamic, and what works today may require adjustment tomorrow. Establishing a culture of recurrent review—where monthly or quarterly performance meetings are standard practice—is essential for keeping the measurement framework responsive and relevant. Regular review cycles allow organizations to recalibrate their KPIs as market conditions, regulatory environments, or internal priorities change. The example of a global retail chain using quarterly reviews to reduce processing times demonstrates that iterative adjustments lead to sustainable improvements over time. These continuous feedback loops validate the initial technological investments and ensure that the CLM system evolves in tandem with the overall business strategy.

In addition, integrating risk management metrics into the measurement framework further enhances strategic decision-making. Contract management is invariably associated with risks due to regulatory non-compliance, disputes, or unforeseen delays. Quantifying these risks through specific metrics, such as the frequency of contractual non-compliance or issues arising from ambiguous language, enables organizations to tackle potential problems before they escalate. We discussed how a healthcare organization's automated compliance tracking system helped to preempt regulatory breaches by highlighting contracts that deviated from standard clauses, thereby averting significant penalties. By treating risk as a measurable component, organizations can proactively protect their financial and operational interests while further cementing the strategic value of their contract management practices.

Economic justification for CLM initiatives also emerged as a central theme. When organizations can explicitly link improvements in contract processing, such as faster turnaround times, reduced administrative costs, and increased revenue from renegotiation, to financial outcomes, the return on investment becomes tangible. One global consumer electronics company successfully reduced its processing costs by 20 percent after modernizing its CLM system, a savings that translated directly into improved operating margins. By articulating such quantifiable benefits, decision-makers can secure further investments in contract management tools and systems, ensuring that successive layers of improvement yield cumulative, measurable gains.

Cross-functional alignment is another critical component of this measurement framework. Although departments like legal, finance, procurement, and customer service may focus on different aspects of contract management, effective performance measurement depends on synthesizing these insights into a unified narrative. Regular cross-departmental meetings and standardized reporting practices ensure that every stakeholder works from the same set of metrics, fostering a culture of shared accountability. A coordinated approach enhances operational efficiency and amplifies the CLM system's strategic impact by ensuring that every improvement is recognized and reinforced across the organization.

In conclusion, the advanced measurement framework we have examined serves as the cornerstone for transforming contract lifecycle management into a strategic function. By establishing a clear baseline, defining granular KPIs, ensuring data integrity, and implementing continuous feedback loops, organizations are well-equipped to convert operational improvements into measurable strategic gains. Automation and advanced analytics provide the technological underpinning that significantly reduces manual errors and supports proactive risk management. At the same time, qualitative feedback and cross-functional alignment ensure that performance improvements are both comprehensive and sustainable.

The insights gleaned from detailed case studies and real-world examples illustrate that measuring success in CLM is not simply an administrative exercise but a strategic imperative informing resource allocation, risk management, and future process enhancements. With a robust measurement framework, every aspect of contract management, from processing times to compliance rates, becomes quantifiable and actionable. This approach enables organizations to identify hidden inefficiencies, swiftly make informed decisions, and adjust their strategies based on real-time data, transforming contracts into actual strategic assets.

As we transition to the next chapter, where we will focus on designing executive dashboards and reporting frameworks, the principles discussed in this subchapter set the stage for a deeper exploration of performance visualization. The executive dashboard represents the practical culmination of these measurement practices, providing a centralized format from which leadership can monitor progress, identify risks, and make strategic decisions promptly. The journey toward fully realizing the benefits of a data-driven CLM system continues by translating these comprehensive metrics into clear, accessible intelligence that aligns operational performance with strategic business objectives.

This subchapter has provided an in-depth exploration of the refined measurement framework essential for driving success in contract lifecycle management. It has emphasized the importance of defining detailed KPIs, ensuring data accuracy, integrating quantitative and qualitative feedback, and fostering a culture of continuous improvement. These elements uniquely contribute to forming a dynamic, comprehensive system that reduces risks, optimizes operations, and enhances revenue capture. Implementing these measurement practices validates the investment in advanced CLM tools and serves as a beacon that guides further investments and process enhancements.

In wrapping up this chapter, it is worth reiterating that measuring success transforms everyday operational data into a strategic resource. By harnessing the power of integrated analytics, continuous review, and cross-functional collaboration, organizations can convert raw contract data into actionable insights that drive short-term performance improvements and long-term strategic growth. The measurement framework is an ongoing journey, it evolves iteratively, adapts to new challenges, and continuously supports the organization's overarching objectives.

As we move forward to the next chapter on designing executive dashboards and reporting structures, the robust measurement framework you have built will serve as the foundation for translating these detailed insights into easily digestible, actionable intelligence. The dashboards will aggregate these metrics, enabling leadership to visualize real-time performance, monitor trends, and respond proactively to emerging challenges or opportunities. These tools will not only validate the effectiveness of current initiatives but will also shape strategic decision-making as you optimize contract management practices further.

In closing, the comprehensive measurement framework we have explored is critical for ensuring that contract management is efficient and strategically impactful. It provides the data-driven foundation for continuously measuring and improving operational performance. Every metric, every KPIs update, and every cycle of feedback loops contributes to a more agile, resilient, and competitive organization. With this framework, you are well-prepared to capture the full benefits of your CLM initiatives, ensuring that each contract contributes to sustained operational excellence and long-term business growth.

With these final insights in mind, we now solidify our understanding of measuring success in contract management and prepare to embark on the next phase of our journey—translating these detailed measurements into dynamic executive dashboards and reporting frameworks that will empower your organization with real-time strategic decision-making capabilities.

CHAPTER 7:

MEASURING SUCCESS

As organizations continue to refine and harness the power of strategic contract management, a new challenge naturally emerges: How to expand these successes into scalable, enterprise-wide solutions that propel growth over the long term. In previous chapters, we have examined how a modern CLM system—backed by advanced technology, data-driven insights, and a culture of continuous improvement—can transform contracts from static legal documents into agile, revenue-driving assets. We have seen case studies where streamlined processes, integrated dashboards, and proactive risk management techniques have not only reduced processing times and compliance breaches but also unlocked hidden revenue streams. Now, the focus shifts to scaling these advantages across broader segments of the organization, and ultimately, across the entire enterprise.

Scaling your contract advantage is about transforming isolated improvements into a systematic, repeatable model that can be applied across diverse business units, geographies, and market segments. It requires taking the best practices and successful pilot projects and integrating them into the organization's very fabric. When contract management is scaled effectively, every contract, whether with a key supplier or a new customer, becomes part of a cohesive strategy that amplifies innovation, flexibility, and financial performance. The goal is to ensure that the strategic benefits of improved contract management are not confined to a single function or silo but are spread throughout the organization, driving competitive differentiation and long-term growth.

Consider, for example, a mid-sized enterprise that initially embarked on a focused initiative to automate its contract renewal process in one business unit. In that limited setting, the company experienced a reduction in renewal cycle times by nearly 40 percent and captured incremental revenue through improved negotiation leverage. Encouraged by these outcomes, leadership scaled the process across all business units. However, scaling came with its challenges. Each unit had its legacy processes, data quality variations, and different readiness levels for technological integration. What began as a controlled pilot quickly evolved into a comprehensive change management project, involving a cross-functional team tasked with standardizing processes, integrating disparate data sources, and training employees across the board. Ultimately, this scaling effort delivered consistent improvements in contract processing across the entire enterprise and engendered a culture of collaboration and continuous improvement. The success of this initiative was measured not only in operational efficiency gains and financial savings but also in the way it brought together teams from legal, finance, procurement, and sales to work toward common strategic objectives.

A central theme in scaling contract management is harmonizing and standardizing processes while preserving the flexibility required to adapt to local conditions. On one hand, standard operating procedures (SOPs) are created to establish a common baseline for contract creation, review, and renewal. On the other hand, organizations must maintain enough flexibility to tailor contracts to the unique needs of different markets, industries, or customer segments. This balance ensures that while processes are consistent enough to generate measurable improvements, they are not so rigid as to stifle innovation or responsiveness. Many organizations have overcome this challenge by adopting a modular approach—developing core standardized processes that serve as a framework, which can then be customized by individual business units based on factors such as regional regulations or specific market conditions.

Scaling contract advantage also means integrating increasingly sophisticated technology across the organization, ensuring every department benefits from the same level of real-time insight and predictive analytics. Earlier chapters demonstrated the value of automated alerts, integrated dashboards, and AI-driven analytics in managing a single portfolio of contracts. However, when scaling these tools across multiple departments, challenges such as data interoperability, uniformity in user training, and the integration with legacy systems come to the forefront. For instance, a successful large enterprise recently embarked on an effort to integrate its CLM solution with its global ERP and CRM systems, creating a central repository of contractual data that could be accessed company-wide. This integration improved the transparency of contract performance across geographies and provided leadership with a unified platform for monitoring key performance metrics. The result was a seamless flow of data that directly informed strategic decision-making at the executive level and allowed individual business units to drill down and address local inefficiencies. By scaling technological integration in this way, organizations can ensure that the benefits of advanced contract management, such as faster processing times, better compliance, and increased revenue from renegotiated terms, are realized on an enterprise-wide level.

Moreover, scaling the contract advantage extends beyond the implementation of technology and standardized processes, it also involves embedding a culture of continuous improvement and accountability throughout the organization. When the benefits of refined contract management are observed in isolated projects, it becomes easier to demonstrate the potential for broader transformation. However, change management on a larger scale requires concerted leadership effort and a strategic plan to overcome resistance. Employees across different regions and functions must be engaged through comprehensive training programs, clear communication, and the establishment of performance-based incentives. For example, one multinational organization implemented an organization-wide change program that brought together representatives from all business functions to share best practices, discuss challenges, and set uniform targets for contract performance. These cross-functional workshops accelerated the adoption of new processes and fostered a sense of shared ownership over the enterprise's contractual success. As a result, the organization saw not just operational improvements but a significant enhancement in employee morale and inter-departmental collaboration, paving the way for sustainable, long-term growth.

In the context of scaling, it is also important to acknowledge that global organizations often face additional complexities. Multiple regulatory frameworks, diverse market conditions, and varying internal competencies can all influence how contract management practices are deployed. To address these challenges, a phased approach to scaling may be necessary. The initial phase often involves piloting new systems in one region or business unit, gathering robust data, and refining the playbook before rolling it out across the enterprise. This phased approach allows for localized adjustments while maintaining a clear, overarching strategy. For example, a large healthcare conglomerate first implemented its advanced CLM system in North America, where regulatory requirements were most stringent. After achieving measurable success, such as reduced compliance breaches and improved supplier terms, the organization gradually extended the same processes to its operations in Europe and Asia. Such an approach ensures that scaling is done methodically, with lessons learned from each phase feeding back to improve the subsequent rollouts. The iterative nature of this process ultimately leads to a comprehensive, adaptable framework that benefits the organization as a whole.

Another critical concept in scaling contract management is the refinement of performance metrics and dashboards that offer real-time, actionable insights across the organization. As contract management processes are expanded, the measurement system must remain agile enough to capture performance comprehensively across various units. Executive dashboards must be customizable so that leaders at global, regional, and local levels can monitor the most relevant KPIs to their operations. For instance, while the worldwide leadership team might focus on overall cycle time improvements and revenue impacts, local managers might be more interested in cancellation rates, speed of approval, or customer satisfaction levels. Ensuring that these metrics are consistently tracked—and that cross-functional teams can drill down into specifics when needed—provides a clear view of how well scaling efforts are performing and where further improvements are warranted. Integrated dashboards, therefore, become critical tools in the scaling process, enabling a seamless transition from pilot projects to an enterprise-wide system.

An anecdote that illustrates the power of scaling comes from a multinational manufacturing company. Initially, the company implemented an automated contract renewal system in one of its key business units. The pilot project yielded impressive results, including a 35 percent reduction in renewal delays and a noticeable increase in cost savings from improved supplier terms. Emboldened by these outcomes, the leadership decided to roll out the system across all business units. However, as the project scaled, the complexities of data integration, varying process standards, and cultural differences between departments became apparent. In response, the company established a centralized office dedicated to CLM oversight, which coordinated training sessions, standardized processes, and technology integration across the board. The coordinated effort led not only to uniform improvements in contract processing times across multiple regions but also to enhanced financial performance and operational synergy. This case is a testament to the fact that scaling, while challenging, is attainable through strategic planning, continuous measurement, and cross-functional collaboration.

Furthermore, scaling your contract advantage necessitates educating and involving everyone from the ground up. A top-down approach is practical only if a bottom-up understanding of the value matches it arrived at through improved contract management. Empowering teams at all levels with the knowledge and tools to monitor and improve their contract practices ensures that localized inefficiencies do not hinder the scalability of processes. This comprehensive engagement includes providing training on new technologies, sharing success stories, and establishing clear communication channels for feedback. In one instance, an international logistics provider significantly improved its contract compliance and reduced operational disruptions by engaging its regional teams through regular workshops and sharing best practices. The inclusive approach not only accelerated the adoption rate but also revealed unique, region-specific challenges that the central team could address more effectively, thereby reinforcing the scalability of the solutions.

Considering these more profound insights into scaling, it becomes evident that the journey from isolated improvements to an enterprise-wide strategy involves many layers. Each component—from data consolidation and process standardization to technological integration and change management—must be carefully managed and aligned with the overall strategic vision. Integrating cross-functional data and feedback loops, in particular, emphasizes that scaling is an ongoing, dynamic process. It is not sufficient to replicate the successes of a pilot program; the entire organization must continuously refine and enhance its contract management practices. Moreover, scaling is an iterative journey that requires ongoing adjustments in response to internal performance metrics, external market conditions, and emerging technological innovations.

This subchapter has provided a deep dive into the numerous facets of scaling a robust contract management system. We have explored how a unified data ecosystem, refined performance metrics, configurable dashboards, and continuous training and change management combine to transform isolated successes into a scalable, enterprise-wide model. The real-world examples we discussed illuminate the challenges and triumphs organizations face as they expand their advanced CLM practices beyond pilot projects and into the core of their business operations. The key takeaway is that scaling your contract advantage is not merely about replication. It is about evolving processes, integrating technology, and fostering a culture of widespread collaboration and continuous improvement.

As we conclude this discussion and prepare for the next phase of our narrative, the move toward scaling is a vital step in securing long-term competitive advantage. The systems, processes, and cultural shifts that have yielded measurable benefits in isolated settings must now become standard practice throughout the organization. By doing so, contracts are elevated from administrative necessities into strategic instruments that drive revenue, mitigate risk, and support proactive decision-making across every enterprise level.

With these insights in mind, we now set the stage for the next chapter, where the focus will shift from scaling operational capabilities to measuring and demonstrating the ongoing success of these initiatives. The subsequent discussion will delve into developing executive dashboards and reporting frameworks, tools that are essential in translating real-time data from a scaled CLM system into actionable intelligence. This transition will enable leaders to monitor progress effectively, adjust strategies dynamically, and ensure that every improvement in contract management contributes to the organization's broader strategic goals.

In conclusion, scaling your contract management framework is a multifaceted endeavor that requires thoughtful integration of technology, standardization of processes, and vigorous engagement from all levels of the organization. It is a process that transforms isolated wins into an ongoing engine of growth system that is agile enough to adapt and robust enough to support enterprise-wide success. The insights and best practices covered in this subchapter illustrate that when scaling is approached methodically and strategically, the results are transformative: faster contract processing, improved compliance, higher revenue capture, and a strengthened competitive position in the marketplace.

As you reflect on these more profound insights into the challenges and strategies of scaling contract management, you can envision a system in which every aspect of contract performance is cohesively managed across the organization. With a broad-based, scalable approach in place, your organization is well-positioned to harness the full strategic potential of its contracts. With these foundational elements established, we now prepare to transition to the next phase of our journey—measuring and reporting the success of these initiatives through executive dashboards and performance reporting systems that will further empower strategic decision-making across the enterprise.

:::

- KEY METRICS AND REPORTING FOR CLM -

Organizations that have transformed isolated contract management improvements into a broader competitive strategy now face the critical challenge of scaling these successes across the entire enterprise. This subchapter introduces the theme of scaling the contract advantage, articulating how isolated wins in contract optimization can be systematically replicated throughout every business unit, region, and process to drive sustainable growth. Drawing on industry examples and practical methodologies, we examine how processes, technology, and culture must align to create an enterprise-wide system in which contracts are managed efficiently and actively contribute to strategic outcomes.

Initial successes have been realized in many companies through focused projects that redesigned contract processing, standardized legal documents, and introduced technology-driven workflows. For instance, one mid-market enterprise improved its contract renewal speed and reduced administrative costs within a single business unit. The team achieved results by introducing automated alerts and standardized review processes, cutting processing time by nearly 40 percent. While these achievements proved promising, they also revealed that the real power of contract management lies in expanding those isolated successes into a comprehensive system, in a way that every contract across the organization carries the same strategic weight and efficiency.

Scaling contract management is fundamentally about creating repeatable, robust systems that are flexible enough to address local nuances but standardized sufficient to deliver consistent outcomes. A central part of this effort involves carefully mapping the current contract processes across all departments. This diagnostic phase goes beyond simply collecting data about processing times or compliance rates; it entails a detailed examination of how contracts are initiated, reviewed, negotiated, signed, administered, and eventually renewed or terminated within each organization segment. By comparing these processes across different business units, organizations can identify not only best practices and success stories from pilot projects but also common barriers and inefficiencies that, if unaddressed, will continue to hinder performance on a larger scale.

One instructive example is a large multinational corporation initially implementing an automated contract renewal system in its European division. There, the system improved tracking of renewal dates and provided real-time status updates to both legal and finance teams. Recognizing the benefits, the company planned to extend the system to its North American and Asian operations. However, the expansion revealed several challenges. While the European division enjoyed high data interoperability and uniform adherence to standardized processes, other divisions used legacy systems with inconsistent data formats, making integration far more complex. To scale successfully, the company had to reconcile these differences through a phased approach that involved reengineering data capture methods, standardizing procedures, and remediating legacy system issues. This example highlights that scaling is not merely a replication of a successful process, it's a careful integration of improvements into an overarching framework that must consider the unique characteristics of various business units and regions.

One of the core elements of scaling the contract advantage is establishing a set of standardized procedures that work as the backbone for the entire organization. Standard operating procedures (SOPs) should be designed to address every stage of the contract lifecycle. This includes initiating negotiations, documenting terms with clarity, executing contracts, and managing renewals. When every part of an organization follows the same SOPs, it creates an environment of predictability and transparency. For instance, one company reduced errors in contract submissions by instituting a unified document review checklist that every department used. As a result, inconsistencies in terms and conditions were minimized, and corrective actions became more straightforward to implement globally. Such standardization is crucial for ensuring consistency and enabling the integration of technology that can automate and monitor these processes effectively.

Technology plays a central role when scaling contract management. In the early stages, many organizations benefit from pilot programs that demonstrate the value of a new CLM system on a small scale. However, as these systems are rolled out across the enterprise, integrating them with existing technologies such as enterprise resource planning (ERP) and customer relationship management (CRM) platforms becomes essential. The goal is to create an interconnected environment where contract data flows freely between different business functions. This interoperability is critical: when the same data is accessible to procurement, finance, legal, and even operational departments, decisions are based on a comprehensive view of contract performance. Consider a manufacturing firm that linked its CLM platform to its ERP system. This integration allowed the company to correlate contract performance with production and inventory data, enabling it to negotiate better pricing or adjust supply chain strategies in real time. When scaling, the technology must not remain siloed; instead, it should enhance an enterprise-wide approach to contract management that improves reporting, accountability, and strategic planning.

Scaling also requires a significant cultural shift. In many organizations, contract management has traditionally been seen as the exclusive responsibility of the legal department. However, all relevant stakeholders must be involved to spread the benefits of refined contract processes across the organization. This means engaging finance, procurement, sales, and customer service teams in the contract management process. Cross-functional collaboration ensures that contracts support the overall strategic objectives of the business and that insights gained in one department can benefit others. A compelling example is a retail conglomerate establishing a dedicated, cross-departmental contract management committee. This team regularly reviewed contract performance metrics and shared the best practices, which led to improvements in contract turnaround times, supplier negotiations, and customer satisfaction levels. The committee's work underscored that scaling contract management is as much about breaking down internal silos as it is about implementing new processes and technology.

Another primary consideration when scaling the contract advantage is changing management. Moving from localized, often manual processes to an advanced, standardized system inevitably meets resistance. Employees accustomed to specific workflows may find the transition disruptive. Hence, a comprehensive change management plan is essential. This plan should include detailed training programs, clear communication strategies, and mechanisms for gathering ongoing feedback from all levels of the organization. Lessons learned from pilot projects and early implementations should be documented and shared widely. When employees understand the strategic rationale behind changes and see firsthand how improved contract management contributes to overall business performance, resistance diminishes, and adoption increases. For example, after rolling out a new CLM system in one region, one enterprise organized training workshops and follow-up sessions for teams in all areas. The result was rapid adoption of the system and a notable increase in process efficiency and employee satisfaction across the organization. In scaling contract management, nurturing an inclusive and transparent culture enhances the success of technological and procedural integrations.

Refining performance metrics and executive dashboards as organizations scale becomes even more critical. Not only must incoming data from various business units be aggregated accurately, but it must also be actionable. Executive dashboards that offer real-time insights into contract performance allow senior management to monitor progress, identify areas for improvement, and respond quickly to emerging issues. When scaling, these dashboards need to be customizable, enabling global, regional, and local teams to view KPIs most pertinent to their segments. For instance, while a worldwide view may focus on overall contract cycle times and revenue recovery figures, local teams might track specific metrics such as turnaround time for regional contracts or compliance adherence in local markets. The flexibility of these reporting tools is crucial to ensure that the benefits of improved contract management are realized at all levels. A customizable dashboard can transform isolated data into an enterprise-wide narrative that supports strategic decision-making, ensuring that every part of the organization works towards common goals.

Risk management remains a vital component throughout the scaling process. As the number of contracts and interdependencies increases, so does the risk potential, whether from non-compliance or misaligned vendor relationships. Scaling requires that organizations develop a robust framework for monitoring and mitigating these risks. This can be achieved by incorporating risk measures into the standard performance metrics discussed earlier. For example, tracking the frequency of contractual disputes or non-compliances can help identify trends requiring immediate corrective action. One case in point involves a healthcare organization that, after scaling its CLM system, noticed an increase in compliance-related issues in one business unit. With an established risk management protocol, the organization quickly addressed these issues through revised training and updated contract templates. Such proactive risk management strategies are critical in ensuring that scaling does not dilute the quality of contract performance and that any emerging risks are managed systematically.

Financial justification for scaling is another factor that drives its successful implementation. When the improvements yielded by a new contract management system in one division are quantified, such as reduced cycle times, improved supplier terms, or increased revenue from renegotiated contracts, they can serve as the basis for broader investment. Documenting these successes provides a clear return on investment (ROI) narrative that convinces stakeholders across the organization of the strategic value of scaling. For example, a multinational reported that its pilot project saved significant operational costs and led to revenue increases that far outweighed the initial costs, prompting the program's expansion to all business units. When scaling initiatives can be tied directly to measurable financial benefits, they gain the necessary momentum and support from executive leadership to be implemented enterprise-wide.

Scaling also requires attention to local adaptation. While a standardized approach is essential for consistency, it is equally vital to accommodate regional and industry-specific requirements. Organizations must plan for uniformity and flexibility by adopting a modular framework for their CLM practices. This approach allows core processes to remain consistent while providing room for localized customization. For instance, a global corporation might standardize its contract review process while allowing for regional adjustments in terms of regulatory compliance. This ensures that local teams have the autonomy to modify processes as necessary without compromising the organization's overarching objectives. Such a modular approach minimizes friction and creates an environment where improvements can be effectively scaled while addressing specific local challenges.

Finally, the success of scaling contract management efforts strongly depends on the alignment of technological, process, and cultural initiatives. When scaling becomes a coordinated effort involving cross-functional teams, consistent training, unified performance metrics, and flexible yet standardized processes, the organization benefits from improved operational performance and strategic coherence. The journey from isolated pilot successes to an enterprise-wide system is iterative, requiring continuous monitoring, adaptation, and the willingness to refine processes based on new insights and feedback. By integrating these elements effectively, organizations improve the efficiency of their contract management practices and establish a competitive advantage that can drive sustainable growth.

In conclusion, scaling contract management is a complex but essential process for modern organizations seeking to transform tactical wins into enduring competitive advantages. The journey involves establishing standardized practices, integrating advanced technology, ensuring cross-functional collaboration, and deploying change management strategies to create a cohesive, enterprise-wide model. Organizations can ensure that every contract is managed to deliver maximum strategic value through detailed segmentation of performance metrics, robust risk management, customizable executive dashboards, and a culture of continuous improvement. The experiences and examples discussed here underscore the multifaceted nature of scaling, illustrating that it is not simply a replication of successful pilot projects but a strategic transformation that requires uniformity, adaptability, and sustained commitment across all levels.

As we step toward the next phase of our narrative, the focus will shift from scaling operational capabilities to quantifying and showcasing the success of these initiatives. The forthcoming chapter will center on designing executive dashboards and reporting frameworks that simplify performance data visualization. These tools will enable leaders to monitor progress in real time, adjust strategies dynamically, and ensure that every improvement in contract management translates directly into tangible business results. In this way, scaling is not an end in itself but a critical step in a larger journey toward making contract management an integrated, proactive, and profit-driving enterprise function.

In summary, this subchapter has explored the intricacies of scaling the contract advantage, demonstrating the need for standardized processes that are flexible yet consistent, robust integration of technology for unified data flow, a strong emphasis on change management and continuous training, and the importance of measurable performance indicators that align with strategic objectives. The case studies and examples discussed illustrate that while scaling presents specific challenges, these can be overcome through careful planning and a modular approach that balances global consistency with local flexibility. The resulting system offers streamlined processes, proactive risk management, and quantifiable financial benefits across the organization.

By adopting such an approach, organizations are well-prepared to convert isolated contract management successes into an enterprise-wide system that significantly improves operational efficiency and contributes to sustainable growth. The principles outlined here provide a roadmap for turning every contract into a strategic asset, ensuring that as your organization grows, so too does its contract management practices' quality, consistency, and effectiveness.

With these insights in hand, you are now ready to transition to the next chapter, which will focus on measuring the long-term impact of these scaling efforts through executive dashboards and advanced reporting systems. These tools will bridge the gap between operational efficiency and strategic decision-making, providing a comprehensive view of performance that supports continued evolution and competitive advantage.

This concludes our discussion in this subchapter on scaling the contract advantage. The foundational elements of process standardization, technological integration, cultural change, and rigorous performance measurement come together to create a model that is not only scalable but also adaptable and strategically sound. As you reflect on these principles, consider how each component can be systematically applied within your organization to drive continuous improvement and lasting results in contract management.

⁙

- DESIGNING EXECUTIVE DASHBOARDS FOR STRATEGIC INSIGHTS -

In deepening our exploration of scaling the contract advantage, we must move beyond the high-level concepts and examine how organizations can operationalize these ideas to achieve consistent, enterprise-wide success. This subchapter delves into the detailed strategies and methodologies that underpin the systematic scaling of contract management best practices. We will discuss how technology integration, process standardization, and cultural alignment can be practically implemented across diverse business units. Through illustrative examples and insightful analysis, this discussion reveals the intricate balance between global consistency and local flexibility—a balance that is the hallmark of scalable contract management solutions.

One of the foremost challenges in scaling contract management is the diverse nature of operational practices across different departments, regions, and business units. What works in one segment often does not translate seamlessly to another due to variations in legacy processes, regulatory environments, and market conditions. Organizations must first perform a detailed cross-functional analysis of their existing contract processes to overcome this. This diagnostic phase is not simply a matter of auditing average cycle times or compliance rates; it requires a granular mapping of each step in the lifecycle of a contract, from initiation to renewal. For example, a multinational firm discovered through a comprehensive process mapping exercise that its procurement division employed a highly efficient electronic approval workflow. In contrast, its sales division relied on a more informal, paper-based review. The discrepancy created significant delays when contracts passed between these divisions. By documenting these differences, leadership was able to design a standardized process that respected the unique needs of each unit while ensuring a consistent global standard. This approach underscores that scaling begins with understanding the diversity within the organization and then working to harmonize key aspects without stifling the local adaptations that add value.

Standardization is closely tied to the successful integration of technology. As discussed in previous chapters, technology provides the backbone for modern contract lifecycle management. However, scaling technology across an enterprise presents its own set of challenges. Adopting a single, unified CLM platform for a company with multiple business units must account for variations in data formats, user competencies, and system infrastructure. Achieving interoperability between new systems and existing legacy platforms is a critical step in this process. Consider a global manufacturing company that embarked on a CLM modernization project. Initially, its European branches deployed a cloud-based CLM solution that significantly streamlined contract renewals and enabled automated alerts, rapidly reducing cycle times. However, when this system was introduced in North American units, integration issues arose because many of these units were still reliant on legacy software that did not easily communicate with the new platform. To resolve this, the company invested in middleware solutions and data conversion tools that allowed the disparate systems to interact smoothly. The result was an enterprise-wide CLM environment where data flowed seamlessly, enabling cohesive reporting and strategic analysis at the global level. This case illustrates that scalable technology integration requires investment in new tools and the careful bridging of old and new systems.

Another critical element in scaling is the focus on key performance indicators (KPIs) and the refinement of performance measurement. Scaling benefits are fully realized when organizations can track improvements consistently across all units. A single business unit's efficiency gains are substantial but must be aggregated to show a clear, measurable return on investment at the corporate level. To this end, organizations should establish core KPIs—such as average contract cycle time, renewal rates, compliance metrics, and revenue recovery from renegotiations—that are uniformly defined and monitored. However, these global KPIs must also be broken down into sub-metrics that reflect local variations. By doing so, a financial manager in a regional office can see that while the overall cycle time might be 30 days, certain types of contracts in their region may take 35 days, indicating an area for targeted improvement. This dual-level measurement provides a high-level perspective for executives and granular insight that can drive localized process enhancements.

Equally important is data consolidation into executive dashboards that offer real-time insights. As scaling progresses, decision-makers need accessible, dynamic tools that display aggregated metrics from across the enterprise. Effective dashboards serve as the nerve center for global contract management, showing trends over time and highlighting deviations that require intervention. For instance, one enterprise's dashboard allowed global leadership to monitor a sudden increase in dispute-related delays across a specific region, prompting an immediate investigation into that unit's review processes. These dashboards must be customizable to accommodate the varying needs of global, regional, and local teams. In doing so, they ensure that scaling does not dilute the visibility of performance metrics or create rigid silos that hide as much as they reveal.

Change management plays a fundamental role in the process of scaling. Even if technology is implemented flawlessly and processes are standardized, the overall success of scaling depends on the willingness of employees to embrace new ways of working. Resistance to change is common, particularly in large organizations with long-established practices. To overcome this, organizations must couple their scaling initiatives with robust training programs, open communication channels, and incentive structures that clearly demonstrate the new system's benefits. One notable example involved a retail conglomerate that launched an enterprise-wide CLM enhancement initiative. The company organized a series of cross-departmental workshops where employees could voice concerns and see demonstrations of the new system's capabilities firsthand. These workshops facilitated smoother adoption of the new processes and technology and contributed to a cultural shift that emphasized innovation and continuous improvement. When employees at every level see how improved contract management directly benefits their work and the organization's success, the scaling process becomes a shared goal, accelerating its success.

Beyond internal processes, scaling contract management must address external relationships, including suppliers, customers, and partners. As organizations expand their contract management systems, the same rigorous standards and processes applied internally must also be communicated to and adopted by external stakeholders. This external alignment ensures that contracts remain consistent, mutually beneficial, and strategically sound. For example, a multinational logistics company faced challenges when regional offices negotiated supplier contracts with varying terms and performance benchmarks, leading to inconsistencies in service levels and pricing. The company could harmonize supplier agreements globally by standardizing key contract terms and integrating vendor management protocols into its CLM system. This improved supplier performance, built trust, and facilitated smoother negotiations, demonstrating how scaling internal processes can extend benefits outward to reinforce strategic partnerships.

A modular approach to scaling is another significant insight that emerged during our exploration. Rather than attempting to enforce a rigid, one-size-fits-all process across the entire organization, scaling needs to be implemented in modules that allow for local customization while adhering to core global standards. This modular strategy can be particularly effective in multinational companies where business practices and regulatory requirements differ dramatically between regions. For instance, a pharmaceutical company operating in various countries might institute a global CLM framework that outlines key contract terms and approval processes, yet allows for modifications to comply with local drug regulation policies. This approach preserves the integrity of the global strategy while granting sufficient flexibility to address local needs. Modular scaling thus bridges the gap between uniformity and adaptability, ensuring that the best practices proven in one context can be successfully adapted to others.

The financial impact of scaling cannot be overlooked. Demonstrating a clear return on investment is crucial for securing ongoing support from executive leadership. When a scaled CLM initiative delivers measurable improvements, such as shorter contract cycle times, lower administrative costs, and increased revenue from bet-ter-negotiated terms, it provides the financial justification for further investments and consolidation of processes. A case in point comes from a large consumer electronics firm that reported a 20% reduction in contract process-ing costs after scaling its advanced CLM system across all business units. This cost saving and increased rev-enue capture from renegotiated contracts significantly improved the company's bottom line. Such quantifiable financial benefits help to reinforce the strategic value of scaling and encourage a continuous effort to embed these practices across the organization.

Risk management remains a constant priority throughout the scaling process. As the volume of contracts increases and processes become more integrated, the complexity of risk monitoring grows accordingly. Scaling must include a robust, enterprise-wide risk management framework that standardizes how risk is measured and mitigated. This involves setting up alerts for potential compliance breaches, monitoring contractual disputes, and tracking the frequency of non-performance issues across depart-ments. A healthcare organization, for example, expanded its risk management protocols as it scaled its CLM system and noticed that a particular business unit was experienc-ing higher rates of compliance deviations. By addressing these issues through targeted training and procedural ad-justments, the organization was able to reduce risk, lower associated costs, and ensure that the integrity of the scaled system was maintained.

Furthermore, scaling contract management is deeply in-tertwined with the concept of performance visibility. As processes and technology are deployed across larger segments of the organization, it becomes increasingly important to maintain a clear, unified view of overall performance. Integrated dashboards play a critical role by consolidating data from multiple sources and presenting it in an accessible format. These dashboards allow global leaders to track high-level metrics and enable local managers to drill down and examine specific areas that need attention. When every business unit sees its performance in the context of the larger organizational goals, it fosters a sense of accountability and shared purpose that drives overall improvement.

The journey of scaling contract management is iterative by nature. It requires continuous refinement, as improvements implemented in one phase often reveal new areas for optimization when applied on a broader scale. The feedback loop—capturing lessons learned, adjusting processes based on performance data, and incorporating employee and vendor feedback—becomes indispensable. The agile nature of this process ensures that scaling is not a one-off project but an ongoing transformation that evolves alongside market dynamics, regulatory changes, and internal innovations. The iterative approach means that each scaling phase builds on the last, leading to cumulative benefits that enhance the organization's competitive position in the long run.

Lastly, it is essential to address the human element in scaling. Sustaining improvements across an enterprise-wide system depends on the active participation of all employees. Leadership must ensure that the scaling process includes comprehensive change management, robust training, and clear communication. In one notable example, an international logistics provider conducted periodic cross-functional workshops to encourage knowledge sharing and address emerging challenges. These sessions not only bolstered employee morale but also contributed to a smoother, more integrated rollout of updated CLM practices, demonstrating that technological and process innovations can be scaled more effectively when people are engaged.

In summary, scaling your contract management advantage involves a multifaceted approach that integrates the best practices and technological solutions identified in earlier stages. Detailed process mapping and standardization provide the foundation for consistent operations, while integrated technology ensures that data flows seamlessly and is accessible in real time. Cross-functional collaboration, robust change management, modular customization, and continuous feedback loops collectively create an environment where scaling is possible and sustainable, resulting in improved operational efficiency, reduced risk, and tangible financial benefits.

By adopting these strategies, organizations can expand localized successes into an enterprise-wide system that transforms contracts into strategic assets. The scalability of these initiatives is measured not only by replicating improvements across business units but also by adapting to diverse regulatory, market, and cultural environments. When every contract across the organization is managed with a common standard yet tailored to specific local needs, overall performance improves, strategic risks are mitigated, and competitive advantages are amplified.

These more profound insights into scaling emphasize that success in contract management is an ongoing journey.

Each scaling phase builds upon the previous one, creating an integrated, agile, and responsive system equipped to drive growth and deliver measurable strategic value. The efforts to standardize processes, integrate advanced CLM technology, and manage change across diverse business units are all crucial components of this journey. Moreover, the financial benefits realized through reduced cycle times, lower administrative costs, and better-negotiated terms justify continuous investment in scaling initiatives.

As you reflect on these strategies, the key takeaway is that scaling contract management transcends mere expansion—it is about fostering an organization-wide culture where strategic contract management becomes ingrained in every operational process. This holistic integration ensures that each contract is processed efficiently and contributes positively to the organization's long-term strategic objectives. The pathway to a truly scalable system lies in balancing global standardization with local flexibility, ensuring that while best practices are maintained across the board, regional specialties and requirements are duly integrated.

In conclusion, this subchapter has deeply explored the key strategies and practical insights required for scaling contract management effectively. From granular process mapping and robust technological integration to cross-functional alignment and adaptive change management, every element plays a role in transforming isolated improvements into a cohesive, enterprise-wide system. The examples and methodologies discussed demonstrate that while scaling poses significant challenges, it offers substantial rewards in enhanced operational efficiency, reduced risks, and measurable financial gains.

As we transition into the final chapter of our journey, the insights on scaling serve as a critical link between internal operational excellence and the broader strategic vision. The subsequent chapter will build on these foundations by addressing how to measure the long-term impact of these scaling initiatives through executive dashboards and reporting frameworks. This next phase will translate all the integrated insights from our discussion into actionable intelligence that informs real-time strategic decision-making at the highest levels of the organization.

In summary, scaling your contract management practices is a multifaceted endeavor that requires strategic planning, technological integration, and cultural transformation. It is about replicating isolated successes across multiple business units while accommodating the unique challenges of different regions and markets. The comprehensive approach outlined here illustrates that when organizations adopt an iterative, adaptable strategy, they create a robust framework that supports continuous improvement and sustainable competitive advantage. The foundation laid by these scaling initiatives enables the organization to harness the full strategic potential of its contracts, ensuring long-term operational excellence and growth.

With this understanding, you are now well-equipped to advance further into our narrative. As we transition to the next chapter, the focus will shift towards measuring and demonstrating the success of these transformative initiatives through executive dashboards and comprehensive reporting systems. These tools will offer a clear, real-time view of performance improvements and strategic impacts, consolidating all the benefits discussed thus far into actionable, quantifiable metrics that drive future success.

Thus, as we bring this subchapter closer, we reflect on the transformative power of scaling in contract management. Beyond simply expanding processes, scaling creates a culture where excellence is replicated and continuously refined across the organization. The insights and best practices detailed here provide a roadmap for turning localized wins into a pervasive, strategic advantage. With a scalable contract management framework, every contract becomes an opportunity to drive growth, mitigate risks, and enhance the overall competitive position. As you move forward, these insights will guide you in ensuring that your organization remains agile and responsive in an ever-changing market landscape and that every contract contributes to your long-term strategic objectives.

⁜

- CREATING A CULTURE OF CONTINUOUS IMPROVEMENT -

Throughout this chapter, we have explored the multifaceted process of scaling the contract advantage—from replicating pilot successes to establishing an integrated, enterprise-wide framework that leverages technology, standardized processes, and a culture of continuous improvement. Our discussion examined how isolated wins in contract management can be expanded into scalable systems that deliver consistent benefits across all business units and geographies. We analyzed detailed case studies and real-world examples that underscored the importance of process mapping, technology integration, cross-functional collaboration, and adaptive change management in transforming contract management into a strategic asset that fuels revenue growth, mitigates risks, and enhances operational efficiency.

One of the central lessons throughout this chapter is that scaling is not a simple replication of a successful process—it is an iterative and evolving journey that combines global standardization with local adaptation. Initially, we discussed the need for a thorough diagnostic phase in which organizations map out every step of the contract lifecycle. This detailed examination allows decision-makers to understand the current state of operations, identify bottlenecks, and reveal inherent inefficiencies. By segmenting the contract process into clearly defined stages— such as drafting, legal review, negotiation, execution, and renewal- each department can pinpoint its specific contribution to the overall performance. We examined how one multinational firm uncovered discrepancies between its streamlined European division and paper-based practices in its North American offices. This prompted a phased, customized rollout that ultimately harmonized practices.

The chapter then delved into the vital role of technology in scaling contract management. Modern contract lifecycle management (CLM) platforms, when integrated with other enterprise systems such as ERP and CRM, facilitate a unified data ecosystem where contract data flows seamlessly across departments. This integration provides leadership with real-time, actionable insights via executive dashboards that consolidate key performance indicators such as cycle time, renewal rates, compliance levels, and revenue recovery from renegotiations. After bridging legacy systems with cloud-based solutions through middleware, we saw how a global manufacturing company achieved a truly integrated CLM environment that allowed data to be processed in real time and decisions to be made swiftly. The technological transformation reduced manual errors and administrative overhead and shifted the contract management function from a reactive process to a proactive, intelligence-driven system.

A critical element for successful scaling is standardization balanced with flexibility. Establishing standard operating procedures (SOPs) for every stage of the contract lifecycle provides a common baseline that can be leveraged across the enterprise. One company's experience with a unified document review checklist highlighted how standardization minimizes inconsistencies and streamlines the process, ensuring that contracts meet established quality standards. Yet, at the same time, we emphasized the importance of a modular approach that allows local business units to adapt core processes based on regional or market-specific requirements. For instance, global companies must respect varying regional regulatory frameworks while maintaining consistency in contract language and performance metrics. This balance between uniformity and local customization is essential to scale success without stifling innovation or responsiveness to local market pressures.

Another cornerstone of our discussion was the crucial need for cross-functional collaboration. Historically, contract management was confined to legal departments, but scaling requires engaging finance, procurement, sales, and customer service teams. Cross-functional committees, integrated review meetings, and coordinated change management efforts foster an environment of shared ownership. A notable example was provided by a retail conglomerate that established a dedicated contract management committee comprising representatives from all key departments. Their collective efforts enhanced supplier negotiations, improved contract cycle times, and fostered stronger interdepartmental coordination, improving employee morale and strengthening operational transparency. This shared accountability ensures that scaling efforts are not viewed as isolated projects but are integral to the overall corporate strategy.

We also discussed the importance of robust change management throughout the scaling process. As organizations roll out new technologies and standardized processes across diverse units, resistance to change can impede progress. Companies must invest in comprehensive training programs, effective communication strategies, and feedback mechanisms to overcome these challenges. When employees understand the strategic benefits of improved contract management methods and see concrete efficiency and risk reduction improvements, they become more motivated to adopt these changes. For example, an international logistics provider successfully boosted its system-wide adoption by organizing cross-functional workshops and establishing regional training hubs. These initiatives improved user proficiency and laid the groundwork for a culture that embraces continuous improvement across all levels.

Financial considerations remain a driving factor in scaling contract management. When initial pilot projects demonstrate significant operational savings, such as lower processing costs, faster contract cycles, and increased revenue from renegotiated terms, these tangible benefits provide a persuasive ROI narrative. After scaling its streamlined CLM process, one global consumer electronics firm reported a 20 percent reduction in contract processing costs, alongside higher revenue realized from improved supplier terms. Such clear financial benefits justify the investment in scaling initiatives and encourage further investment in technology and process optimization across the organization.

Risk management must be revisited as scaling expands the volume and complexity of contractual relationships. Organizations can monitor and mitigate risks in real time by integrating risk measurements such as the frequency of compliance breaches, dispute occurrences, and non-performance rates into the performance metrics. One healthcare organization, for instance, scaled its automated compliance tracking system to flag deviations across multiple departments, thus preventing regulatory violations and significant potential penalties. Integrating risk metrics ensures that scaling does not compromise the organization's risk management objectives but rather strengthens them as scaling accelerates.

The iterative nature of scaling was highlighted as a continuous journey rather than a one-off project. As each scaling phase reveals new opportunities and challenges, organizations must remain agile, constantly refining processes, adapting technologies, and updating performance metrics. Regular review cycles, supported by well-integrated executive dashboards, allow leadership to monitor progress and adjust strategies promptly. For example, a multinational retail chain used quarterly performance reviews to identify local bottlenecks and refine its standardized processes, leading to incremental improvements that compounded over time. This continuous feedback loop ensures the scaling process is dynamic and responsive, allowing organizations to remain competitive and adapt to evolving market conditions.

Interoperability between different technology systems plays a significant role in scaling success. Modern CLM solutions must seamlessly integrate with legacy systems, ERP, CRM, and business intelligence platforms to create a holistic, connected data environment. This integration streamlines internal processes and enriches decision-making by providing a comprehensive view of contract performance and associated business outcomes. A global manufacturing enterprise that successfully integrated its disparate systems was able to correlate contract performance data with production metrics, which enabled more accurate forecasting and better negotiation with suppliers. The success of such integration underscores that scalable technology solutions must be designed with interoperability at their core.

Finally, a modular approach that balances global standardization with regional flexibility proved to be a crucial theme. Organizations must implement standardized processes where possible, yet provide sufficient room for local adaptations. This approach is particularly important for multinational companies that operate under different regulatory frameworks and market conditions. By adopting scalable, modular systems, companies can maintain the core benefits of improved contract management while still accommodating local nuances. The example of a global pharmaceutical company that standardized key contractual terms across all regions but allowed for regional adaptations to meet local regulatory requirements demonstrates that flexibility is key to successful scaling.

This subchapter has provided a deep dive into the core strategies for scaling contract management practices across an organization.

Key elements include:

- Conducting a comprehensive diagnostic to map diverse processes and identify inefficiencies.

- Establishing standardized operating procedures as a baseline for consistent contract management.

- Integrating advanced technologies, including CLM systems, ERP, and CRM, to create an interoperable data environment.

- Implementing a modular approach that allows for global consistency coupled with local flexibility.

- Fostering cross-functional collaboration and robust change management to support enterprise-wide adoption.

- Refining performance metrics and utilizing comprehensive executive dashboards to track progress and drive continuous improvement.

- Embedding effective risk management practices and quantifying financial benefits to validate the scaling efforts.

As we weave together these insights, scaling your contract management function is a multifaceted, strategic endeavor. Each element—from technology integration to cultural alignment—contributes to creating an enterprise-wide ecosystem where every contract is managed precisely and aligned with broader strategic goals. The successful scaling of contract management transforms isolated departmental wins into a sustainable, competitive edge that enhances efficiency, reduces risk, and drives quantifiable financial improvements.

Moreover, as you continue to build and refine your scalable contract management strategy, the lessons learned from these detailed initiatives provide a robust foundation for further innovation. The iterative nature of scaling means that every phase builds upon the previous one, resulting in cumulative benefits that extend throughout the organization. Whether through standardized processes that ensure consistency across business units or integrated dashboards that deliver real-time performance insights, each component plays a critical role in shaping an agile, responsive, and strategically aligned system.

The journey of scaling contract management is not without its challenges. Variations in legacy systems, cultural resistance, and the need for continuous training can pose obstacles that require thoughtful planning and dedicated resources. Yet, the comprehensive examples and case studies discussed in this subchapter testify to the transformative potential of a well-executed scaling strategy. They demonstrate that when organizations commit to systematic scaling, the enhancements are profound—improvements in contract cycle times, stronger negotiation outcomes, and a more significant competitive advantage that positions the organization for long-term success.

As we conclude this discussion, remember that successful scaling is an ongoing process that demands regular review and continuous adaptation. It requires a balance of global standardization and local customization, supported by integrated technology and fortified by a culture of collaboration and accountability. The financial, operational, and strategic benefits realized through scaling validate the initial investments and lay the groundwork for further advancements in contract management capabilities.

In conclusion, scaling your contract management function across the enterprise is a critical strategic goal, transforming isolated successes into a robust, integrated system. By meticulously mapping processes, standardizing procedures, integrating advanced technologies, and fostering collaboration across all levels, organizations can achieve an enterprise-wide transformation that drives efficiency, reduces risks, and unlocks sustainable value. The insights shared in this subchapter—from detailed diagnostic approaches and technology integrations to effective change management and risk mitigation—provide a comprehensive roadmap for scaling contract management. These strategies ensure that each contract is processed effectively and contributes to the organization's strategic financial and operational goals.

As we transition to the final chapter, the groundwork laid in our scaling discussions will serve as the steppingstone to the next focus: measuring and reporting on the long-term impact of these transformative initiatives via executive dashboards and reporting frameworks. The subsequent chapter will consolidate our insights into clear, actionable intelligence that enables decision-makers to monitor progress, refine strategies, and sustain competitive advantage in an ever-evolving market landscape.

The comprehensive framework for scaling contract management that we have built here ultimately paves the way for a more efficient, agile, and financially robust contract management function. With every process standardized, every technology integrated, and every stakeholder engaged, the full potential of contract management emerges as a strategic asset that propels organizational growth and mitigates risk. As you reflect on these detailed strategies and insights, imagine a future where every contract contributes systematically to your organization's success, regardless of origin. This is the essence of scaling—transforming isolated improvements into lasting, enterprise-wide competitive advantages.

With these foundational elements in place, you are now well-equipped to advance to our final chapter, where the focus shifts to measuring and communicating success using executive dashboards and robust reporting systems. These tools will ultimately translate the comprehensive, scaled improvements into clear, quantifiable outcomes, ensuring that real-time data and actionable insights back every strategic decision.

In summary, this subchapter has provided a deep, strategic exploration of scaling contract management across the enterprise. The key themes—process standardization, technological integration, modular adaptability, robust change management, and data-driven risk and performance measurement—interconnect to form a cohesive framework that transforms contract management into a pervasive strategic asset. As you look back on these insights, take heart in the notion that scaling is not merely an operational goal but a strategic imperative that, when executed effectively, can drive significant efficiency gains, reduce risks, and generate measurable financial returns.

With these strategies in mind, the journey toward full-scale contract management is well underway, setting the stage for the next chapter where you will learn how to capture and utilize these improvements through executive reporting. This final transition will ensure that every insight, every performance metric, and every strategic advantage gained from scaling is clearly communicated and continuously refined, ultimately positioning your organization for enduring success in a competitive marketplace.

CHAPTER 8:

SCALING YOUR CONTRACT ADVANTAGE

In today's competitive business world, converting isolated contract improvements into organization-wide competitive advantage is not only an operational priority but a strategic necessity. This final chapter focuses on scaling your contract advantage, ensuring every contract becomes a powerful, lasting asset contributing to long-term growth and sustainability. This chapter offers a comprehensive blueprint for transforming the successes achieved through modern contract lifecycle management (CLM) into scalable, enterprise-wide practices that drive efficiency, reduce risk, and produce a quantifiable return on investment.

This book examined how a customer-centric approach, robust technology tools, and data-driven performance measurement can transform contract management from a fragmented administrative function into a strategic asset. We have seen how proactive risk management, standardized processes, integrated dashboards, and continuous improvement create a resilient framework for managing contracts effectively locally or nationally. Now, the journey moves to the next phase—ensuring these innovations are replicated, refined, and harmonized across the enterprise.

Scaling your contract advantage fundamentally bridges the gap between the pilot successes and an enterprise-wide system. It begins when isolated wins, such as automation reducing processing times by 40 percent in one division or a cross-functional collaboration lowering compliance risks in another segment, are formalized into repeatable, standardized processes applicable to every business unit. In our exploration, we have seen that these improvements, while beneficial on a small scale, represent only a portion of the potential competitive edge. To build sustainable growth, companies must integrate these best practices into a comprehensive framework that spans every facet of their operations, regardless of regional differences or legacy system disparities.

A primary focus in scaling contract management is developing a unified, enterprise-wide standard. This requires thoroughly mapping and analyzing existing contract processes across all departments and regions. For instance, a multinational corporation might find that its European units have embraced electronic approvals while its North American or Asian divisions still rely on manual workflows. By conducting a detailed diagnostic across the organization, leadership can identify the pockets of success and areas of inefficiency. This baseline audit is an essential precursor to scaling, as it clarifies which elements of the contract lifecycle can be standardized and where flexibility is needed to meet local requirements.

Once this comprehensive assessment is completed, the challenge becomes one of standardization. Implementing standard processes, such as using identical review checklists, establishing uniform governance protocols, and developing centralized data collection methods, creates a cohesive and predictable environment across the enterprise. Yet, standardization must never come at the expense of local adaptability. A modular approach enables organizations to define core global standards while allowing individual business units the flexibility to adapt elements for regional or industry-specific conditions. This balance is critical—for instance, an international financial institution may standardize its renewal procedures but provide its regional teams the autonomy to tweak negotiation strategies to reflect local market conditions. In this way, scaling fosters both consistency and responsiveness.

Technology remains the linchpin in scaling contract management effectively. Modern CLM systems, when integrated with enterprise resource planning (ERP) and customer relationship management (CRM) platforms, create a comprehensive ecosystem where data flows seamlessly from one department to another. In the early chapters, we explored how such integration provides real-time, actionable insights through executive dashboards and automated alerts. Now, at scale, these systems must be configured to handle increased volumes of contracts, diverse types of agreements, and varying regional requirements without sacrificing performance or data integrity. A successful scaling initiative might involve deploying middleware solutions that facilitate data exchange between legacy systems and modern cloud-based platforms, ensuring that all business units operate from a single, reliable source of contract data. This holistic digital integration improves operational efficiency and empowers decision-makers at every level by providing a consistent, reliable picture of contract performance across the organization.

Cross-functional collaboration is another cornerstone of scaling. Historically, contract management was confined to the legal department, but the modern enterprise recognizes the value of engaging finance, procurement, sales, and customer service teams. When every department understands how contract performance impacts overall business outcomes through enhanced cash flow, improved supplier terms, or bolstered customer satisfaction, the entire organization stands to benefit. Scaling, therefore, requires building a culture of shared ownership. For example, a retail conglomerate that established a cross-departmental contract management committee experienced reduced processing times and improved interdepartmental alignment, leading to smoother supplier negotiations and greater customer retention. Such initiatives underscore that the collective impact of scaling is far greater than the sum of its parts.

Effective change management is vital as organizations scale their contract management practices. Transitioning from fragmented, legacy systems to a standardized, technology-driven framework invariably encounters resistance. Employees accustomed to long-established processes might view change as disruptive, particularly when new systems require learning and adaptation. Therefore, a comprehensive change management plan must accompany scaling initiatives. This should include targeted training programs, ongoing support, open forums for feedback, and well-defined incentive structures that underscore the tangible benefits of the new practices. In one illustrative case, a multinational logistics provider implemented regional workshops and a centralized support desk to help employees transition smoothly to the new enterprise-wide CLM system. The proactive approach led to high adoption rates and a noticeable uplift in process efficiency—a clear indication that scaling can be achieved more rapidly and effectively when people are fully engaged.

Furthermore, scaling contract management necessitates a robust risk management framework integrated across all business units. As contractual volume increases and data becomes more dispersed across a vast enterprise, potential risks, such as non-compliance, inconsistent terms, or unanticipated contractual disputes, can emerge unexpectedly. Scalability demands that risk management processes be standardized while remaining flexible enough to address local nuances. Automated systems that flag risks, combined with cross-functional interdepartmental reviews, ensure that emerging issues are identified and rectified promptly. For example, a healthcare conglomerate expanded its compliance monitoring functions by scaling its CLM system across different regions, thereby reducing the incidence of regulatory breaches and safeguarding its reputation. By quantifying risk-related metrics and incorporating them into performance dashboards, organizations gain a proactive edge in mitigating threats before they escalate.

As scaling progresses, performance measurement becomes even more critical. Comprehensive executive dashboards that aggregate data from various business units allow leadership to monitor the overall impact of CLM initiatives in real time. These dashboards should be designed to provide high-level overviews and detailed drill-down capabilities to address strategic issues on both macro and micro levels. A retail chain, for instance, used its updated dashboards to identify regional discrepancies in contract processing times. The insights prompted targeted interventions that resolved local inefficiencies and contributed to an overall improvement in the enterprise-wide benchmark. Integrating such performance metrics ensures that the scaling process is continuously monitored and re-fined—a necessity for sustaining long-term benefits.

Financial validation is another crucial aspect when scaling contract management. Demonstrating a clear return on investment helps secure ongoing support from senior management and justifies allocating resources for ongoing improvements. When the financial benefits, such as reduced processing costs, increased revenue from better-negotiated terms, and lower risk exposure, are quantified and linked directly to strategic outcomes, they make a compelling case for enterprise-wide scaling. For example, a global consumer electronics firm documented a 20 percent reduction in contract-related costs after scaling its CLM initiatives. These cost savings, coupled with improved revenue capture through enhanced renegotiations, provided a clear financial benchmark that reinforced the strategic value of the expanded CLM system.

The iterative nature of scaling is also essential to understand. Scaling is not a one-time project; it is an ongoing process of improvement that requires regular review cycles, feedback loops, and agile adjustments in response to emerging challenges and opportunities. Organizations must be prepared to continuously refine their processes, update their technology systems, and adjust their performance metrics as the business environment evolves. This long-term commitment to continuous improvement ensures that the scaled CLM system remains effective and aligned with the organization's strategic objectives over time.

In addition to these technical and operational considerations, a modular approach to scaling plays a significant role in ensuring success across diverse environments. A modular strategy allows core processes to be standardized at an enterprise level while still permitting local customization to address regional requirements or specific market conditions. For instance, a pharmaceutical company might adopt the best global practices for contract review but allow its regional offices the flexibility to modify certain administrative aspects to comply with local regulatory standards. This balanced approach of international uniformity and local customization ensures that scaling is efficient and contextually relevant.

As we examine the dynamics of scaling further, it becomes clear that the integration of technology, process improvements, and cross-functional collaboration forms a multifaceted ecosystem that transforms contract management into a strategic, scalable asset. The challenges of aligning disparate systems, overcoming resistance to change, managing risks, and validating financial performance are significant but surmountable. Organizations can establish a scalable contract management framework that delivers consistent, enterprise-wide improvements through careful planning, sustained executive commitment, and iterative refinement.

The insights and examples provided in this discussion illustrate that successful scaling produces cumulative benefits that extend far beyond isolated improvements. When every contract is managed with a common standard, supported by integrated technology and enriched by cross-functional cooperation, the strategic advantages multiply. Improved operational efficiencies lead to quantifiable cost savings, while enhanced risk management and revenue optimization contribute to stronger financial performance and competitive positioning.

This subchapter has provided a detailed exploration of the strategies and methodologies essential for scaling contract management practices across the entire organization. We have examined the importance of baseline diagnostics, process standardization, technology integration, robust performance measurement, cross-functional collaboration, adaptive change management, and a modular approach. Each of these elements plays an integral role in ensuring that the benefits of improved contract processes are replicated consistently across all business units and regions. The collective outcome is an enterprise-wide system that enhances efficiency, reduces risk, generates significant financial returns, and positions the organization for sustained growth in a competitive landscape.

As you reflect on these insights, the key takeaway is that scaling the contract advantage is a strategic imperative, transforming localized improvements into systemic, measurable, and sustainable competencies. Every refined process, every integrated technology solution, and every collaborative effort contributes to an agile framework that can adapt to the evolving demands of our global business environment. The journey toward scalable contract management is iterative, dynamic, and ongoing—it is a continuous pursuit of excellence that, over time, turns everyday contract operations into a fundamental driver of strategic success.

Looking ahead, the efforts to scale provide the necessary foundation to transition to the next phase of our journey, where we will focus on measuring and reporting the long-term impact of these initiatives. The forthcoming chapter will detail how executive dashboards and reporting frameworks translate these integrated efforts into clear, actionable intelligence for strategic decision-making. These tools will enable leaders to monitor enterprise-wide performance in real time, refine processes continuously, and further solidify the competitive advantages established through scalable contract management.

In closing, this subchapter has illuminated the intricate process of scaling the contract advantage. This process requires precision in standardizing processes, agility in technological integration, and a commitment to fostering a collaborative, data-driven culture. The journey from isolated wins to a fully scalable contract management system is complex. Still, as the examples and methodologies have demonstrated, it is a vital step toward achieving long-term, sustainable success. With each element working in concert—from cross-functional meetings and adaptive change management to comprehensive performance measurement—the full potential of contract management emerges as a pervasive strategic asset that drives operational excellence and financial growth across the entire enterprise.

As we transition to the final chapter, remember that the scalability of contract management rests on the balance of standardization and flexibility, robust technological infrastructure, and unwavering commitment to continuous improvement. These principles ensure that every contract contributes effectively to the organization's strategic objectives, regardless of origin or designation. With the scalable system in place, organizations are equipped to navigate market complexities, mitigate risks proactively, and confidently seize emerging opportunities.

With these foundational insights established, our next chapter will concentrate on translating these integrated scaling efforts into robust executive dashboards and reporting frameworks. These reporting tools will allow decision-makers to visualize performance data across the enterprise, tighten feedback loops, and confidently steer strategic initiatives. In doing so, every improvement realized through scaling will be communicated and optimized in real time.

Thus, as we conclude this subchapter on scaling the contract advantage, take with you the understanding that true scalability transforms every contract into a catalyst for growth, risk reduction, and long-term competitive superiority. The principles of standardization, technological integration, cross-functional collaboration, and adaptive change management collectively lay the groundwork for a future-ready contract management system. This scalable framework underpins immediate operational gains and builds a resilient foundation for sustained strategic success in an ever-changing business landscape.

⁂

- STRATEGIES FOR CONTINUOUS IMPROVEMENT AND GROWTH -

As we arrive at the final stage of our exploration, we focus on how the achievements and practices cultivated throughout this book can be embedded deeply into the organizational framework, ensuring that the competitive advantage extends and endures. Building upon the dramatic gains novel approaches have delivered in isolated business units or specific departments, this concluding chapter spotlights the practical imperative of transforming those focused successes into a system-level strategy. By doing so, contract management evolves from an occasional source of operational efficiencies to a dynamic, enterprise-wide force that propels growth, curbs risk, and enhances every layer of business performance.

This subchapter introduces the main themes that underpin this final step. We will scrutinize companies' strategies to weave contract management improvements into their broader corporate fabric, so that every contract, regardless of origin or complexity, is managed with precision and a clear link to leadership's vision. Achieving this requires more than replicating processes that proved effective in trials or pilot programs. It entails carefully analyzing each business segment's needs, crafting adaptable frameworks that fit local realities, layering in robust data analytics, and building a strong sense of shared ownership among stakeholders across the enterprise.

One of this final chapter's fundamental themes revolves around creating a unified enterprise environment for contract management. Throughout this book, we have witnessed how pilot initiatives—such as reducing the time to finalize supplier contracts or increasing the transparency of compliance protocols—yield significant benefits in targeted areas. However, once leaders decide to roll out these methods across multiple business units or global divisions, they discover that the complexities of scale demand a more holistic, carefully orchestrated plan. This plan must consider variances in technology infrastructures, the maturity of existing processes, and the cultural contexts within which contracts are negotiated and executed.

Consider, for instance, a financial services group that implemented a targeted workflow automation tool within its North American arm. The pilot project led to sharper compliance oversight, shorter approval windows, and more precise tracking of renewal dates—ultimately delivering quantifiable revenue gains. However, when the enterprise sought to extend the same approach to its European or Asian divisions, it encountered incompatible legacy systems, language-specific contract nuances, and different regulatory requirements. The pilot's successes,, therefore,, could not be merely "copied and pasted" into these regions. Instead, the corporation had to integrate flexible solutions suited to local markets while retaining consistent global standards for key contractual components. This real scenario demonstrates how scaling the contract advantage requires a blend of uniformity and adaptability, a recurring theme we will explore further.

A parallel issue emerges when organizations realize the importance of cross-functional collaboration in scaling contract processes. A single business function—often legal—no longer "owns" end-to-end contract oversight once a company commits to enterprise-wide improvements. Finance, procurement, sales, product development, and other stakeholders must now see themselves as equal participants in shaping, monitoring, and refining contracts. This distributed sense of responsibility often challenges traditional organizational structures. Grasping the opportunities in these cross-departmental synergies, however, can yield extraordinary breakthroughs. When finance, for example, is actively engaged in contract negotiations from the outset, it can insert vital clauses that align with the organization's risk appetite and financial objectives. Similarly, procurement's early involvement can help finalize more favorable pricing and supplier terms, or sales can ensure that evolving customer needs are accounted for before execution. The net effect is a contract that fully serves broad strategic goals, rather than being confined to legal compliance or narrower departmental aims.

Another core theme in this chapter addresses leadership's role in championing a culture of continuous improvement. The transformation of contract management into a widespread driver of operational and strategic value requires unflagging support from top executives. We have underscored in prior chapters that building momentum behind organizational changes hinges on transparent communication, well-orchestrated training programs, and accessible feedback mechanisms. Leadership must clearly articulate how the contract advantage dovetails with broader goals such as market expansion, cost containment, or quality enhancements. When employees understand that each contract, whether it governs the purchase of office supplies or defines a major client engagement, can incrementally strengthen overall business objectives, they become motivated to adopt and refine the new systems. In one instructive case, a global manufacturing conglomerate established monthly town-hall gatherings where executives reviewed contract performance metrics alongside quarterly financial results. This repetitive exposure to how contract management improved cost containment and compliance demystified the process. It reinforced the idea that contract performance was central to executive priorities—an alignment that accelerated organization-wide adoption.

Closely related is the theme of balancing standardization with range and diversity. While standardized processes reduce complexity and inconsistency, an enterprise spanning multiple regions and markets must accommodate local nuances. Organizations need a "unified but flexible" contract management system. This often takes the form of a tiered approach, where core processes—like negotiated legal language, compliance checks, and basic approval workflows—remain constant, but specific details—such as currency exchange clauses or region-specific standard clauses—are adapted to local needs. Striking this equilibrium fosters global cohesion while preserving the ability to address local market demands.

Underpinning all these themes is the importance of robust analytics and data visibility. The final mile of scaling the contract advantage depends on the organization's capacity to gather, synthesize, and act upon the wealth of data generated across its expanded contract ecosystem. Comprehensive dashboards, tracking everything from contract cycle times and renewal rates to compliance metrics and revenue recovery, become indispensable. They enable managers and executives to pinpoint emerging issues before they escalate, spot trends that might warrant strategic adjustments, and measure progress toward enterprise-wide targets. We have seen how these dashboards clarify previously opaque processes, bridging the distance between offices in different geographies or business functions that rarely interact.

Finally, this subchapter places particular emphasis on the theme of ongoing evolution. Even as organizations reach a mature phase in their contract management strategy, the business environment and internal structures will continue to shift. Acquisitions, spin-offs, expansions into new markets, or significant shifts in regulatory policy can rapidly alter the landscape for contracts. Ensuring that the contract advantage remains robust and relevant requires a built-in capacity for evolution—regular reviews of SOPs, periodic updates to technology tools, and a supportive organizational culture that sees change not as a disruption, but as part of routine operations. Embracing iteration ensures that processes stay aligned with strategic objectives, technology remains cutting-edge, and the workforce's skills do not stagnate.

Consider that an enterprise might develop a world-class contract renewal process, only to acquire a new division heavily reliant on paper-based systems and archaic review workflows. Instead of forcing the new division to adopt methods that may not be entirely suitable, the enterprise might gradually adapt the global approach to incorporate the new division's unique environment. The result is a measured but consistent extension of best practices, ensuring minimal disruption while preserving the clarity and efficiency of a standardized contract lifecycle. Over time, the organization's capacity for iteration and adaptation broadens the competitive advantage and cements it as a durable, strategic function that thrives under various scenarios.

This initial subchapter of our final chapter aims to lay out these crucial themes, providing a roadmap for how organizations can expand their contract success from localized improvements to a fully integrated, enterprise-wide system. The following sections will delve into specific avenues for scaling, discussing how to identify pockets of excellence and replicate them systematically, balance standardization with local adaptability, secure leadership commitment, and maintain a culture of continuous improvement that fuels sustainable growth. We will also examine how advanced analytics and robust dashboards are deployed differently at scale, ensuring that leadership retains real-time visibility into contract performance across every organization segment.

By understanding these foundational principles, readers can appreciate the scope of the undertaking: scaling is neither an incremental addition nor a one-time replication of a pilot program, but a strategic metamorphosis that must be carefully managed at every stage. This subchapter thus sets the tone for the concluding segments of our work, where we vividly illustrate how the contract advantage, fine-tuned through technology, process excellence, cultural transformation, and data-centric insights, can be leveraged across the enterprise. In doing so, organizations lay the groundwork for immediate operational gains and lasting competitive distinction.

As you progress through this final chapter, remember that scaling is a natural continuation of the building blocks we have established throughout. From forging a customer-oriented contract approach and developing robust technological underpinnings to embedding a results-driven performance measurement culture, each preceding chapter supplies the necessary tools for this culminating effort. The synergy between these components drives the ability to expand contract success across business lines, geographies, and product portfolios, creating a cohesive environment where every contract underscores the organization's purpose and value.

From here, the remaining sections in this chapter will illustrate precisely how to orchestrate this expansion, drawing further on real-world examples to demonstrate the challenges and triumphs that arise during enterprise-wide scale-ups. By the end, you will possess a pragmatic framework for ensuring that every contract, from minor supplier agreements to high-stakes deals, is executed swiftly, safely, and strategically across the entire organization. This consistent approach enhances the bottom line and positions contract management as a visible pillar of corporate strategy, reinforcing a culture that seeks continuous improvement and welcomes innovation at every turn.

In conclusion, this subchapter sets the stage for an in-depth exploration of enterprise-wide scaling of contract management initiatives. It introduces the cardinal themes of unified enterprise environments, cross-departmental collaboration, flexible standardization, robust analytics, and continuous evolution. Each of these aspects contributes to a tapestry of best practices that ensure organizations replicate successes and perpetually refine and reinforce them. As you move forward, keep these reference points in mind: Synergy among technology, processes, and culture; the vital role of local adaptability under global standards; and the integral function of leadership and ongoing measurement in sustaining the contract advantage.

Ultimately, scaling is the gateway to a long-term, strategic shift in how contracts drive business objectives. When done thoughtfully, it recasts previously narrow departmental improvements into an overarching framework that lifts performance across the enterprise. This approach prevents fragmentation, fosters synergy, and creates an ongoing cycle of excellence. In the upcoming sections, we

delve deeper into tangible strategies, exploring how to systematically align each business unit under a shared vision
for contract management while respecting local dynamics. This final phase cements the contract advantage and
ensures it remains a cornerstone of growth and resilience
for years to come.

⌗

- FUTURE-PROOFING YOUR BUSINESS WITH CLM -

Building on the themes introduced in the first subchapter
of this final chapter, we now look more closely at how organizations can systematically integrate contract improvements throughout the enterprise. Achieving this level of
coordination involves a deliberate strategy that addresses each layer of the organization—technology, processes, people, and culture—so that every department, region,
and function operates under a unified vision. This deeper
discussion emphasizes the criticality of cohesive frameworks, shared accountability, and continuous refinement
to ensure that business units embrace and build upon successful contract management practices instead of revert-
ing to individually customized, disconnected routines.

One of the central topics in scaling contract management
is the persistent tension between local autonomy and central oversight. On the one hand, organizations desire the efficiencies and clarity of standardized processes, metrics,
and tools. On the other hand, local business units—whether defined by geography, function, or market segment-

often have valid reasons for keeping certain aspects of contract management tailored to their specific needs. The optimal solution usually lies in creating a core "template" for managing contracts (encompassing essential steps such as legal review protocols, approval workflows, and compliance checks) while retaining flexibility where contextual nuances matter. A retail conglomerate, for instance, may adopt uniform scheduling and renewal procedures for most of its contracts across multiple regions. However, it allows certain divisions leeway to incorporate local currency fluctuations or region-specific regulatory clauses. By distinguishing which processes demand absolute uniformity and which can be locally adapted, the enterprise ensures scale consistency without stifling local teams' practical requirements.

Establishing this balance early in the scaling process is easier said than done. It requires leadership to define the "non-negotiables"—the elements of contract management that are core to corporate governance, risk management, and strategic alignment—and to identify realms where local refinement is permissible. Executives and process owners should collaborate to document these guidelines in a clear, accessible fashion, ensuring that each business unit understands which actions must be in strict compliance and which can be adapted based on local or industry-specific conditions. This clarity helps avoid confusion when new policies or technologies are introduced. One global manufacturing organization found it immensely helpful to develop a "Contract Management Playbook" that specified the universal steps all units had to follow, accompanied by supplemental sections for regional variations. This single reference source eased the rollout of updated workflows and minimized the conflict arising from committees wrestling over what is or is not mandatory.

A second concept in enterprise-wide scaling centers on the implications for risk management. As contract processes extend into new regions or incorporate additional lines of business, the risk potential—regulatory, financial, or reputational—often grows proportionately. Therefore, any robust plan for scaling must include a consistent approach to identifying, assessing, and mitigating these risks. Similar to standardizing procedures, risk mitigation strategies must balance global uniformity and local responsiveness. For example, a healthcare conglomerate that has expanded into multiple countries may require all divisions to perform the same baseline compliance checks during the contract drafting phase to ensure alignment with corporate risk thresholds. However, each regional unit may build on that baseline by adding extra checks for local laws or region-specific operational complexities. By standardizing a core layer of risk assessment while still allowing region-specific additions, the organization benefits from comprehensive coverage without imposing an overly rigid system that could hinder adaptability.

Moreover, advanced analytics can play a significant role in scaling risk management. As businesses adopt integrated CLM platforms, they can track universal risk factors (such, overall compliance metrics, contract disputes, or non-performance rates) and local indicators (such as region-specific regulatory changes or unique supply chain vulnerabilities). Dashboards that aggregate such data in real time become vital tools for leadership and functional managers. A multinational finance institution might use these dashboards to monitor contract volumes, renewal rates, and compliance metrics across numerous markets simultaneously, receiving alerts whenever a particular region reports a spike in contract disputes or compliance lapses. By proactively flagging these anomalies, the organization ensures that issues are addressed before they escalate into significant liabilities.

A third key topic in scaling involves the cultural shift needed to embed contract management practices into the day-to-day granularity of all departments. While leadership can establish guidelines and technology can streamline processes, success ultimately hinges on the willingness of employees to adopt these new methods. Consequently, strong change management support is integral. This process encompasses comprehensive training programs that outline how the scaled system affects each department's responsibilities and objectives; open forums or "town halls" where concerns can be aired and feedback exchanged; and a structured approach to resolving conflicts or misunderstandings. The motivation behind these efforts is twofold: first, to ensure that every employee appreciates the strategic rationale behind scaled contract practices, and second, to create a sense of shared ownership wherein challenges are collectively tackled. A leading logistics provider famously conducted iterative, round-table sessions across various regions during its global CLM rollout. These sessions provided direct channels for localized teams to inquire about new workflows, propose refinements, and sync with the core project team, leading to robust adoption and minimal friction.

It is also crucial to note that scaling contract management must be supported by carefully defined performance indicators tailored for cross-organizational visibility. Earlier chapters emphasized how dashboards and examinations of key performance indicators (KPIs) could drastically improve localized decision-making and accountability. When scaling, those dashboards often need to be expanded or reconfigured to accommodate enterprise-wide data's broader scope and complexity. This might involve designing tiered reporting structures that permit high-level executives to see an aggregated "organization-wide" snapshot while mid-level managers drill down into region-specific metrics. For instance, a high-level view could show that the average contract cycle time has dropped from 30 days to 25 days across the enterprise. A more localized lens, however, might reveal that while two divisions have impressively reduced their cycle times to below 20 days, one lagging department remains stuck at 35 days. This granular insight can prompt focused interventions and spread best practices from high-performing areas to those encountering difficulties. By ensuring that these metrics and dashboards remain visible, real-time, and easily interpretable, the organization fosters an environment of continual improvement even at scale.

Connected to that point is the concept of "pockets of excellence," which refers to those departments or regions that have excelled disproportionately in implementing contract best practices. Instead of confining these successes to one area or function, scalable strategies identify, codify, and replicate these pockets of excellence across the larger ecosystem. For instance, if the procurement team in one location has devised a particularly efficient negotiation workflow that shortens approval times while securing favorable terms, that approach should be systematically documented and broadcast across the company. This dissemination of proven methods forms a critical part of scaling, as it prevents duplication of effort and leverages internal expertise for maximum organizational benefit. The challenge often lies in establishing the channels for knowledge transfer—for example, scheduling periodic summits or clocking up "virtual roadshows" that highlight success stories, detailing the underlying process innovations, and guiding other teams in replicating or adapting them.

Another dimension that warrants attention is integrating strategic supplier and customer relationships into a scaled contract management framework. When scaling, organizations often discover that better-managed contracts present an opportunity to improve external partnerships. Suppliers may gain better clarity regarding performance expectations or scheduling, resulting in fewer delivery errors or unplanned disruptions. Meanwhile, customers may face fewer obstacles in finalizing deals, leading to stronger satisfaction and loyalty. Emphasizing these external benefits can, in turn, reinforce internal alignment, as employees observe firsthand the positive impacts on revenue generation and brand reputation. For instance, a pharmacy retailer that integrated its contract processes with key suppliers found that deliveries became more predictable and costs stabilized. Seeing these externally driven wins, internal teams grew even more invested in ensuring consistent compliance with the standardized processes.

Yet, this synergy with external partners introduces complexities. Each partner likely brings its own systems, timelines, and compliance needs, meaning that an enterprise must manage not only its transformation but also the points at which these external systems interact with internal ones. Maintaining clarity and open communication can mitigate these challenges, tying them back to the fundamental principle of alignment that underlies successful scaling. By defining universal guidelines for external collaboration, like specifying that all vendor or customer contracts must use standard templates plus local "annexes"—and creating digital portals for real-time obligations tracking, the enterprise fosters transparency and reduces confusion among all parties.

Throughout this discussion, it is worth reiterating that scaling the contract advantage is fundamentally iterative. After establishing processes, technology integrations, and policy frameworks, organizations commonly discover new issues or inefficiencies as the system is extended across broader scopes. This is not a sign of failure but a natural aspect of continuous improvement. Early-phase successes should be treated like a living laboratory: each improvement that worked in a small environment is tested against the complexities of a large-scale rollout, refined, and made more robust as implemented in multiple contexts. A feedback loop capturing lessons from these rollouts is vitally important, whether through scheduled retrospectives or curated user feedback from diverse departments. By feeding these lessons back into the process, the scaling approach remains dynamic and resilient, better equipped to handle growth, mergers, acquisitions, or expansions into new global markets.

Additionally, it is valuable to emphasize the role of leadership in sustaining momentum during scaling. Strong executive advocacy can override local or departmental inertia that might hamper broad-based integration. Leadership can ensure that scaling remains an organizational priority by visibly supporting contract best practices, aligning them with corporate goals, and encouraging cross-functional dialogue. This visibility helps unify disparate factions around a single, goal-oriented mission. In large enterprises, doubt or resistance can emerge if staff members perceive conflicting signals—one business leader might champion robust contract oversight while another might push for ad-hoc quick solutions that bypass established procedures. Clear executive alignment, manifested in consistent messages and policies, goes a long way toward eliminating such mixed signals and uniting everyone behind the scaled approach.

In analyzing these elements—local autonomy versus global consistency, strategic risk management, comprehensive analytics, cultural engagement, pockets of excellence, iterative refinement, and leadership alignment—it becomes evident that scaling is not just an extension of pilot projects but the forging of a cohesive organizational identity around contract management. With every iteration, the enterprise learns, adjusts, and standardizes anew, reinforcing an environment where contracts move beyond clerical tasks and become strategic assets that inform many decisions, from budget allocation and vendor selection to customer satisfaction and compliance strategy.

As a final layer of understanding, it is crucial to recognize that "scaling" often leads to emergent synergies. When an organization fully embraces integrated contract structures, automation, analytics, and cross-departmental engagement, new opportunities can arise, such as synergy between supply chain optimization and contract terms or the integration of advanced forecasting models that track inventory data and contract renewal patterns. These emergent benefits can exceed the sum of the initial pilot's achievements. A software corporation once realized that combining contract analytics on renewal timelines with CRM data on customer usage trends could proactively suggest contract modifications that boosted customer satisfaction and prevented churn, effectively turning an internal optimization into a direct business advantage. This phenomenon illustrates how scaling fosters innovation, interplay, and expanded benefits that were not initially anticipated.

In summary, scaling your contract advantage requires structured frameworks, robust leadership support, and a flexible approach that acknowledges local nuances. Organizations must engage in multifaceted strategies—refining standardized SOPs, seamlessly integrating advanced CLM platforms, forging cross-functional collaboration, and embedding iterative learning cycles. Throughout this discussion, we have seen how each dimension builds upon the others to sustain a scalable contract management culture that yields enhanced performance metrics, risk mitigation, and revenue growth.

With this expanded view, readers can appreciate the depth of planning and coordination required to move from discrete success stories to large-scale operational transformation. The following sections will synthesize these principles into a cohesive blueprint, providing additional guidance on identifying and addressing obstacles during expansion and ways to systematically measure outcomes aligned with broader corporate goals. Ultimately, scaling the contract advantage is an ongoing endeavor—an iterative mission to unify various parts of the organization behind a single, strategic approach to contract management. The synergy engendered by such scaling offers immediate, quantifiable returns (in terms of cost reductions, faster contract cycles, or reduced compliance issues) and the longer-term intangible benefits of forging a thoughtful, data-driven culture.

With these strategies, organizations can confidently enter new markets, adopt emerging technologies, and evolve in shifting regulatory environments. Contracts, which were once relegated to a misunderstood back-office function, have become a unifying thread that runs through every department, ensuring consistent governance, dependable results, and continuous advancement. This synergy is a testament to the power of scaling: not simply replicating proven methods, but refining them so they flourish in the unique contexts of each division, region, and business partnership.

Thus, as we progress to the concluding phase of this final chapter, remember that scaling the contract advantage is ultimately about forging robust, enterprise-wide frameworks that merge the universal with the particular. By harnessing global uniformity and local intelligence, companies make contract management a living expression of their values: agile, oriented to excellence, and responsive to evolving challenges. The following subchapter will delve into the practical blueprint for implementing such frameworks and highlight how real-time dashboards, advanced analytics, and collaborative governance structures can ensure that growth, efficiency, and risk management remain locked as the organization matures.

In the upcoming sections, we will systematically review how to bridge the final gap between departmental improvement and total organizational alignment. We will outline the tactics for weaving contract management best practices into daily operations, clarifying responsibility at each departmental level, and persistently reinforcing the synergy that yields cross-functional gains. The end goal, as always, is to convert every contract into a strategic mechanism that fosters cost efficiency, compliance assurance, and revenue generation across the business. By applying the structured insights provided here, leaders and teams alike will be well-positioned to secure the contract advantage at scale, assuring that operational excellence, financial health, and innovation-inspired resilience define the future of their enterprise.

⁙

- THE LONG-TERM BENEFITS OF A PROACTIVE CLM APPROACH -

As we conclude this final chapter on scaling your contract advantage and, by extension, bring this book to a close, the discussion has illuminated a clear path forward for organizations seeking to transform contract management into a business pillar. We have seen how local pilot successes can serve as the blueprint for organization-wide expansion, careful planning and flexible approaches generate sustainable improvements, and cross-functional collaboration fosters an enduring culture of continuous refinement. In this last subchapter, we will summarize those insights, offer predictions for the next phase of contract management evolution, and encourage you to maintain the momentum you have built throughout your journey.

Scanning through the chapters, recurring themes emerge: the strategic imperative of viewing contracts as more than administrative documents, the centrality of data-driven tools and analytics, and the need to balance standardization with local customization. In our most recent discussions, we delved into how enterprise-wide scaling demands not just replicating lessons from successful pilot projects, but a nuanced interplay of governance, technology, and leadership that actively reshapes daily operations across every department. By anchoring contract management within broader business objectives, each contract can be aligned with the company's strategic trajectory, transforming them from rudimentary obligations into instruments of revenue, risk control, and stakeholder confidence.

Forward-thinking organizations gradually realize that contract management holds a value proposition far beyond cost savings: it can nurture brand reputation, underpin compliance efforts, and propel business growth. Whether through restructured workflows, automated alerts, or more innovative negotiation strategies, contracts can be a competitive differentiator. For instance, a software firm mines contract data to predict renewal timelines and usage patterns might discover new revenue streams through up-sell or cross-sell offers. Conversely, a pharmaceutical company that systematically tracks contract performance with suppliers can maintain steady inventory to meet clinical trials, avoiding costly—perhaps even life-threatening—disruptions. These pragmatic examples illustrate the tangible impacts that scaled contract management can have on everyday operational and strategic decisions.

As organizations integrate scaled practices across multiple units, they should also monitor how changes affect the entire contractual lifecycle, both inside and outside the organization. Internally, employees benefit from cross-pollinated ideas, advanced analytics, and integrated dashboards that consolidate performance metrics into centralized, easily interpretable formats. Teams see the immediate upshots of well-managed contracts: shorter approval times, improved compliance rates, more transparent accountability, and, ultimately, more confident leadership decision-making. Externally, the consistent application of best practices to supplier and customer relationships fosters trust, reduces disputes, and breeds loyalty, all of which count toward building a reputable profile in the marketplace. The cross-functional synergy gained in scaling thus spills onto external partnerships, leading to healthier supply chains, more satisfied customers, and deeper collaborative opportunities.

Redesigning your organization's approach to contract management also entails a fresh look at talent. As the contract advantage becomes embedded into daily routines, employees versed in data analysis, change management, legal compliance, and negotiation tactics will find themselves increasingly valuable. Some forward-looking companies are streamlining roles and processes and expanding opportunities for roles like contract analysts or data scientists. These professionals can continuously refine the system based on feedback and performance metrics, ensuring that scaling efforts remain vibrant. This attention to upskilling and continuous learning is crucial, as new regulations, market pressures, or internal policy shifts might crop up, requiring agile adjustments to contract workflows.

In the future, several trends will likely shape the ongoing

evolution of contract management. Chief among these is the proliferation of advanced technologies. We have high-lighted how rapid improvements in cloud computing, process automation, and AI-driven analytics reshape contract review, negotiation, and performance monitoring practices. Looking ahead, more specialized use cases for artificial intelligence, such as machine learning algorithms that predict regulatory changes or clause disputes, are likely to gain traction. Another possibility is the greater application of blockchain or distributed ledger technologies, which, in theory, can create a credible, tamper-proof record of each contract revision, offering new levels of security and trans-parency. Although adoption remains nascent, these trends hint that the advanced tools available to large organiza-tions today may become standard for midsize and even small enterprises in the coming years.

Additionally, regulatory changes will continue to influence contract management strategies. In many regions, height-ened concerns over data privacy, environmental sustain-ability, and fair labor practices push companies to embed greater scrutiny into each contract. At scale, these obliga-tions could result in global or multi-regional compliance frameworks that demand quick responses and thorough documentation. Enterprises with refined, flexible contract management systems will be best positioned to adapt, seamlessly updating templates and workflows each time new rules or guidelines enter force. Being able to respond swiftly helps organizations avoid legal repercussions and fosters goodwill among investors, customers, and em-ployees who value ethical, transparent practices.

On a cultural level, we can anticipate organizations strengthening their commitment to cross-functional dialogue around contracts. Over time, this shift in mindset—treating contracts as strategic assets rather than necessary evils—reinforces the notion that responsibilities and successes are shared. For instance, finance, legal, sales, and procurement each have overlapping stakes in a well-constructed contract. The enterprise that institutionalizes a cross-departmental forum or committee to review, refine, and scale contract-related best practices can use these gatherings to solve real-time issues, adopt uniform solutions, and accelerate collective learning. Through iterative cycles, collaboration fosters an environment of accountability, so that every function, from marketing to product development, recognizes and proactively manages parts of the contract management process relevant to their operations.

From our experience, transformation is often accompanied by growing pains, especially in large or diversified organizations. Technology rollouts can falter if not implemented with care; employees uncertain about new tools and expectations might revert to old methods, or poorly aligned leadership agendas may hamper progress. Yet if there is one overarching lesson from this book, these obstacles can be surmounted with careful planning, consistent messaging, and a willingness to adapt. Detailed frameworks, advanced dashboards, iterative training, and the constructive use of performance metrics all present proven methods for surmounting transitional challenges. By tying improvements in contract management to tangible financial or operational gains, organizations sustain the impetus for performing incremental, ongoing enhancements, forging a cycle of consistent progress that rarely recedes.

Amid this complex environment, we trust that the principles, case studies, and strategic guidelines covered herein provide a sturdy foundation for your continued journey. The methods of process mapping, data integration, modular standardization, risk measurement, cross-functional alignment, and iterative refining described across these chapters are universal enough to remain relevant. Regardless of geography, industry, or corporate maturity, they can be tailored to fit an organization's particular culture and constraints. Continued learning and flexible application of these insights are vital. In time, your organization will find that contract management evolves naturally from a departmental afterthought into a fulsome, enterprise-wide discipline that underpins resilience, fosters incremental improvements, and nurtures new competitive opportunities.

In conclusion, the most pivotal takeaway is that the journey of contract management should never be a static or finite campaign. Ensuring the contract advantage is an ongoing process that thrives on iterative feedback, emergent innovations, and a spirited curiosity about what can still be optimized. As new norms in technology or regulation arise or your corporate strategies adjust to suit new market realities, the contract management system—duly integrated, scaled, and data-enriched—will serve as a robust response framework. This capacity to pivot effectively, grounded in consistent and accurate data, will undoubtedly remain a critical determinant of business success in the uncertain landscapes ahead.

Looking forward, I expect to see further consolidation of contract analytics platforms with broader enterprise resource planning tools, forging an even more unified ecosystem where strategic vision, operational data, and risk management strategies converge seamlessly. As artificial intelligence matures, it will likely be harnessed to optimize contract language, clauses, and timetables in ways that surpass current manual or semi-automated processes. By preemptively scanning for potential disputes, AI accelerates contract drafting and mitigates costly forms of operational friction. All these factors point to a future where the contract advantage becomes fully embedded into corporate DNA, as ubiquitous and essential as basic supply chain management or financial controls.

Through these next steps and eventual evolutions, the spirit of the contract advantage endures as both a mindset and a culture—one where each stakeholder, from frontline staff to executive leadership, appreciates and stewards the value inherent in well-orchestrated contracts. As a result, contract processes evolve from an item on a to-do list to a shared strategic enabler that fosters synergy, broad-based accountability, and perpetual growth. Consider how your enterprise might harness expanded dashboards that compile global performance data, identify synergies between sales forecasts and supplier capacity, or leverage advanced alerting for risk hotspots. The possibilities soon multiply when management sees contract management as a bond linking the entire value chain, rather than a separate, bureaucratic overhead.

As this final subchapter and the book draw to a close, we extend our sincere encouragement for your ongoing business journey. The steps, examples, and frameworks provided across all chapters aim to inspire and equip you to cultivate a holistic, scalable, and future-resilient contract management environment—one that truly integrates into your business's overarching mission. Whether you are a chief executive championing cross-departmental synergy, a procurement lead restlessly optimizing vendor terms, a legal officer targeting foolproof compliance, or a finance director longing for uniform contract data to inform your forecasts, the contract advantage remains within reach. Each department, each regional unit, and each employee can play an active part in nurturing it.

Looking ahead, your continued success hinges on upholding the same principles that guided you this far: a willingness to adapt processes and technology as markets shift; steadfast leadership that consistently communicates strategic goals; an unyielding focus on measurable performance; and a robust culture that celebrates continual learning and open collaboration. Even as you celebrate early victories, never lose sight of how ephemeral these gains can be if the impetus for improvement dwindles. Instead, strive to keep refining, integrating, measuring, and adjusting, thus creating a durable platform that naturally attracts additional enhancements and fosters innovation.

In delivering these final insights, we trust you have gained the knowledge and inspiration to make contract management an enduring cornerstone of your organization's growth agenda. The frameworks outlined herein—encompassing everything from the earlier steps of diagnosing contract chaos, reorienting your culture, and implementing new technologies, to now consolidating best practices and scaling them—form a cohesive guide for your transformation. By studying and harnessing these dimensions over time, you lay the groundwork for a sustainable, intelligent contract approach that buffers against uncertainty and sparks new possibilities for business development.

As we release you from these pages and into the ongoing

evolution of your enterprise, remember that each contract stands as an artifact of where your organization is today and a lens on future aspirations. Every renewal, renegotiation, compliance checkpoint, instance of advanced analytics, or AI-driven assistance is a stepping stone that collectively molds your competitive posture in a shifting marketplace. Seize the contract advantage by internalizing these lessons, committing to continuous improvement, and fostering an environment where innovations emerge readily and improvements endure.

With that, we close this volume by underscoring our confidence that you possess both the roadmap and the resolve to capitalize on the contract advantage for years to come. Equipping every department with the capacity to refine, measure, and scale contract management ensures that your enterprise remains nimble amid regulatory changes, global competition, and evolving customer expectations. The future belongs to organizations that lean into analytics, collaboration, and holistic thinking—qualities that become second nature in a fully realized, enterprise-wide contract culture. We applaud your progress thus far and encourage you to carry forward the momentum, forging your own stories of operational excellence, meaningful innovation, and unstoppable strategic growth. May this blueprint serve you well on your ongoing journey, and may every contract fulfill the role of a pivotal strategic instrument in your mission to thrive in the modern business world.

VOLUME II

METHODOLOGY,
FRAMEWORKS, AND
IMPLEMENTATION TOOLS
& PLAYBOOKS
FROM
A PRACTITIONER'S
EXPERIENCE

CONTRACTS AS A BUSINESS ASSET™

The Strategic Reframing of Contract Lifecycle Management in the Value-Centric Enterprise

*"Contracts are not relics of legal tradition.
They are the source code of modern commerce."*
— *From* The Contract Advantage™

Contracts form the connective tissue of every business. They articulate intent, allocate value, assign risk, govern relationships, and hold parties accountable. No material business function - procurement, sales, service, partnerships, product delivery—can operate without contracts. Yet, despite their criticality, contracts remain among the most misunderstood, mismanaged, and strategically underutilized business instruments in today's enterprise.

Too often, organizations treat contracts as legal documents to be filed away after signature. They are considered administrative hurdles—necessary evils to fulfill regulatory obligations or avoid litigation risk. This perception is dangerously incomplete. When approached as **living, data-rich, strategic assets**, contracts can drive revenue realization, reduce operational friction, increase customer satisfaction, and unlock organizational agility.

This chapter introduces the book's central premise: **Contracts as a Business Asset™.** It is a theory grounded in operational experience, executive insight, and real-world impact. More than a label, it is a fundamental reframing of the role contracts play within the modern enterprise.

I. The Misalignment Between Contract Importance and Investment

Despite the universal dependence on contracts, most organizations invest minimal thought or strategic oversight into how contracts are designed, negotiated, executed, tracked, and renewed. The contradiction is stark:

- Contracts define how a company makes money but are rarely treated as revenue infrastructure.

- Contracts define obligations to customers - yet they are seldom integrated with customer success or product teams.

- Contracts define risk boundaries - yet they are often manually handled, inconsistently versioned, and poorly tracked.

This disconnect results in inefficiencies, leakage, and strategic risk. It leaves organizations vulnerable to delayed revenue recognition, supplier disputes, compliance breaches, and poor customer experiences. Worse still, these inefficiencies are normalized, as if contract dysfunction is simply the cost of doing business.

But it doesn't have to be.

II. Reframing Contracts: From Static Documents to Dynamic Value Systems

The most dangerous assumption in contract management

is that contracts are static records. Contracts are dynamic systems; they change in relevance, value, and risk the moment they're signed.

A contract is not an endpoint. It is the starting point of performance. It sets into motion a series of dependencies, deliverables, milestones, and risk exposures that evolve over time. Every clause is a node of intent. Every obligation is a lever of trust. Every renewal is an opportunity for optimization.

This recognition reframes the contract from being a form of legal compliance to a form of **value realization**.

When this reframing occurs, three strategic questions emerge:

1. Are we designing contracts to enable and protect customer outcomes?

2. Are we managing contracts in a way that enhances operational performance?

3. Are we using contract intelligence to anticipate risk and capture opportunity?

For most companies, the answer today is no. But this is also an opportunity.

III. CLM as a Core Component of Product Infrastructure

If a product cannot be delivered without a contract, then the contract is not peripheral to the product but part of it.

Contracts define pricing models, delivery windows, support SLAs, subscription terms, and liability protections.

They are as integral to the customer experience as UX design or service quality. And yet, contract creation is rarely integrated into product design, customer success operations, or go-to-market strategy.

This is a critical omission.

When CLM is repositioned as **product infrastructure**, the contract becomes a user experience in and of itself:

- A responsive, adaptive contract experience shortens deal cycles.
- A clearly articulated contract improves trust and accelerates onboarding.
- A performance-monitored contract strengthens renewals and deepens relationships.

In this way, contracts become continuity tools—not just between legal teams but also across the product, finance, customer, and delivery functions.

IV. The Cost of Siloed, Reactive Contract Management

The financial consequences of poor CLM are not speculative - they are measurable and persistent. Consider the following real-world costs experienced by companies across sectors:

- **Revenue Leakage:** Deals close, but payments stall due to vague obligations or missed billing triggers.
- **Missed Renewals:** Service agreements lapse without review, leaving value on the table or customers churned.
- **Margin Erosion:** Outdated pricing terms remain

in effect for years due to overlooked renegotiation windows.

- **Regulatory Fines:** Obligations under GDPR, HIPAA, or other frameworks are embedded in contracts, but go untracked.

- **Legal Risk:** Key liability or indemnity clauses are inconsistent or missing, exposing the enterprise to litigation.

According to years of experience, my benchmark would be:

- Companies lose between **5% and 15% of contract value annually** due to poor CLM practices.

- Even mid-market organizations report **millions in avoidable losses** per year tied to contract inefficiency.

- The average **cycle time to close** a complex B2B contract exceeds **30–45 days**, delaying revenue capture and product delivery.

More broadly, the opportunity cost is immense:

Slow contracting hampers innovation, misaligned contracts undermine partnerships, and invisible contract data limits strategic foresight. In effect, contract dysfunction is organizational dysfunction.

V. The Case for a Strategic CLM Model

So, what does strategic CLM look like?

It begins with a principle: **contracts are assets, not artifacts**. That means contracts must be:

- **Designed** with purpose

- **Structured** for automation
- **Monitored** continuously
- **Integrated** with business systems
- **Measured** for performance

Strategic CLM transforms contracts into a closed-loop system - one that begins at initiation and ends only when all obligations have been fulfilled and insights have been harvested.

This approach aligns with broader trends in the modern enterprise:

- **Customer-centricity**: Contracts reflect the customer journey, not internal bureaucracy.
- **Data-driven operations**: Contracts become analyzable, queryable assets—like any other record system.
- **Platform integration**: CLM systems connect to CRM, ERP, billing, procurement, and compliance tools.
- **Real-time oversight**: Dashboards and alerts replace static PDFs and email chains.

Ultimately, contracts become **living systems** - intelligent, integrated, and aligned with strategic objectives.

VI. Contract Touchpoints Are Customer Touchpoints

In many industries, the contract is the first and last impression a customer receives. The negotiation sets the tone, the language sets the expectations, the performance monitoring sets accountability, and the renewal sets the trust.

And yet, contracts are still drafted and delivered in jargon-laden language, managed through email, and buried in document repositories.

This gap matters.

Consider the downstream effects:

- Customers experience delays because contract approvals stall.
- Sales teams lose momentum because legal redlines delay closings.
- Implementation teams miss deliverables because contract terms weren't surfaced.
- Support teams struggle because SLA triggers were not automated.

These moments add up—and they compound over time. A single missed SLA can sour a relationship. A delayed onboarding can kill expansion. A confusing renewal term can create churn.

In short, CLM is not a legal function but **a customer experience function.**

VII. Contracts as Drivers of Enterprise Agility

The future of business is unpredictable. Organizations must navigate regulatory flux, supply chain instability, shifting customer demands, and global economic headwinds.

Static, inaccessible contracts are ill-equipped for this environment.

Agile businesses require agile contracts. That means:

- **Terms that can evolve**
- **Performance metrics that are monitored**
- **Risk clauses that trigger action**
- **Partnerships that adapt**

Contracts should not just record agreements—they should **inform decisions**.

That's why strategic CLM includes:

- Machine-readable clause libraries
- Real-time performance triggers
- Risk alerts and exception handling
- Dynamic renewal workflows

In this model, contracts help organizations respond to change—not react to crises. They become tools for resilience.

VIII. Technology as Enabler—Not Solution

CLM software has matured dramatically in recent years. Platforms now offer:

- Clause version control
- Redline tracking
- AI-assisted obligation extraction
- E-signature integration
- Role-based approvals
- API-driven interoperability

But software alone is insufficient. Without executive sponsorship, process redesign, and cultural alignment, even the best tools fail.

Strategic CLM success depends on:

- Clear governance structures
- Cross-functional collaboration
- Unified KPIs
- Process standardization
- Change management

The goal is not to automate chaos—it is to build a new foundation.

Contracts must move from folders to frameworks. From archives to assets. From obligations to opportunities.

IX. The Organizational Mandate

The burden of change does not fall solely on legal teams. True transformation requires broad participation.

- **Legal** must design for scale, not perfection.
- **Sales** must adopt contract planning as pipeline hygiene.
- **Procurement** must negotiate for flexibility, not just price.
- **Finance** must model contract terms into revenue forecasts.
- **Operations** must track obligations as performance metrics.
- **IT** must integrate CLM into the enterprise architecture.

Every function touches contracts. Every function must benefit from better CLM.

What Comes Next: Diagnosing the Broken Model

This section introduces the conceptual foundation of Contracts as a Business Asset™, a theory that reframes contracts from legal necessities into levers of value, agility, and customer alignment. We've also outlined what strategic CLM looks like and why transformation is essential.

In **Part 2**, we'll step into diagnostic mode.

We'll examine the **symptoms and systems** that perpetuate contract chaos:

- Why manual workflows persist
- How silos block performance
- Where ownership breaks down
- What cultural patterns reinforce stagnation

This is not an indictment - it's an invitation. Only by confronting the broken pieces can organizations begin to rebuild.

❊ ❊ ❊ ❊

CONTRACTS AS A BUSINESS ASSET™

Diagnosing the Dysfunction – The Anatomy of a Broken CLM System

"The inefficiencies of traditional contract management aren't just annoying.
They're expensive, reputationally damaging, and strategically limiting.
But most of all—they're avoidable."
*— **From** The Contract Advantage™*

While Part 1 reframed contracts as dynamic business infrastructure, Part 2 uncovers the real, persistent challenges that keep organizations stuck in outdated models. The failure to modernize CLM is not due to a lack of awareness; most leaders know something is broken. What's missing is visibility into how deeply the dysfunction has embedded itself across teams, systems, and culture.

Let us now make the invisible visible.

I. Contract Management as an Organizational Pain Point

In the typical enterprise, contracts suffer from low visibility, unclear ownership, inconsistent enforcement, and disconnected oversight. These symptoms appear across every stage of the contract lifecycle:

- **Initiation**: Business teams scramble to find the right templates. Legal redlines from three years ago are used again "just because they worked before."

- **Negotiation**: Terms are manually tracked in email threads. Each counterparty edits a different version of the document.

- **Execution**: Contracts get signed—sometimes late, sometimes with errors—and are immediately forgotten.

- **Storage**: PDFs are saved on local drives, SharePoint folders, or buried in document management systems with no naming standard.

- **Monitoring**: There's no automated tracking. Deadlines are missed. Renewals auto-trigger without review.

- **Renewal/Amendment**: Deals are either lost or blindly renewed without evaluation, pricing adjustments, or risk recalibration.

Every one of these stages creates friction. Taken together, they form a continuous cycle of operational drag.

II. Five Root Causes of CLM Dysfunction

The breakdown in contract operations isn't just the result of bad habits. It is rooted in **five systemic failures** that repeat across industries and verticals.

1. Siloed Ownership and Accountability Gaps

Contracts touch every department—but no single leader owns their performance. Legal creates the language. Sales initiates the deal. Finance invoices. Ops delivers.

Procurement negotiates terms.

Yet when something goes wrong—an SLA is missed, a renewal triggers without review, or a vendor underdelivers—everyone points elsewhere.

In this environment, no one is accountable for the contract's lifecycle. And without ownership, performance deteriorates.

Strategic Insight: Contracts must have cross-functional ownership models, with clear accountability mapped to value delivery and milestone compliance.

2. Over-Reliance on Manual Processes

Contracts are still managed like it's 2003:

- MS Word templates are copied from old files.
- Redlines are passed through email chains.
- Final documents are printed for wet signature and scanned back into disorganized folders.
- Approvals rely on "nudges" in Slack or email.

These manual processes are inefficient, error—prone, hard to audit, and completely opaque.

They create opportunity for:

- Version control errors
- Forgotten approvals
- Missed deadlines
- Incomplete clause updates
- Misapplied terms

Strategic Insight: A modern CLM system replaces inconsistent handoffs with structured, transparent, automated workflows that preserve institutional memory.

3. Lack of Contract Visibility and Traceability

One of the most common phrases heard in any contract audit is: *"We couldn't find it."*

- Where is the original agreement?
- What version was signed?
- Who approved the exception?
- When is it up for renewal?
- What are the penalties for delay?

The fact that these are even *questions* reveals the depth of dysfunction.

This visibility gap is not just a search problem, it's a strategic risk. Organizations routinely:

- Miss critical renewal dates
- Fail to enforce contractual penalties
- Renew vendors with subpar performance
- Overlook exposure buried in expired obligations

Strategic Insight: Contracts must be mapped, indexed, and monitored as performance instruments—not passive documents.

4. Cultural Resistance to Reengineering

Every executive nods when told their CLM needs improvement. But when the solution demands cross-functional alignment, behavioral change, and investment in new processes, resistance emerges.

Why?

- Contract management has long been treated as "legal's job"
- Stakeholders fear loss of control
- Change disrupts ingrained habits
- CLM transformation requires funding, but is rarely budgeted for

This resistance is not about contracts. It's about organizational inertia.

Strategic Insight: CLM reform is as much about leadership alignment and change management as it is about technology and templates.

5. No Strategic Link Between Contracts and Business Outcomes

In most companies, contracts are not treated as performance levers. They are not integrated into KPIs, used to forecast risk, or referenced in customer satisfaction scoring.

This is the ultimate failure—**the separation of contracts from value creation.**

As a result:

- No one reviews whether customer obligations were delivered on time
- Vendor scorecards omit contractual compliance metrics

- Product teams don't validate if what was promised is deliverable
- Finance teams forecast without incorporating contractual escalators or penalties

Strategic Insight: Contract terms must be surfaced, quantified, and linked to real-time business objectives, just like any other operating metric.

III. Operational Backlogs and the Crisis of CLM Overload

As companies scale, the volume of contracts increases exponentially. What begins as a manageable process becomes a backlog.

- Sales teams delay closings due to overloaded legal reviews.
- Procurement slows down onboarding because third-party paper takes too long to vet.
- Customer teams fail to deliver commitments because they never reviewed the contract scope.

This contract overload becomes self-reinforcing:

- The more delayed contracts are, the more exceptions pile up.
- The more exceptions pile up, the more escalations are needed.
- The more escalations are needed, the more the system grinds to a halt.

The result: Deals die. Relationships strain. Internal teams burn out.

Strategic Insight: CLM processes must be **scalable by design**, leveraging automation, smart templates, and routing logic, not people as workflow engines.

IV. The Human Cost of CLM Failure

Beyond financial leakage, there is a deeper cost: **human exhaustion**. Teams are forced to:

- Search across 5 systems to find the right clause
- Repeat the same approval steps for each new deal
- Re-negotiate the same exceptions over and over
- Manually update spreadsheets with dates and obligations
- Field urgent escalations due to last-minute contract changes

These inefficiencies sap morale, erode trust across departments, and make work harder than necessary.

And they are entirely preventable.

Strategic Insight: High-performance organizations invest in systems that respect people's time—CLM included.

V. Real-Life Scenarios: How Broken CLM Erodes Value

Let's make this tangible with composite examples from client engagements:

- A **$300M software company** auto-renewed a $1.2M vendor agreement for another 3 years. Why? The contract was buried in a SharePoint folder, and the renewal clause was triggered 90 days before expiration—with no alert.

- A **fast-scaling logistics firm** delayed onboarding a key supplier by 6 weeks due to internal confusion around indemnity language. During the delay, they missed $500K in potential revenue due to service gaps.
- A **B2B SaaS enterprise** lost a major customer because the original contract did not reflect changes agreed to in a scope call. The implementation failed. The customer churned. No one had updated the master agreement.

These stories are not edge cases. They are everyday failures that compound until they threaten the enterprise.

VI. What This Tells Us

The persistent underperformance of contract systems is not a technology problem. It is not a legal problem. It is not a process problem.

It is a strategic problem.

It is the failure to see contracts for what they are: **living, multi-functional systems** that govern how value is promised, delivered, measured, and protected.

The same dysfunctions will persist until organizations make that shift, no matter what CLM platform they purchase.

⁜⁜⁜⁜

CONTRACTS AS A BUSINESS ASSET™

PART 3

Building the Future-State CLM Framework

*"Contracts are not a supporting function. They are core business infrastructure.
They deserve the same design, oversight, and innovation as the products and services they enable."*
— *From The Contract Advantage™*

Parts 1 and 2 explored the philosophical and operational failures embedded in traditional contract lifecycle management (CLM). We defined a new theory:

Contracts as a Business Asset™

and diagnosed the institutional inertia, siloed processes, and broken accountability models that trap organizations in reactive, value-eroding behaviors.

Now, in **Part 3**, we focus on transformation. This is where we shift from critique to construction.

This section outlines the **core architecture of modern CLM**, which is driven by product logic, customer outcomes, and measurable value creation. We do not start with software, we start with strategy.

I. First Principles of Modern CLM

Future-ready contract systems are built on **the first principles** that align with product management, revenue enablement, and operational excellence. These principles govern not only what tools are selected but also how contract systems are designed, governed, and continuously evolved.

1. Customer-Centric Design

Contracts must reflect the customer journey, not internal bureaucracy. Every touchpoint, clause, and obligation should be framed in the context of value delivery, not legal fallback.

This means:

- Using plain language where possible
- Defining success criteria as mutual milestones
- Aligning contract terms with customer experience goals
- Structuring renewals to reward loyalty and incentivize feedback

A contract should be the most clarifying document a customer sees—not the most intimidating.

2. Integrated Ownership Model

CLM is not the responsibility of legal alone. A future-state system embeds contract accountability into every department that creates or fulfills value.

This includes:

- **Sales**: Owns deal structuring and customer expectations

- **Legal**: Owns policy, risk terms, and enforceability
- **Finance**: Owns billing, escalators, and fiscal compliance
- **Customer Success**: Owns delivery milestones and performance
- **Product/Delivery**: Owns the feasibility of what's promised
- **Operations**: Owns tracking, renewal, and optimization workflows

Ownership must be **clearly distributed but jointly accountable**.

3. Data-Driven Governance

Modern contracts are not paper, and they are data. And that data should drive decisions.

Key principles:

- Every clause should be searchable, reportable, and monitored
- Every milestone should be tagged, time-stamped, and surfaced
- Every renewal, escalation, or audit requirement should be tied to automated alerts

A contract without metrics is just a risk. A contract with metrics is a roadmap.

4. Scalability Through Systemization

A scalable CLM model is not dependent on heroic effort. It runs on defined workflows, intelligent automation, and repeatable processes.

This includes:

- Smart templates for standard use cases
- Configurable routing for approvals
- Pre-negotiated clause libraries with fallback logic
- Tiered review levels based on risk profiles
- Integrated signature, storage, and archival processes

Systems don't eliminate human judgment - they **free it** to focus where it matters.

II. The Five Layers of the CLM Transformation Framework™

To operationalize the theory of *Contracts as a Business Asset™*, I've developed a five-layer architecture. This framework reflects not just technology requirements, but the full spectrum of organizational transformation:

1. Contract Strategy Alignment

Purpose, Performance, Positioning

This layer ensures that contract objectives are aligned to business strategy:

- How does each contract type contribute to core KPIs?
- Are we optimizing terms to drive renewals, reduce CAC, or manage cost-to-serve?
- How do contractual frameworks support market differentiation?

This is where CLM meets business modeling.

2. Policy and Clause Governance

Consistency, Risk Mitigation, Negotiation Agility

This layer manages legal integrity, clause versioning, fallback standards, and dynamic approvals:

- What are the core clause families?
- Where can business users self-negotiate?
- What is the escalation path for exceptions?

Governance must balance consistency with agility.

3. Process and Workflow Design

Speed, Transparency, Role Clarity

This layer defines how contracts move through the organization:

- Who initiates?
- What triggers are required for each stage?
- Where does parallelization make sense?
- How is tracking surfaced?

Process must be designed backward from outcomes - not forward from tradition.

4. Technology and System Integration

Automation, Intelligence, Scale

This layer encompasses the CLM platform, CRM/ERP connections, data lakes, and analytics tooling:

- Can systems ingest metadata from executed contracts?
- Can risk scoring be tied to AI clause analysis?
- Are renewals pushed to customer success with context?

Technology must not create another silo—it must connect ecosystems.

5. Performance and Optimization

Feedback Loops, Dashboards, Continuous Improvement

This layer establishes performance metrics, alerts, and review cycles:

- What's our average contract cycle time by contract type?
- Where are exception requests most common?
- Which terms drive renewal success vs. churn?
- Are obligations being met—and tracked?

You cannot optimize what you do not measure. You cannot govern what you cannot see.

III. Redesigning Contracts as Productized Experiences

When contracts are productized, they serve a dual function: enabling value and enhancing trust.

This means designing contracts like you'd design a SaaS product:

- What is the onboarding experience (negotiation)?
- What are the success milestones (obligations)?

- What is the NPS score (renewal satisfaction)?
- What's the churn reason (exit terms, value realization)?

Design Thinking should be applied to contracts, not just customer interfaces.

What language creates friction? What clause triggers confusion? Where do customers hesitate? If you're listening, the answers to these questions are buried inside every negotiation.

IV. Role of the Executive Sponsor

No transformation can be sustained without leadership. CLM transformation must be sponsored not just by Legal but also by the **C-suite**.

The role of the sponsor includes:

- Championing a new vision of contracts as revenue infrastructure
- Funding cross-functional alignment and systems investment
- Embedding contract metrics into board-level reporting
- Holding leaders accountable for contract value outcomes

In high-performing companies, contract performance is reviewed like any other strategic function—monthly, in front of leadership, with KPIs.

V. Building a CLM Transformation Roadmap

CLM transformation is not a switch. It's a staged evolution. Most organizations will follow a three-phase roadmap:

Phase 1: Stabilize

- Inventory and centralize all contracts
- Standardize templates and clause libraries
- Establish contract lifecycle roles and responsibilities

Phase 2: Systematize

- Digitize contract workflows
- Deploy CLM software and integrate with CRM/ERP
- Define performance dashboards and renewal alerts

Phase 3: Strategize

- Align contract terms with customer segmentation
- Embed contract insights into the go-to-market strategy
- Drive continuous clause-level optimization based on data

The goal is not perfection. The goal is **progress with precision**.

VI. The Strategic Payoff

When CLM is transformed, the results are measurable, enterprise-wide, and compounding:

Area	Before	After
Sales	Stalled deals, unclear terms	Accelerated closings, structured playbooks
Legal	Burdened with every draft	Empowered with pre-approved guardrails
Finance	Forecasting without contract inputs	Real-time visibility into financial clauses
Operations	Reactive execution	Milestone-driven delivery with alerts
Customer Experience	Misaligned expectations	Contracts that mirror the journey and outcomes
Risk & Compliance	Hidden exposure	Live dashboards and audit readiness

Strategic CLM doesn't just fix a process. It **elevates the entire organization's performance**.

VII. From Contract Chaos to Contract Confidence

This book opens with a simple premise: contracts are not burdens. They are assets.

But they only become assets when we choose to treat them as such. When we:

- Design with intent
- Track with intelligence

- Manage with precision
- Align with outcomes
- Evolve with feedback

This shift isn't just operational. It's cultural.

When companies embrace *Contracts as a Business Asset*™, they step into a future where every agreement contributes to customer success, financial clarity, and strategic growth.

Epilogue: The Contract Advantage™

You are not reading a theory. You are holding a strategic imperative.

The ideas in this chapter form the foundation for the entire Contract Advantage™ framework. They are not derived from legal manuals or technology whitepapers—but from real work with real teams building real systems that perform.

The chapters that follow will equip you to apply this theory in action:

- With tools
- With playbooks
- With change frameworks
- With metrics that matter

And with the conviction that contracts deserve to be **owned, optimized, and elevated**—because no company can scale what it cannot trust.

CHAPTER 1A

CONTRACTS AS A BUSINESS ASSET™
-THE PRACTITIONER'S NARRATIVE-

FROM CONTRACT CHAOS TO CLM COMMAND:

THE FIELD-TESTED PLAYBOOK BEHIND THE THEORY

BY THE CREATOR OF THE CONTRACT ADVANTAGE™ MODEL

"You don't just lose money through bad contracts.
You lose time, trust, innovation, and the ability to scale what you sell."
— From the Field Notes of a CLM Strategist

PART 1

Why This Chapter Matters

Theory without practice is fragile. This chapter is the ground truth—the evidence base for the theory I've laid out in *Contracts as a Business Asset™*. It distills over two decades of consulting, implementation, and recovery work across global enterprises into the realities that most business leaders feel but struggle to name.

In this chapter, I'll walk you through:

- What contract chaos really looks like in the trenches
- How it erodes performance, one missed term at a time
- Why most CLM investments fail to deliver strategic value
- The transformation method I built to fix it, every time

This isn't a sales pitch. It's a battle-tested process—a system designed not just to solve contract dysfunction but to convert contracts into accelerators of growth, innovation, and customer trust.

I. What Contract Chaos Looks Like in the Real World

You know it when you see it—and when you feel it. Contract chaos isn't some abstract problem. It appears in meetings, audits, backlogs, delays, and frustrated teams. Here's what I've seen consistently in my consulting and diagnostic work, regardless of industry, geography, or company size:

🔁 Siloed Systems Everywhere

Contracts are fragmented across inboxes, shared folders, outdated DMS platforms, and isolated tools. Legal works from one version. Sales uploads another to the CRM. Finance never sees either. There's no single source of truth - only digital silos.

📫 Manual, Non-Trackable Workflows

Approvals vanish into inbox black holes. Routing is improvised, inconsistent, and undocumented. Nobody knows who's holding up the signature—or why it's taking so long. And when the contract finally goes through, there's no audit trail.

🎯 No Linkage to Financial Systems

Revenue-impacting clauses (rebates, escalators, penalties) are signed—but never tracked. Finance is unaware of triggers. Renewals auto-execute without pricing reviews. Value disappears without anyone noticing.

🔒 No Metadata, No Metrics, No Visibility

Most contracts are not digitized at the clause level. You can't search, report, or compare. No one knows how many NDAs are active. Or how many MSAs are expiring next quarter. CLM is flying blind.

🐻 Legal Backlogs and User Workarounds

Legal is overwhelmed. Contract owners stop trusting the process. Teams begin using "unofficial" contracts to move deals forward. The CLM system becomes the blocker - not the enabler. Compliance risk skyrockets, and legal loses control.

These aren't minor frustrations. They are **strategic liabilities**. The longer this environment persists, the more expensive it becomes—financially, operationally, and reputationally.

II. The Hidden Costs You Don't See—But I Do

Leaders usually ask, *"What's the financial impact of our contracting mess?"*

The truth is: it's worse than they think.

Below are the **hidden costs of contract chaos**—many of which only surface when it's already too late:

💰 Revenue Leakage

- Rebate thresholds missed.
- Discount terms forgotten.
- Payment escalators untriggered.
- Renewal clauses ignored.
- Upsell windows bypassed.

These aren't edge cases. They're routine. And they cost millions.

🔍 Audit & Regulatory Exposure

When a subpoena arrives or a compliance audit kicks in, most orgs realize:

"We can't search our contracts fast enough to stay clean."

Without clause-level visibility, you're one poorly timed request away from a high-risk finding—or worse.

⚙️ Operational Bottlenecks

- NDAs are reviewed line by line, every time.
- MSAs are redlined manually—every deal.
- No one uses standard templates because they're outdated or untrusted.

Result: Legal becomes a throughput constraint on the business. Growth slows because contracts do.

⊞ Innovation Drag

- AI governance can't launch without clear IP clauses.
- Procurement platforms stall without clause clarity.
- Product teams can't validate launch criteria buried in contracts.
- Pricing strategy gets locked behind old terms.

Tech roadmaps die waiting for contracts to catch up.

III. The Strategic Cost: Lost Trust

This is the one most leaders overlook - until it's already costing them dearly.

Contract dysfunction creates **distrust across the business**:

- Sales stops using the official process.
- Procurement creates shadow workflows.
- Legal becomes "the bottleneck."
- Executives stop asking for real-time contract data—because it doesn't exist.

And when trust breaks, fixing it takes **radical transparency**, time, and a commitment to rebuilding the system from the ground up.

IV. Real-World Field Cases: How Chaos Costs You Millions

These are anonymized versions of real clients I've worked with—and the hard lessons they learned.

🏛 Case: Global Banking Institution

Problem: A five-year contract backlog led to $9 million unresolved obligations.

Fallout: Vendor transitions delayed. Audit flags triggered. Regulatory heat applied.

My Fix: Built an automated escalation engine using clause-based triggers and performance gates.

Result: Reduced backlog from 5 years to 3 months. Cleared all audit issues. Preserved vendor performance continuity.

🚀 Case: Aerospace Manufacturer

Problem: Procurement, supply chain, and legal teams operating in silos.

Cost: $15M+ in missed supplier rebates. Tier 1 pricing protections are unenforced.

My Fix: Designed an integrated CLM-to-SAP ECC workflow with clause metadata tagging.

Result: Captured and enforced rebate clauses. Automated alerts. Enabled reporting dashboards by supplier. ROI realized in less than one fiscal year.

💡 Case: Global Technology Provider

Problem: Separate CLM systems for direct and indirect procurement. No central clause governance.

Impact: 47% delay rate. Over 1,300 contracts are missing a compliance review.

My Fix: Implemented enterprise-wide playbooks, a unified clause library, and standardized templates.

Platform: Ironclad across global operations.

Result: 3x ROI in Year 1 through compliance capture, faster go-lives, and accelerated vendor onboarding.

These are not exceptions. They are what happens **when contracts are unmanaged at scale**.

V. Why This Happens: The Root Causes

Every one of the failures above stems from **five predictable root causes**:

1. **Contracts are treated as legal artifacts - not business instruments.**

2. **CLM tools are bought for compliance - not value creation.**

3. **Ownership is diffused. No one is accountable for the full contract lifecycle.**

4. **The contract process is disconnected from the enterprise tech stack.**

5. **CLM implementations are handed in to IT instead of strategic operators.**

These root causes aren't failures of intention. They're failures of design.

That's why I created the **Contract Advantage™ Model**—a methodology for realigning contract strategy with business performance, starting with diagnosis and ending with value realization.

⇥ Coming Next in Part 2

In the next section of Chapter 1A, I'll walk you through:

- My **14-day diagnostic approach**
- How I use the **Contract Chaos Index**™ as a strategic scorecard
- The transformation playbook I deploy across every engagement
- The mindset shift from *"compliance tracking"* to *"value orchestration"*

It's not about patching the process. It's about redesigning how value flows through your organization, starting at the contract.

⌗ ⌗ ⌗ ⌗

The Contract Advantage™ Playbook in Action

*"Every broken contract process is a signal.
The question is whether your organization is
listening—and ready to act."*

I. From Theory to Practice: The Contract Advantage™ System

The cases I've shared in Part 1 were not saved by software alone. They were rescued and reengineered by applying a playbook I developed over the years of real-world consulting. That playbook is what I now call the **Contract Advantage™ Model**.

This model is not just a process. It's a mindset shift. It enables companies to move from:

From	To
Firefighting	Forecasting
Silos	Integration
Legal Bottleneck	Cross-functional Enablement
Cycle Time Tracking	Value Lifecycle Management
Document Repositories	Data-driven Decision Engines

The following sections break down the **core components of this methodology** and show how I deploy them in high-stakes, high-velocity environments.

II. The 14-Day Diagnostic: Contract Reality Check™

Diagnosis is mandatory before transformation begins. Most teams don't need another software tool—they need to understand where they are.

My 14-Day Diagnostic process is a rapid, high-visibility engagement designed to uncover:

- Where your contracts live
- How your workflows behave under pressure
- Who owns outcomes
- What you're measuring—and what you're missing
- How much value is leaking (and how fast)

It maps reality, not assumptions.

🔍 Tools I Use in the Diagnostic Phase

- **Contract Chaos Index™** – A proprietary maturity and risk rating scale across 10 CLM categories (see below).
- **Workflow Walkthroughs** – Real-time tracing of how a contract moves from request to archive.
- **System Maps** – Technology stack inventories across CLM, CRM, ERP, and shared drives.
- **Stakeholder Interviews** – Sales, legal, procurement, operations, customer success, finance.
- **Revenue Risk Snapshots** – Identify dollar-at-

risk clauses, missed renewals, and compliance exposure.

This fast, focused analysis reveals the **operational cost of inaction** and sets the foundation for executive buy-in.

III. The Contract Chaos Index™ (CCI)

This is your "FICO score" for contracting maturity. Developed over hundreds of real-world use cases, the **CCI**™ rates your organization across 10 critical domains:

Domain	Diagnostic Focus
1. Contract Visibility	Can you find what you've signed?
2. Clause Consistency	Are key terms standardized or improvised?
3. Approval Workflow	Is there clear routing logic- or chaos?
4. Risk Flagging	Do you surface risky language before the signature?
5. Template Trust	Do business units use them, or avoid them?
6. Renewal Readiness	Do you manage renewals proactively or reactively?
7. Obligation Monitoring	Are you tracking what you've promised?
8. Contract-to-System Sync	Do contract terms map into ERP/ CRM systems?
9. Performance Measurement	Are you measuring contract value or just throughput?
10. Strategic Alignment	Do contracts support? Or distract from core growth priorities?

Each domain is scored on a 0–5 scale and color-coded for clarity:

- **Green (4–5)**: Optimized
- **Yellow (2–3)**: Exposed
- **Red (0–1)**: Risk Zone

At the end, I deliver a Contract Chaos Index heatmap that executive teams *cannot unsee*.

IV. The Contract Advantage™ Playbook: 6 Core Stages

Once the diagnostic is complete, I deploy a **6-stage transformation framework** that is adaptable to the client's maturity, industry, and internal capabilities.

Stage 1: Clarify Value Intent

- Define what "contract value" means for this business
- Establish KPIs that reflect outcomes, not just activities
- Identify value blockers (e.g., deal friction, risk overexposure, revenue leakage)

🏹 *This stage aligns the CLM strategy with executive priorities.*

Stage 2: Map Lifecycle Gaps

- Walk each contract type through the full lifecycle— from request to renewal
- Identify bottlenecks, black holes, and bypasses
- Surface redundant steps, missing approvals, and blind spots

343

⚒ *We don't automate chaos. We redesign it.*

Stage 3: Redesign Governance

- Create clause libraries with fallback logic
- Embed legal policy into workflows - not documents
- Set approval thresholds and owner escalation maps

⚒ *Governance shouldn't block speed. It should enable smart velocity.*

Stage 4: Systemize Performance

- Integrate CLM with CRM, ERP, and document management
- Deploy innovative templates tied to business use cases
- Configure dashboards for real-time visibility

⚒ *Performance is what makes contracts valuable after the signature.*

Stage 5: Operationalize Insights

- Track clause usage, turnaround time, and renewal triggers
- Report on dollar-at-risk and value-realized metrics
- Translate data into action (alerts, exception management, risk scoring)

⚒ *Every contract generates intelligence. Only mature systems use it.*

Stage 6: Embed a Culture of Contract Thinking

- Train cross-functional teams on contract awareness

- Introduce KPIs into team reviews
- Create a shared language for risk, opportunity, and compliance
- Celebrate outcomes—not just legal sign-offs

🔨 *Transformation isn't complete until behavior changes.*

V. The Real ROI of Strategic CLM

Leaders often ask: *What's the ROI of this kind of contract transformation?*

Here's what I've seen consistently:

Impact Area	Measurable Gains
Deal Cycle Time	30–70% faster
Renewal Capture	20–40% increase
Legal Review Volume	50% reduction
Clause Compliance	Near 100% in standardized areas
Operational Load	Reduced by 1,000+ hours annually
Revenue Leakage	Recovered $1M+ in Year 1 for mid-market orgs
Audit Readiness	Transformed from reactive to instant response

But the **qualitative ROI** is just as powerful:

- Sales stops avoiding the process
- Legal stops burning out
- Customers start seeing clarity

- Executives start getting real-time answers
- Risk stops being invisible

Strategic CLM is not a cost center. It is a competitive advantage when it's built right.

VI. Final Note from the Field

Here's what I've learned, over and over again:

The moment an organization starts treating its contracts like it treats its revenue, products, or customer experience, transformation becomes inevitable.

Until then, contract chaos will remain an invisible drag on performance. But the companies that choose to do this work? They outperform. They retain customers. They recover value. And they scale with clarity.

This chapter—and the theory behind it—isn't based on speculation. It's based on 25+ years of trenches, turnarounds, and transformation.

You can build a Contract Advantage™. Now you have the blueprint.

The True Cost of Contract Chaos
Why Inefficiencies, Invisibility, and Inaction Bleed Business Potential

"Every contract mismanaged is not just an operational lapse. It's a strategic leak."
— From the notebooks of a CLM transformation architect

I. The Economic Damage You Can't See—But Feel Everywhere

While most organizations understand that poor contract management creates inefficiencies, few recognize the true scope of the damage. Contract chaos is not an administrative nuisance. It's a multi-dimensional drain on the business: it depletes cash, dilutes trust, paralyzes innovation, and corrodes strategic momentum.

When contracts are disorganized, scattered, and unmanaged, they don't just delay processes - they destabilize performance. And yet, many leaders tolerate this environment because the costs are not always immediately visible. The losses hide in missed renewals, outdated pricing terms, and forgotten obligations. They surface in failed audits, stalled sales, broken partnerships, and misaligned teams. Most damaging of all: They erode an organization's ability to make decisions with confidence and agility.

II. The Financial Fallout of Fragmentation

Companies today rely on contracts to activate revenue, regulate risk, govern relationships, and shape commitments. But when these contracts live in unsearchable folders, undocumented workflows, and manually-driven review cycles, the organization bleeds value daily.

These are not theoretical losses. In my experience leading contract diagnostics and recovery for large enterprises and mid-sized growth firms, I've repeatedly uncovered:

- 💰 **Millions in revenue leakage**: Poorly tracked escalators, lapsed renewals, expired pricing terms
- 🪟 **Sizable compliance exposure**: Undetected violations of payment timelines, regulatory clauses, or scope creep
- ⏳ **Slower deal cycles**: Delays in execution that kill momentum or let competitors get to market first
- 📄 **Budget overages**: Legal review costs balloon as contracts are redlined from scratch without templates or pre-approved language
- ✖ **Missed renegotiation windows**: Opportunities for better terms pass silently without notice

In these cases, the organization pays for contracts twice: once when it signs them, and again in penalties, lost value, and cost overruns when it fails to manage them.

III. The Operational Impacts Are Just as Severe

Contract mismanagement is a systemic, not symptomatic, issue. It touches every corner of the enterprise:

- Legal teams become bottlenecks—not by choice, but by design.
- Sales delays become standard practice—not because of the customer, but because of the process.
- Procurement overpays - not due to market conditions, but due to never revisited terms.
- Finance operates on guesses, not forecasts, because it lacks visibility into contractual obligations.

And all of this persists because **contracts are not treated as active business instruments**. They are left on digital shelves, unable to influence the business because they've been exiled from the operational flow.

IV. Contract Chaos Undermines Strategic Agility

What's often missed in traditional assessments of contract inefficiency is the **strategic opportunity cost**. A disjointed contract environment doesn't just cause rework or lost savings. It erodes the very traits businesses rely on to survive and thrive:

- **Speed to market** is reduced because every product launch or pricing change requires contract rewrites.
- **M&A readiness** is weakened because contract inventories are outdated, incomplete, or scattered.
- **Vendor leverage** is lost because terms aren't benchmarked, renegotiated, or consolidated.
- **Customer trust** deteriorates because contracts feel adversarial, slow, or inconsistent.

Simply put: the chaos doesn't stay contained. It infects performance across product, sales, finance, and delivery

V. From Invisibility to Insight: The Power of Centralization

Contract chaos thrives in the shadows—when contracts are invisible, inaccessible, and unmanaged. The fix starts with **visibility**.

In every successful CLM transformation I've led, the first step was surfacing the full contract ecosystem:

- Where contracts live
- Who owns them
- Which terms are recurring sources of pain or risk
- What obligations have been left unattended
- When critical milestones are likely to be missed

Once these are visible, patterns emerge—and so do opportunities for redesign.

VI. Compliance, Risk, and the Illusion of Control

Another hidden cost of outdated contracting practices is **compliance exposure**. Even in heavily regulated industries, I've seen firms rely on tribal knowledge and spreadsheet tracking to manage critical terms. The illusion of control leads to real-world consequences:

- Regulatory audits uncover undocumented approvals or missing clauses
- Data protection clauses don't align with evolving privacy requirements
- Obligations tied to SLAs, insurance, or subcontracting are breached without notice

These are not hypotheticals. They are common and costly. And the damage doesn't end with fines. It extends to **brand reputation**, **partner confidence**, and **executive credibility**.

VII. The Myth of "We Just Need Better Software"

There's a recurring false belief in many organizations: *"We just need a better CLM platform."* But most contract chaos is not caused by tools - it's caused by misalignment.

I've seen Fortune 500s install best-in-class software that still delivered poor results. Why? Because:

- They digitized broken workflows instead of redesigning them
- They treated contract management as an IT initiative, not a business strategy
- They trained for compliance, not for performance

Technology is a multiplier, not a miracle. Without a clear operating model, better software just accelerates dysfunction.

VIII. The Cost of Doing Nothing

Here's what inaction actually costs:

Hidden Cost Type	Organizational Impact
Missed Renewals	Lost revenue and rework
Manual Approvals	Slower sales, audit gaps
Outdated Templates	Higher legal cost, inconsistent brand risk

Hidden Cost Type	Organizational Impact
Untracked Obligations	Financial penalties, reputation damage
Lack of Clause Insights	Weaker negotiation power, missed optimization

And these aren't one-off issues. They repeat. Monthly. Quarterly. Annually. Silently chipping away at business performance until someone notices—and by then, it's expensive.

IX. Turning the Problem into Possibility

The good news is that contract chaos is fixable. When fixed correctly, **contracts become a revenue engine, a risk governor, and a growth enabler**.

But this shift requires rethinking the role contracts play—not as "legal paperwork," but as living tools for:

- Customer experience
- Product delivery
- Financial forecasting
- Vendor optimization
- Strategic execution

This mindset shift is the first real step in treating **Contracts as a Business Asset™**.

✳✳✳✳

The Quantifiable Business Case for CLM Reinvention

"You don't need a spreadsheet to know something's broken. But when you have one, it becomes impossible to ignore."
— From a client C-Suite conversation on contract reform

I. Every Contract Touches Cash—So Why Don't We Measure It?

It's astonishing how many companies can generate a P&L in minutes, but can't answer questions like:

- How many contracts are up for renewal next quarter?
- How much revenue is tied to unstructured terms?
- Which contracts include missed SLAs, unclaimed rebates, or outdated pricing?

This disconnect reveals a larger truth: **most organizations don't know how contracts affect cash until after the money is gone**.

When unmanaged contracts become passive - documents that sit idle while business is conducted around them. When activated, tracked, and measured, they become **engines of commercial clarity**.

II. The Revenue Leakage Problem

In my diagnostics with enterprise and mid-market companies, I've consistently identified a pattern of **silent revenue loss**—value that disappears not because of market forces, but because of mismanagement. This is revenue leakage.

Common sources include:

- Over-discounting due to unclear deal desk rules
- Renewal auto-executions with outdated pricing
- Escalators and incentives that were never triggered
- Late billing due to untracked milestones
- Misapplied usage tiers or volume commitments

Even conservative analysis shows organizations can leak **1–3% of contracted revenue** annually. For a $100M company, that's up to $3M in yearly silent losses.

And this is before we consider penalties, risk exposure, and service-level failure costs.

III. CLM Is a CFO Concern—Not Just Legal's Domain

The economic logic is straightforward:

- Every contract affects revenue recognition, cash flow, and margin.
- Missed clauses lead to real P&L damage.
- Unmonitored renewals undermine recurring revenue integrity.

Yet in most companies, **contract ownership is functionally isolated in Legal**. CLM doesn't show up in financial dashboards, it's not embedded in deal modeling, and it rarely aligns with the CFO's office.

This is a missed opportunity.

In a Contract Advantage™ operating model, finance teams gain:

- Real-time visibility into revenue-bearing contracts
- Predictive insight into contract-triggered costs and risks
- Governance over terms that affect forecasting and accruals

The shift? From legal compliance to financial command.

IV. A Contract Isn't Closed at Signature—It's Activated

Another common misbelief is that it's done once a contract is signed.

Reality: Signature is Day 0.

The contract activates:

- Billing terms
- Service obligations
- Compliance checklists
- Renewal alerts
- Performance scorecards

But unless these elements are integrated into systems— and managed like operational data—they get lost.

A signed PDF in a SharePoint folder won't generate revenue. An integrated, clause-level activated contract will.

V. The Real ROI of Strategic CLM

What's the upside of getting this right?

Organizations that strategically redesign CLM have consistently reported:

Metric	Lift
Contract cycle time	30–70% faster
Revenue leakage	Reduced by 1–3%
Renewal accuracy	+25–40% improvement
Legal review load	50% fewer inbound requests
Audit readiness	From 4+ weeks to real-time
Vendor performance capture	+30–50% increase

These are not hypotheticals. They are field-tested outcomes across industries—from SaaS to pharma to financial services.

And behind these outcomes is one consistent approach: a shift from **reactive compliance to proactive commercial design**.

VI. Case Insight: A Mid-Sized SaaS Provider

Scenario:

A $75M ARR tech company noticed increasing customer churn—but couldn't pinpoint why.

CLM Reality:

- Contracts were stored in siloed folders
- Renewals occurred without revalidation of value
- Upsell clauses were never activated
- Discounts extended beyond term commitments

Solution:

- Mapped all active contracts into a centralized system
- Aligned customer success with renewal clause timelines
- Created dashboard alerts for renewal, upsell, and churn-risk triggers

Result:

- $1.4M in retained revenue over 9 months
- 17% reduction in churn in the first two renewal cycles
- Full visibility for customer success and finance teams

Lesson: Value isn't lost at contract signature. It's lost in silence.

VII. Why Most Contract Investments Fail to Pay Off

You can spend seven figures on a CLM platform and still fail. Why?

Because value capture doesn't come from software—it comes from **strategic orchestration**.

Common failure modes include:

- Automating existing chaos instead of redesigning the process flow
- Focusing only on legal terms instead of full lifecycle integration
- Leaving contract data out of operational dashboards
- Missing the change management to drive adoption

Strategic CLM is not an IT implementation. It's a **cross-functional redesign of how business is promised, delivered, and measured**.

VIII. Quantifying the Unquantified

Want to make the business case to your board, CFO, or CEO?

Here's what I recommend as a **CLM ROI Model** for internal business case framing:

Metric	Formula	Purpose
Annual Revenue Leakage Estimate	(Total Contracted Revenue) × 1–3%	Identify recoverable revenue
Cycle Time Recovery	(Avg contract cycle days saved) × (# of deals per year)	Accelerate time-to-cash
Legal Cost Reduction	(Hours saved from pre-approved language) × (Hourly cost of Legal)	Free legal to focus on strategy

Metric	Formula	Purpose
Risk Cost Avoidance	# of prior-year audit issues × average remediation cost	Avoid compliance exposure
Renewal Optimization	% of missed renewals × avg deal value	Reclaim recurring revenue

This model is part of the financial underpinning of *The Contract Advantage*™ theory. When contracts are governed as business assets, these metrics are not hypothetical—they're measurable, and they scale.

IX. Contracts Are Not Paperwork—They Are Value Chains

The biggest shift companies must make is psychological, not procedural.

Contracts are not documentation.

They are **value chains in motion.**

Every clause is a node. Every milestone is a trigger. Every renewal is an inflection point.

Every term affects risk, reward, revenue, and reputation.

If you can see them that way, you can begin managing them as such. And when you do, **you stop managing contracts and start commanding them.**

☑ What's Next: The Strategic Redesign Framework

In **Part 3 of Chapter 2**, I'll walk through the blueprint for strategic redesign:

- The four elements of a contract-centric operating system
- Key principles for redesigning CLM around customer, cash, and compliance
- The executive role in enforcing the model
- How Contracts as a Business Asset™ becomes a living, measurable system

❖ ❖ ❖ ❖

PART 3

Designing the Business System Around Contracts as Assets

"Every contract carries opportunity. The only question is whether your systems are designed to realize it - or ignore it."
— The Contract Advantage™ Method

I. Why System Design Matters More Than Software Selection

Once companies recognize the hidden costs of contract dysfunction and the measurable benefits of strategic CLM, they often rush to implement technology.

That's where many fail.

Technology without structure accelerates chaos. A new platform layered over fragmented processes only automates confusion. What's needed isn't just a tool—it's a **contract-centered operating system**.

This chapter outlines a business's four core design elements that treat contracts not as artifacts but as assets.

II. The Four Elements of a CLM-Centric Operating System™

These pillars represent a unified strategy for elevating contract management from legal hygiene to commercial advantage.

1. Strategic Alignment

Contracts must reflect—and reinforce—the organization's strategic objectives.

This means:

- Pricing models aligned to customer value realization
- Escalation clauses linked to service performance metrics
- Renewal structures tied to lifecycle milestones
- IP, data, and liability terms aligned with product and compliance roadmaps

In short, contracts must do more than protect the business. They must **propel it**.

2. Lifecycle Governance

Contract lifecycle management is not a stage - it's a continuous system. Each phase must be owned, measured, and optimized.

Stage	Strategic Design
Initiation	Guided intake aligned to business priorities
Drafting	Smart templates with clause logic libraries
Review & Approval	Role-based routing with escalation rules
Signature	Digital, secure, and auditable

Stage	Strategic Design
Post-Signature	Integration with ERP/CRM systems
Performance	Obligation tracking and KPI monitoring
Renewal	Predictive triggers, pricing updates, and renegotiation

Each handoff is a moment of risk—or a moment of leverage.

3. Cross-Functional Ownership

CLM is not "owned" by legal. It is **co-owned by every function** that drives or fulfills contract obligations:

- **Sales** – owns commercial integrity
- **Legal** – owns enforceability and governance
- **Finance** – owns fiscal alignment and forecasting
- **Customer Success** – owns post-sale delivery triggers
- **Procurement** – owns vendor value assurance
- **Operations** – owns SLA execution and milestone delivery

Successful companies build a **contract steering committee** or governance council. This ensures oversight without bureaucracy, and velocity without chaos.

4. Performance Visibility

Contracts must be visible not just as documents, but as **data-rich business intelligence sources**.

This means:

- Clause-level tagging and metadata extraction
- Dashboards for obligations, expirations, and escalations
- Contract value realization metrics
- Renewal pipelines with predictive indicators
- Role-specific alerts for key triggers

When contract performance becomes visible, **management becomes proactive**.

III. Designing the CLM Experience Like a Product

To unlock full value, companies must begin designing their contract systems like customer journeys or product interfaces.

Ask:

- What's the user experience for internal teams initiating contracts?
- Where does confusion or friction appear?
- What terms consistently create negotiation deadlock?
- Where are people bypassing the official process?
- What behaviors signal trust—or distrust—in the current system?

Organizations can map and resolve contract friction using Design Thinking or Product Management frameworks, just like a product team eliminates bugs in a feature release.

IV. The Role of the Executive in CLM Reform

No transformation sustains without leadership commitment. The executive sponsor plays a pivotal role in:

- Framing contracts as a strategic priority, not a compliance task
- Funding system redesign and cross-functional training
- Embedding contract metrics into boardroom dashboards
- Aligning KPIs to contract performance (cycle time, renewal rate, value capture)
- Holding leaders accountable to behavioral change, not just process change

In Contract Advantage™ engagements, the most successful transformations came from **C-level sponsorship**, not functional delegation.

V. Principles for CLM System Redesign

Here are the core principles I've applied across successful transformations:

1. **Design from the outside in** – Start with customer, partner, or vendor experience.
2. **Automate decisions, not just steps** – Build logic into routing, approval, and clause selection.
3. **Make contract data operable** – It should influence actions, not just be stored.
4. **Treat exceptions as intelligence** – Track which claus-

es are always redlined, and fix them.

5. **Build for scale, not heroes** – No CLM system should rely on memory, persistence, or favors.

VI. What Success Looks Like

When fully activated, Contracts as a Business Asset™ reshapes enterprise performance:

Dimension	Before	After
Visibility	Contracts scattered and inaccessible	Centralized, searchable, monitored
Velocity	Manual routing and late-stage delays	Streamlined, automated, and tracked
Value	Terms unused, obligations missed	Obligations met, clauses optimized
Governance	Legal bottlenecks	Cross-functional accountability
Intelligence	No insight into clause performance	Clause-level analytics and forecasting
Growth	Contracts limit scale	Contracts enable agility and innovation

VII. A Final Strategic Reframe

The goal of contract transformation is not to eliminate legal risk. That's the floor. The real goal is to **unleash business performance**.

When contracts become strategic infrastructure, they:

- Accelerate sales and renewals

- Clarify delivery and reduce disputes
- Strengthen relationships with vendors and partners
- Forecast revenue with greater accuracy
- Track and manage risk in real time
- Help the enterprise scale with speed and integrity

This is the business case behind *Contracts as a Business Asset™*: Not compliance or control, **but value, velocity, and visibility.**

Chapter 2 Summary: From Chaos to Command

This chapter diagnosed the economic, operational, and strategic damage of fragmented contract systems and made the business case for transformation.

You've seen:

- The hidden cost structure of unmanaged contracts
- How revenue, margin, and reputation erode silently
- The ROI of treating contracts as data, not documents
- A repeatable framework for CLM system design and executive leadership

In Chapter 2A, we move from discussion to deployment. You'll see the **Contract Operating Playbook** I use to implement these principles at scale, backed by the tools, scorecards, and diagnostic frameworks developed over 25+ years of enterprise transformation work.

❉ ❉ ❉ ❉

CHAPTER 2A

-THE PRACTITIONER'S NARRATIVE- UNLOCKING VALUE BY DEFEATING CONTRACT CHAOS BY THE CREATOR OF *THE CONTRACT ADVANTAGE*™ MODEL

"Contracts either fuel innovation - or they choke it. There is no neutral."
— From the Fieldwork of *the Contract Advantage*™ System

Why This Chapter Matters

The theory behind Contracts as a Business Asset™ becomes truly transformative when applied to the field. This chapter details the real-world patterns, failures, and opportunities I've uncovered over two decades of helping organizations regain control over their contract functions.

Contract chaos isn't merely an operational inconvenience. It directly threatens business growth, revenue capture, innovation velocity, and strategic execution.

This chapter is not theoretical. It is built from the ground up—from lost rebates and broken audit trails to stalled product launches and crushed stakeholder trust.

Contracts cannot be treated as administrative afterthoughts if you want to scale with confidence. They must be operationalized as dynamic, measurable assets.

I. What Contract Chaos Looks Like in the Wild

The symptoms are alarmingly consistent across industries, regions, and operational models. Here's what I have witnessed repeatedly:

◇ Siloed Systems

Contracts are scattered across inboxes, personal drives, DMS platforms, and even physical filing cabinets. Legal, Sales, Finance, and Procurement each work from conflicting versions of "truth."

◇ Manual, Non-Trackable Workflows

Approvals routed by email, with no trail. Bottlenecks appear without visibility. Contracts languish, lost between stakeholders with no accountability.

◇ No Linkage to Financial Systems

Revenue terms, rebate triggers, and renewal obligations are signed—but not surfaced, not integrated, not tracked.

◇ Absence of Metadata and Metrics

Most organizations cannot answer simple questions like:

- How many active NDAs are in force?
- How many MSAs have an upcoming renewal clause?
- Which contracts include termination for convenience?

Lack of clause-level metadata means no reporting, no KPIs, no leverage.

◇ **User Distrust and Legal Backlogs**

Without reliable systems, frontline users lose trust. Sales-people create workarounds. Procurement improvises. Legal is inundated—and resented.

This is the ecosystem where opportunity dies silently.

II. The Financial Reality: Real-World Field Cases

Here's what these patterns cost in the real world, drawn from my direct engagements:

🏛 Global Banking Institution

Challenge: 5-year contract backlog with $9M in unresolved financial obligations.

Impact: Delayed vendor transitions, audit exposure, and reputational risk.

Solution: Implemented automated clause-driven escalation flows.

Result: Cut backlog from 5 years to 3 months. Recovered visibility and regulatory footing.

🚀 Global Aerospace Manufacturer

Challenge: Disconnected contracting across supply chain, procurement, and legal.

Impact: $15M in missed Tier 1 rebates. Pricing protections are unenforced.

Solution: Built a CLM-to-SAP ECC integration with renewal triggers and performance dashboards.

Result: Rebate capture enabled. Dashboarded vendor tracking deployed. Realized seven-figure value recovery.

💡 Global Technology Provider

Challenge: Fragmented CLM platforms; compliance gaps in over 1,300 contracts.

Impact: 47% delay rate in contract finalizations; regulatory risks rising.

Solution: Standardized clause library. Unified playbooks. Implemented enterprise-grade CLM system (Ironclad).

Result: Tripled ROI in Year 1 through faster launches, better governance, and vendor onboarding acceleration.

These are not anomalies. These are the predictable costs of neglect.

III. Hidden Costs That Compound Over Time

Even organizations that sense inefficiency often miss the full iceberg beneath the surface:

💰 Revenue Leakage

Unclaimed rebates, outdated pricing escalators, late renewals, and missed upsells sap millions quietly.

🔍 Audit and Regulatory Risk

Organizations are one surprise audit away from disaster without traceability at the clause level.

⚙️ Operational Bottlenecks

Manual redlining and legacy workflows create internal

gridlock that strangles deal velocity and project execution.

⊞ Innovation Drag

Enterprise system integrations fail because contracts are disconnected from ERP, CRM, and digital transformation efforts.

Every quarter, this chaos persists, opportunity cost compounds, and competitors gain ground.

IV. The Strategic Erosion of Trust

Perhaps most dangerously, unmanaged contract chaos erodes internal trust:

- **Sales** stops using the process.
- **Procurement** creates shadow contracting practices.
- **Executives** lose visibility and confidence in operational controls.

Once trust fractures, it demands radical transparency and re-architecture to heal. Left unattended, it metastasizes into cultural dysfunction that no amount of software can repair.

V. Why This Happens: Core Failure Points

Across every broken system, I diagnose the exact root causes:

Core Failure	Impact
CLM tools bought for compliance, not commercial value	No business adoption
Contracts treated as legal risks, not business levers	Stifled innovation
No lifecycle ownership beyond Legal	Fragmented responsibility
No linkage to enterprise tech stack	Data isolation and manual rework
CLM initiatives delegated to IT	Loss of strategic focus and business credibility

This is why **The Contract Advantage™ Model** was built: to rewire these systemic errors from the ground up.

VI. My Transformation Blueprint: From Chaos to Command

Every engagement starts with a diagnostic sprint. Within the first 14 days, I assess:

- Contract volume vs. operational resource capacity
- Percentage of contracts with unenforced financial clauses
- Average time from draft to signature
- System architecture touchpoints (and their integrations or gaps)

- Stakeholder sentiment on visibility, control, and trust

From this, I generate a **Contract Chaos Index™**, a proprietary health score that forms the baseline for roadmap creation and execution.

VII. Contracts as Innovation Engines

Reframing contracts from obstacles to enablers opens entirely new conversations:

Function	CLM Impact
Product Launches	Faster market entry, cleaner SLA frameworks
Vendor Innovation	Clearer IP, licensing, and incentive alignment
Expansion Strategies	Pre-baked renewal and upsell clauses
Customer Success	Embedded milestone and health score triggers
AI Governance	Explicit rights management and compliance
Revenue Forecasting	Clear renewal, rebate, and escalation pipelines

Bad contract systems don't just lose money.

They **delay strategy** and **choke growth**.

VIII. Practitioner's Theory-Into-Practice Checklist

To operationalize these insights, I guide leadership teams to take these first steps:

🛠 Foundational Checklist:

- ☐ Map all systems and repositories where contracts live.
- ☐ Audit 50 randomly selected contracts for missed obligations or renegotiation windows.
- ☐ Interview legal, finance, and sales about top bottlenecks and pain points.
- ☐ Identify three high-risk clauses with direct financial or operational exposure.
- ☐ Calculate your organization's initial **Contract Chaos Index™**.

This baseline isn't optional. It's mandatory for any serious transformation initiative.

IX. Summary: What This Chapter Unlocks

- Contract dysfunction is a strategic growth barrier, not just a legal problem.
- The real-world economic impact is measurable in millions, often compounding yearly.
- Fixing CLM is not about software installation. It is about redesigning your business infrastructure for trust, velocity, and value realization.
- The theory of **Contracts as a Business Asset™** is not aspirational. It is executable.

✘ Theory Into Practice Checklist

- ☐ Audit how contracts are perceived across departments
- ☐ Identify the last time contract data drove a business decision
- ☐ Create a Strategic Contracting Pyramid™ Map for your org
- ☐ Book a mindset briefing with Legal + Finance + Operations
- ☐ Define 3 new metrics that would prove CLM is a growth driver

CONTRACTS AS A BUSINESS ASSET™ SHIFTING THE MINDSET: FROM LEGAL ADMIN TO STRATEGIC ASSET

PART 1

The Conceptual Failure of Traditional Contract Management

Introduction: The Mindset Crisis in Contract Management

In most organizations today, contracts are not managed as the strategic, dynamic assets they truly are. They are relegated to the periphery—treated as administrative formalities, legal shields, or bureaucratic hurdles to "get the deal done."

This limited, reactive view of contracts — as isolated legal documents, detached from business strategy and customer experience — fundamentally cripples the organization's ability to unlock growth, safeguard margins, manage risk, and sustain competitive advantage.

The crisis in contract management is not primarily a tool, template, or process. It is a **crisis of mindset**.

At a systemic level, organizations have failed to see contracts for what they truly are: **living instruments of business performance**.

Until this conceptual failure is addressed head-on, no automation, digitization, or departmental optimization will solve the underlying dysfunction.

This chapter presents a call to rethink, from first principles, the role of contracts in the enterprise. They should not be seen as defensive paperwork but as **strategic, revenue-activating, relationship-governing assets** that sit at the center of sustainable value creation.

I. Diagnosing the Legacy Mental Model: Contracts as Defensive Artifacts

Most organizations' prevailing mental model of contracts is deeply flawed and dangerously outdated. In this model:

- **Contracts are primarily about legal protection** — constructed to minimize liability, not to maximize opportunity.

- **Contracts are finalized at signature**, instead of being activated as operational blueprints.

- **Contracts live within Legal departments** — rather than being integrated into the business functions they enable.

- **Contracts are reactive instruments** — triggered only when a dispute, failure, or audit demands attention.

This traditional conception stems from an era when the pace of business was slower, markets were less volatile, regulatory complexity was manageable, and customer expectations were static.

That world no longer exists.

Today's business landscape demands **velocity, transparency, adaptability, and customer centricity** — qualities the legacy contract management mindset actively undermines.

II. The Organizational Symptoms of Contract Myopia

The failure to reconceptualize contracts manifests in consistent, measurable ways across organizations of every size and industry:

- **Revenue leakage** from unmanaged pricing escalators, discounts, renewals, and rebates

- **Extended sales cycles** due to fragmented review processes and unclear ownership

- **Increased risk exposure** through missed compliance obligations and contractual blind spots

- **Damaged customer relationships** caused by inflexible or opaque contract terms

- **Operational bottlenecks** created by manual routing, redlining, and approval delays

- **Siloed knowledge** with different departments maintaining isolated versions of "the truth"

- **Audit failures and regulatory penalties** stemming from undocumented commitments

These are not random or incidental. They are the **systematic, predictable consequences** of treating contracts as static legal documents rather than as living business frameworks.

III. The Inadequacy of Technology Alone

Many organizations, recognizing some surface-level dysfunction, attempt to solve the problem through technology procurement—purchasing CLM (Contract Lifecycle Management) platforms with the hope that automation alone will fix systemic contract issues.

This almost always fails.

Technology cannot, by itself, correct a flawed mental model.

- **If the organization still views contracts narrowly, no CLM tool can unlock their strategic value.**
- **If cross-functional ownership remains absent, technology merely digitizes the existing dysfunction.**
- **If contracts remain isolated from revenue strategy, customer journey design, and risk governance, automation makes inefficiency happen faster.**

This misplaced faith in "tech as savior" results in millions wasted on underutilized

systems, poor adoption rates, and ultimately, organizational disillusionment with transformation initiatives.

The critical prerequisite is not new software. It is a **new philosophy**.

IV. Contracts as Strategic Infrastructure: A Reframed Vision

A truly modern view understands that:

- **Contracts are not just legal documents—they are operating systems.**

- **Every contract embodies commercial strategy, customer intent, vendor alignment, and regulatory navigation.**

- **Contracts are dynamic entities—meant to evolve, adapt, and inform ongoing business decisions.**

- **Contract performance metrics are not legal KPIs - they are core business KPIs.**

When contracts are architected and managed accordingly, they no longer serve as friction points. They become **accelerators of growth, agility, and trust**.

This reframing is not optional for organizations seeking to lead in volatile, customer-driven, innovation-intensive markets. It is a **strategic imperative**.

V. From Reactive to Proactive: The Core Mindset Shifts Required

To transition from administrative chaos to strategic command, organizations must adopt the following fundamental shifts:

Traditional Mentality	Strategic Mindset
"Contracts protect us legally."	"Contracts unlock revenue, loyalty, and operational clarity."

Traditional Mentality	Strategic Mindset
"The contract is done at signature."	"The contract activates at signature."
"Legal owns contracts."	"Business units co-own contract value realization."
"Technology will fix this."	"Mindset, governance, and visibility precede technology."
"Compliance first, business second"	"Business outcomes and compliance are integrated goals."

Traditional Mentality	Strategic Mindset
"Contracts protect us legally."	"Contracts unlock revenue, loyalty, and operational clarity."
"The contract is done at signature."	"The contract activates at signature."
"Legal owns contracts."	"Business units co-own contract value realization."
"Technology will fix this."	"Mindset, governance, and visibility precede technology."
"Compliance first, business second"	"Business outcomes and compliance are integrated goals."

These shifts are not mere attitudinal adjustments. They demand structural, operational, and cultural transformation across the enterprise.

VI. The Stakes: What Organizations Risk Without Mindset Reform

Failure to shift the contract management paradigm carries increasingly severe consequences:

- **Strategic Drift**: Contracts misaligned to current market or regulatory realities cause operational misfires.

- **Customer Churn**: Opaque, cumbersome, or punitive contracts alienate customers and partners.

- **Revenue Atrophy**: Untapped escalators, missed renewals, and unmanaged rebate programs silently erode top-line performance.

- **Competitive Lag**: Organizations unable to flexibly renegotiate, adapt, or innovate contractually fall behind faster-moving rivals.

- **Enterprise Fragility**: Poor contract management undermines audit readiness, acquisition due diligence, investor confidence, and regulatory standing.

These are not future risks. **Present realities are** already undermining enterprises that fail to upgrade their view of contract management.

VII. Contracts as Embedded Strategic Infrastructure

In leading organizations, contracts are not external to strategy - they are strategy, operationalized.

Every contractual term embodies decisions about:

- How value is created and shared
- How risk is allocated and managed
- How trust is institutionalized between parties
- How flexibility is preserved for future adaptation
- How financial, operational, and customer outcomes are realized

Contracts become the codebase of commerce—not static documents, but dynamic systems guiding the enterprise.

When seen this way, contracts are no longer legal instruments. They are **embedded infrastructure**, governing daily transactions, revenue flow, service delivery, and customer relationship management.

VIII. The Business Functions Contracts Directly Shape

Strategically managed contracts influence every critical business domain:

Function	Contractual Impact
Sales	Defines pricing flexibility, deal velocity, margin preservation
Finance	Anchors revenue recognition, accruals, and contingent liabilities
Procurement	Manages supplier performance, pricing protections, and compliance risk
Customer Success	Establishes deliverables, renewal conditions, escalation procedures
Product Development	Clarifies intellectual property rights, service level agreements
Compliance & Risk	Structures regulatory adherence and risk mitigation mechanisms
Executive Leadership	Enables strategic mergers, acquisitions, partnerships, and divestitures

No significant business outcome is untouched by the contracts an organization manages, or fails to manage.

Yet, these connections are often invisible, unmeasured, or misunderstood.

IX. From Business Risk to Business Opportunity

The traditional view of contracts fixates on loss avoidance:

- Prevent breach
- Limit damages
- Reduce exposure

The strategic view focuses on opportunity realization:

- Capture upsell and cross-sell value
- Accelerate cash flow
- Institutionalize customer loyalty through performance governance
- Optimize vendor relationships for innovation and cost leverage
- Navigate regulatory change with built-in agility clauses

Risk management remains essential—but it becomes only one dimension of a broader value-creation model.

Organizations that master this shift reframe contracts from passive risk control instruments into **active drivers of revenue, innovation, and market agility**.

X. Leadership's Role in Contract Mindset Reform

True contract management transformation cannot be delegated downward. It demands explicit ownership and visible commitment at the senior leadership level.

Executive leaders must:

- **Frame contract excellence as a business outcome**, not a legal department achievement.
- **Tie contract performance metrics to strategic KPIs**: revenue velocity, customer retention, risk mitigation, cost optimization.
- **Resource cross-functional CLM enablement initiatives**, including governance frameworks, platform integration, and staff training.
- **Model the mindset shift** by treating contracts as dynamic operational tools—not bureaucratic necessities.

Without this top-down strategic framing, contract reform efforts falter—relegated once again to legal compliance silos, procedural tweaks, and eventual organizational disillusionment.

Leadership sponsorship is not a "nice to have." It is the determining factor of success or failure.

XI. Integrating Contracts Into Core Business Planning

In contract-forward organizations, contract considerations are embedded **upstream** in strategic decision-making - not retrofitted after operational plans are underway.

Examples include:

- **Product launches**: contract frameworks for SLAs, licensing rights, customer success guarantees, and compliance triggers are developed during product planning, not post-market.

- **Mergers and acquisitions**: Target due diligence includes contract data mapping, obligation assessments, and integration planning, not just legal review.

- **Sales enablement**: negotiation playbooks, clause libraries, and customer journey-aligned contracting are integrated into CRM and deal desk operations from the outset.

- **Revenue forecasting**: renewal schedules, pricing escalators, and contingent revenue clauses are systematically tied into financial models.

Contracts are not "after the fact."

They are **central inputs into strategic and operational planning**, and they should be treated with the same seriousness as financial, marketing, and product strategies.

XII. Contract Performance as a Board-Level Metric

In a fully mature Contracts as a Business Asset™ model, boards and executive teams demand visibility into:

- **Revenue protected and expanded through contract governance**

- **Risk exposure mapped across contractual obligations**

- **Contract cycle time trends and operational efficiency improvements**

- **Audit readiness and regulatory alignment statistics**

- **Customer satisfaction correlations with contract experience metrics**

Contract performance moves from an invisible function to a visible, measured, strategically reported dimension of enterprise health.

This elevation fundamentally changes how organizations perceive, prioritize, and resource contract management, shifting it from a back-office afterthought to a boardroom strategic lever.

XIII. Designing the Contract Advantage™ Operating Model

Transitioning from a fragmented, reactive contract environment to an integrated, strategic asset-based system demands a **purpose-built operating model**.

This model must unify people, processes, systems, and metrics under a single goal:

Maximize business value through the proactive management of contractual assets.

At its core, the **Contract Advantage™ Operating Model** requires the following foundational pillars:

Pillar	Description
Strategic Intent Alignment	Contracts mirror and advance enterprise goals, not just compliance standards
Cross-Functional Ownership	Shared responsibility across Legal, Sales, Finance, Procurement, and Operations
Data-Driven Visibility	Clause-level metadata extraction, contract lifecycle KPIs, real-time performance dashboards

Pillar	Description
Technology Enablement	Integrated CLM, CRM, ERP, and analytics platforms with user-centric design
Governance and Accountability	Formalized structures for contract design standards, playbooks, risk matrices, and exception handling
Continuous Improvement Loop	Agile-driven updates to templates, clauses, workflows, and systems based on measurable feedback

Without all six pillars, partial improvements degrade over time into fragmented "point fixes" that fail to drive systemic transformation.

XIV. Key Principles for Successful Transformation

Organizational transformation toward contracts-as-assets is not merely structural - it is cultural, behavioral, and strategic.

The following key principles must guide all change efforts:

1. Think Commercial First, Compliance Always

While legal compliance remains critical, contract systems must first be designed to:

- Accelerate revenue
- Improve customer experience
- Enable operational velocity
- Capture upsell, renewal, and rebate opportunities

Compliance is not abandoned; it is embedded—**but it no longer dominates the architecture** to the exclusion of commercial outcomes.

2. Contracts Activate at Signature, Not Terminate

Signature marks the beginning of contractual value realization—not its conclusion.

Post-signature management becomes a **core business function**, including:

- Obligation tracking
- SLA performance management
- Renewal opportunity maximization
- Commercial renegotiation optimization

Lifecycle tracking is mandatory—not optional.

3. Embed Contract Metrics Into Enterprise Performance Dashboards

If contract KPIs remain isolated within Legal or Procurement departments, business value remains invisible.

Instead, contract metrics must appear alongside financial, sales, operations, and risk dashboards.

Examples include:

- Contract cycle time vs. sales pipeline velocity
- Renewal capture rate vs. customer churn rate
- SLA compliance vs. NPS (Net Promoter Score) movement
- Risk exposure delta vs. audit remediation costs

Contracts become integrated performance data sources—not hidden technical artifacts.

4. Govern Through Clear Rules, Escalate Through Exceptions

Overregulation of standard contracts creates friction. Under-regulation invites chaos.

Leading organizations balance these forces by:

- Pre-approving clause libraries and fallback positions
- Automating approval routing for low-risk deals
- Escalating only true risk exceptions for human review
- Auditing workflows regularly for drift and bottlenecks

This model minimizes legal load while maintaining governance integrity.

5. Treat CLM Technology as the Nervous System, Not the Brain

Technology should connect and inform decision-making—not attempt to replace human strategy.

The function of CLM platforms is to:

- Store contracts securely and accessibly
- Surface metadata for analytics and action
- Automate lifecycle workflows and alerts
- Enable searchability, auditability, and compliance tracking

Strategy, leadership, and business design must remain in command.

XV. The Evolution of Organizational Roles

The shift toward a Contracts as a Business Asset™ model redefines key enterprise roles:

Role	Traditional Model	Strategic Model
Legal	Guardian of compliance	Architect of opportunity and risk balance
Sales	Creators of "one-off" deals	Drivers of commercial consistency and velocity
Finance	Passive approvers of revenue impact	Active monitors of contract revenue performance
Procurement	Price negotiators	Value lifecycle managers
Customer Success	Post-sale service responders	Contractual health score owners

These role evolutions demand both **upskilling** and **cultural adaptation**—supported by executive leadership, not isolated departmental training efforts.

XVI. Maturity Stages of Contract-Centric Transformation

Organizations typically progress through predictable stages in their contract management maturity:

Stage	Description
Reactive	Contracts managed case-by-case, no systemic strategy
Fragmented Improvement	Individual departments optimize isolated workflows

Stage	Description
Coordinated Modernization	Technology adoption across multiple functions with basic visibility
Integrated Command	Unified CLM strategy across departments with real-time contract intelligence
Strategic Orchestration	Contracts are embedded into enterprise strategy, innovation, customer success, and financial performance at boardroom level

The ultimate objective: achieve **Strategic Orchestration**, where contracts serve as living engines of value creation across the enterprise ecosystem.

XVII. Vision of the Future-State Enterprise

In organizations that fully adopt the Contracts as a Business Asset™ model:

- **Contracts are visible and actionable at all leadership levels.**
- **Revenue, margin, and risk signals are captured contractually in real time.**
- **Customer journeys are supported, not hindered, by contractual experiences.**
- **Innovation is enabled through flexible, agile contractual frameworks.**
- **Compliance is proactive, embedded, and automated—not disruptive.**
- **Operational agility and market responsiveness are contractually reinforced.**

In short, contracts no longer constrain the enterprise.

They empower it to **scale quickly, innovate confidently, and build enduring, trusted relationships with** customers, vendors, regulators, and partners.

Conclusion: The Strategic Imperative Ahead

The transformation from contracts as administrative burdens to contracts as strategic assets represents one of the most potent, underutilized levers available to organizations today.

This transformation cannot be achieved through technology purchases alone. It demands:

- **A reengineering of mindset at every level of leadership and operations.**
- **An operating system designed to treat contracts as living frameworks of commercial strategy.**
- **An unrelenting commitment to visibility, velocity, value, and accountability.**

For those willing to undertake this shift, the rewards are profound:

Sustainable growth, resilient operations, trusted relationships, market leadership, and enterprise agility in a volatile world.

This is the future of contract management.

This is the foundation of *The Contract Advantage*™.

And this is the pathway to realizing the full potential of **Contracts as a Business Asset**™.

❋ ❋ ❋ ❋

▨ CHAPTER 3A –

THE PRACTITIONER'S NARRATIVE TURNING MINDSET INTO SYSTEMS: ARCHITECTING THE CONTRACT ADVANTAGE™

Introduction: Contracts as Cultural Infrastructure

In high-performing enterprises, contracts are not static artifacts managed after-the-fact by Legal departments.

They are dynamic architectures of organizational behavior— shaping decision-making, accelerating revenue, mitigating risk, and operationalizing customer trust.

When contracts are appropriately designed, governed, and activated, they embed strategic priorities into the daily execution of the business.

When neglected, they become silent saboteurs of speed, value realization, compliance, and customer satisfaction.

This chapter offers a practitioner's blueprint for building contracts not as passive formalities, but as **dynamic business assets** that drive operational and strategic excellence.

Part I. Diagnosing the Mindset Failure

Across decades of advisory work, I have consistently encountered five entrenched myths that sabotage contract management transformation:

Myth	Dangerous Impact
"Contracts are Legal's responsibility"	Strategic detachment, siloed ownership
"CLM is a necessary cost center"	Underinvestment, low executive visibility
"If we're not sued, it's working"	Latent risk and missed value capture
"We'll fix it post-implementation"	Structural technical debt
"Contracts don't affect revenue."	Loss of upsell, cross-sell, renewal leverage

These myths create organizational behavior patterns where contracts:

- Are **invisible to commercial strategy**
- **Disconnected from enterprise data streams**
- **Underleveraged for margin protection and upsell**
- **Become operational bottlenecks** rather than accelerators

Mindset—not technology—remains the root cause of most CLM failures.

Part II. Case Studies: Transformation Through Mindset Reframing

🏥 Healthcare System: From Compliance to Revenue Engine

- **Challenge**: CLM viewed solely as a compliance artifact. Finance had no visibility.
- **Solution**: Executive education, cross-functional roadmap, and finance integration.
- **Result**:
- Revenue risk proactively projected
- Provider renegotiations triggered on obligation alerts
- Contract-derived revenue optimization → **32% ROI lift**

✈ Global Aerospace Firm: Contracts as Operational GPS

- **Challenge**: Sales perceived contracts as legal slowdowns. No operational linkage.
- **Solution**: Clause tagging integration into ERP and sourcing workflows.
- **Result**:
- Engineering sourced materials earlier
- Cost variability reduced by **27%**
- Contract data embedded into production planning

In both cases, **technology followed strategy**, not the reverse.

Part III. The Strategic Contracting Pyramid™

I developed the **Strategic Contracting Pyramid™** to model organizational contracting maturity:

Level	Characteristics
Level 1: Administrative CLM	Templates, routing, Legal-centric control, static documents
Level 2: Operational CLM	Integrated workflows, clause metadata, linked systems (Procurement, Finance, CRM)
Level 3: Strategic CLM (Asset-Based)	Real-time dashboards, predictive obligations, revenue optimization, customer experience integration, enterprise-wide visibility

Most organizations stagnate at Level 1 or 2.

True transformation only occurs at Level 3, where contracts become living systems of enterprise value creation.

Part IV. What Asset-Based Contracting Looks Like in Practice

In strategically mature enterprises, CLM systems serve as:

- **Revenue forecasting engines** (using renewal triggers, escalator clauses, performance credits)
- **Compliance risk radars** (with SLA breach detection, proactive remediation alerts)
- **Negotiation accelerators** (with dynamic fallback clauses and negotiation playbooks)
- **Vendor relationship scorers** (performance-to-com-

mitment analytics)

- **Customer experience validators** (contracts tied to SLA delivery and NPS tracking)

Contracts stop being barriers—and start becoming **instruments of operational trust, velocity, and foresight**.

Part V. Legal's Role in the Asset-Based Model

In this evolved architecture:

Traditional Legal Role	Reimagined Strategic Role
Gatekeeper	Risk architect and enablement strategist
Bottleneck to execution	Partner in commercial velocity
Isolated reviewers	Designers of contract frameworks for growth

Legal moves from reactive risk aversion to proactive value facilitation—protecting the enterprise while enabling scalable commercial execution.

Part VI. Executive Leadership Alignment: The Inflection Point

In every successful transformation I have led, a pivotal moment occurs: **Executive Buy-In.**

In Leadership Alignment Sessions, I deliver:

- Financial analyses of latent value hidden in contracts
- Forecasts on how improved visibility drives

revenue lift

- Risk models showing how early breach detection slashes compliance costs
- Journey maps linking contract experience to customer retention metrics

After these sessions, executives stop asking, "Why CLM?" and start asking, "How fast can we scale it?"

This reframing from **cost center** to **revenue engine** is essential.

Part VII. Metrics That Actually Matter

In strategically aligned organizations, contract management KPIs shift radically:

Traditional Metrics	Strategic Metrics
Contract turn-around time	Value recovered per renegotiation cycle
Contract volume processed	% of contracts linked to finance reporting
Legal risk events	Renewal forecast accuracy rates
Compliance breach incidents	Cross-functional collaboration index

Performance measurement becomes Revenue-Centric and Customer-Centric, not Volume-Centric.

Part VIII. Your Role: Becoming the Catalyst for Change

Leaders inside organizations must be the catalysts who:

- Audit organizational contract perceptions
- Expose the disconnect between contracts and commercial outcomes
- Map their organization's position on the Strategic Contracting Pyramid™
- Facilitate executive briefings linking contract value to business KPIs
- Redefine success metrics beyond speed and volume to value and outcomes

If you are reading this, you are likely already positioned to ignite the transformation your organization needs.

DISCUSSION SECTION
CUSTOMER-CENTRIC CONTRACTING:
BEHAVIORAL DESIGN FOR
REVENUE VELOCITY

Introduction: Contracts as Customer Experience

It's a common blind spot: Organizations spend millions refining their product UX, customer onboarding, and support experience—yet the **contract experience** remains dense, slow, and opaque. Why?

Most companies still view contracts as **internal compliance artifacts**, not as **external trust signals**.

But make no mistake:

To your customer, the contract is the first real experience they have with your back office.

If it's confusing, slow, or overly defensive, it communicates who you really are.

This chapter's discussion and practitioner narrative build the strategic, behavioral, and operational foundations of Customer-Centric Contracting™.

I'll show how contract architecture drives deal velocity, customer satisfaction, and retention, and why behavioral economics, design thinking, and systems integration are now essential tools for contract leaders.

Part I. Theoretical Foundation: Contracts as Behavioral Design

1. *From Legal Formalism to Behavioral Contracting*

Traditional contract theory, rooted in legal formalism (Posner, 1973), treats contracts as rational, objective agreements between two risk-conscious parties. But real-world contracting involves humans, who are subject to emotion, misperception, and friction.

As advanced by legal scholars like Wilkinson-Ryan (2017), **Behavioral Contract Theory** argues that **contracts' form, language, and flow affect performance.** In other words:

- Complexity reduces follow-through
- Hidden clauses undermine trust
- Redlining fatigue increases churn
- Delay signals internal dysfunction

In my global implementations, I've repeatedly seen contract design influence:

- Whether a customer signs at all
- How they behave post-signature
- Whether they renew or escalate at term

Customer-Centric Contracting is not just "nicer legal."

It's **Applied Behavioral Economics.**

2. *Design Thinking and CLM*

Design thinking, as pioneered by IDEO and the Stanford

School (Brown, 2009), urges us to center user experience in every system we build. In contracting, this means:

- Understanding how customers interact with your agreements
- Mapping friction points
- Prototyping and testing clause language
- Designing for clarity, not just compliance

When I apply this methodology, I often redesign MSAs and NDAs using:

- Modular structures
- Plain language tiering
- Guided intake
- Fallback clause visualization
- Time-to-close as a customer satisfaction metric

These aren't just efficiencies - they're **revenue enablers.**

Part II. Contracts as Drivers of Commercial Trust

At their core, contracts encode **the trust calculus** between two parties:

- Will you deliver what you promise?
- Will I get support if something breaks?
- Will your team respond in time?
- Will my terms be respected?

In B2B deals, especially at enterprise scale, the contract experience determines whether a customer sees you as:

- A collaborative partner
- A rigid vendor
- A bureaucratic black hole

A Forrester study (2021) found that 63% of enterprise buyers abandoned deals due to slow or unclear legal processes. Nevertheless, most CLM strategies focus inward: Speed or Compliance, not **Customer Clarity or Control**.

Customer-Centric CLM changes that.

Part III. Architecture of a Customer-Centric CLM System

To operationalize this theory, I've built the **Customer-Centric CLM Framework™**,

used with clients across technology, finance, aerospace, and healthcare. It consists of five pillars:

3. *Audience-Specific Templates*

Each customer segment (Enterprise, Mid-Market, Public Sector) receives tailored templates aligned to their language, priorities, and governance style.

4. *Tiered Clause Logic*

I implement fallback trees that:

- Reduce escalations
- Enable guided self-service
- Offer choices in commercial and compliance terms

This reduces redlines by 47% on average.

5. *Guided Authoring UX*

Customers and sales teams generate contracts through user-friendly forms that:

- Ask plain-language questions
- Trigger clause blocks
- Flag risk
- Auto-assign reviewers

No PDF stitching. Just intelligent design.

6. *Embedded Visibility*

Every stakeholder (sales, legal, procurement, customer success) sees contract status in real time. There are no more "Where is it?" emails or spreadsheets.

7. *Post-Signature Enablement*

Contract data flows into CRM, CS tools, billing, and renewal engines. Obligations don't just sit—they inform.

This is the infrastructure of **customer-aligned trust delivery.**

Part IV. Real Case Study: Building Trust Through Design

🔍 Client: Global FinTech Platform (anonymized)

Initial Issues:

- Customers received dense MSAs with 30-day legal delays
- Sales cycles extended beyond fiscal targets

- No visibility into clause negotiation trends
- Low customer satisfaction with onboarding

Intervention:

- I redesigned the contract experience using behavioral insights
- Introducing three customer-aligned MSA templates
- Built guided clause fallback with integrated redline data
- Tied contract close status to onboarding automation

Results:

- Time-to-sign dropped by 63%
- Deal renewal forecast accuracy rose by 39%
- Customers began referencing "ease of contract" as a differentiator in NPS surveys

Lesson: Good contract experience *is* brand experience.

Part V. The Business Case: Contracts and Revenue Acceleration

In high-growth environments, every "day" matters.

Poor contract experience kills:

- Pipeline velocity
- Revenue realization
- Renewal predictability
- Upsell trust

In one SaaS company I worked with, simply reducing

clause review time by 48 hours led to **$4.3M in quarter-end saves**.

Why? Because the contracts cleared in time to book revenue.

CLM is not just legal ops. **It's revenue ops.**

Part VI. The Post-Signature Opportunity: Contracts as Customer Data

Once signed, most contracts disappear into archives. But in future-ready systems, they become:

- SLAs tracked in CX dashboards
- Renewal alerts in CS workflows
- Expansion flags based on usage patterns
- Compliance signals in ESG reporting

Customer-Centric CLM integrates contract data into the broader customer system.

It connects the dots between **what was promised** and **what is delivered.**

That is not just compliance. It is **experience accountability.**

Part VII. Culture Change: Sales + Legal + Product = Trust

To implement Customer-Centric CLM, I often lead a cross-functional "CLM Enablement Sprint."

We:

- Walk through current templates
- Interview customers about friction

- Review clause redline analytics
- Rebuild from the outside in

When Legal, Sales, and Product co-own contracting, the result is not only faster deals - it's **higher customer confidence** and lower churn.

Part VIII. Summary: A System of Trust, Not Just Terms

Customer-Centric Contracting isn't a feature. *It's a philosophy*.

- It shifts focus from risk to relationship
- From protection to perception
- From language to experience
- From paperwork to partnership

When the contract *feels* customer-aligned, it reinforces what your brand promises.

And when it doesn't, it becomes the very first broken promise.

In the next chapter, we turn inward - examining how the right CLM technology enables these experiences to scale across teams, geographies, and growth trajectories.

A - THE PRACTITIONER'S NARRATIVE SECTION CUSTOMER-CENTRIC CONTRACTING: DESIGNING FOR GROWTH, NOT JUST GOVERNANCE

The contract is the first user-experience your customer has with your back office.
Make it frictionless, relevant, and responsive –
or lose their trust before the deal closes.

I. From Compliance to Customer Strategy

Contracts are too often designed around what the company needs to protect, not what the customer needs to achieve.

That's a mistake.

Every negotiation, redline, and delay sends a message to your customer - **and most companies are sending the wrong one.** The traditional approach to contracting is company-centric: designed to reduce internal risk, routed through internal bottlenecks, optimized for internal compliance.

But that model breaks down in a world where speed, flexibility, and trust drive growth.

This chapter introduces a new approach: **Customer-Centric Contracting**™—a framework I've developed and applied across global companies to shift contracting from a legal checkbox into a **revenue and relationship accelerator**.

II. What Customer-Centric Contracting Really Means

A customer-centric contract isn't just a faster contract. It's a smarter one.

It's a contract that:

- Speaks in the customer's terms, not internal jargon
- Aligns with their buying process, not your approval grid
- Builds trust by being transparent, relevant, and responsive
- Embeds flexibility for how the relationship may evolve
- Automates transparency - so no one asks, "Where is my contract?"

In short, customer-centric contracting makes your customer feel like you are already doing business together before they sign.

III. The Business Case for Customer-Centric CLM

Here's what I've proven, time and again:

Customer experience doesn't stop at the website. It continues inside the contract.

🖼 The Cost of Neglect:

- Delayed revenue recognition because of contract complexity

- Lost deals from slow redlines and over-lawyering
- Renewals skipped due to unclear terms
- Missed upsell opportunities from opaque agreements

🗺 The Value of Focus:

In one global FinTech implementation, I redesigned their contract templates to match the customer's operational language. We removed 40% of the legalese and used modular clause logic tied to use-case tiers. The result?

- 60% faster time-to-close
- 87% improvement in user satisfaction (tracked via post-signature surveys)
- Over $4.2M in recovered volume rebates from more precis tracking terms

IV. How I Build Customer-Centric CLM: The Playbook

To operationalize this strategy, I created the **Customer-Centric CLM Playbook™**, a modular framework that includes:

◇ 1. Audience-Aligned Templates

Templates customized for buyer types: B2B enterprise, SMB, government, vendor-partner, etc. Each includes pre-approved language tailored to that audience's expectations and regulatory standards.

◇ 2. Tiered Clause Libraries

Clauses aren't static - they're dynamic based on:

- Deal size

- Risk level
- Industry type
- Customer lifecycle stage

I build clause matrices and fallback trees that legal can bless once, and sales can execute without waiting.

◇ 3. Guided Authoring & Dynamic Workflows

I implement innovative smart intake forms with conditional logic that:

- Pre-fills based on opportunity stage
- Routes to the right reviewers
- Locks risky terms unless escalated
- Tracks every edit for audit and learning

◇ 4. Visibility at Every Touchpoint

Dashboards show where every contract is:

- In-flight
- At risk
- Blocked
- Approved

These are shared with sales, legal, customer success, and finance - not buried in CLM logins no one uses.

V. Case Study: Redefining Customer Experience Through Contract Design

🌍 Client: Global SaaS Platform (name withheld, under NDA)

Problem: Their contracts were built by Legal for Legal. Even standard NDAs took 14 days to process. Customers complain about being "lawyered" into delay.

My Intervention:

I rebuilt the entire contracting structure—starting with customer intent. I interviewed actual customers. I mapped the deal cycle from their side. Then I rebuilt templates, automated self-service flows, and made contract status a shared KPI between Sales and Legal.

Impact:

- NDA execution time dropped from 14 days to <2 hours
- MSA close rate improved by 38%
- Sales teams began collaborating with Legal—rather than circumventing them

VI. Integrating Customer-Centricity into Enterprise Systems

Customer-centric CLM only works when it integrates with the rest of your stack:

- **Salesforce**: Triggers contract creation based on deal stage
- **ERP (SAP/Oracle)**: Syncs contract terms with in-

voicing, fulfillment, and revenue recognition

- **Customer Success Platforms**: Connect SLA clauses to actual performance data
- **Procurement & Finance**: Tracks rebate clauses and payment terms in real time

When I build system architectures, I ensure **contracts aren't standalone systems - they're connected nodes in your enterprise data fabric:**

One source of truth, one seamless experience.

VII. Governance Meets Growth

Let me be clear: Customer-centric does **not** mean "customer-is-always-right."

It means designing contracts that **create alignment, not friction**.

By enabling customers to understand their obligations, engage transparently, and see you as a partner, not a negotiator, you build loyalty, not just compliance.

Governance still matters. But now it becomes an enabler, not a barrier.

VIII. Metrics That Prove It Works

These are the metrics I track in Customer-Centric CLM transformations:

- Time-to-Sign by contract type
- Clause negotiation frequency (and reasons)
- Renewal uplift tied to customer satisfaction

- Cross-functional friction score (measured by escalations and cycle time)
- % of contracts with shared clause visibility across departments

IX. Summary: Why This Chapter Is the Tipping Point

You've now moved from mindset to method. **Customer-Centric** contracting isn't a theory. It's a system I've built, refined, and implemented globally.

You now have:

- The playbook framework
- The real-world cases
- The metrics that matter
- The integration strategies

In the next chapter, we'll take this even further. Now that you understand what to build, I'll show you **how to scale it - across tools, teams, and territories.**

⚒ Theory Into Practice Checklist

- ☐ **Interview three customer-facing teams on contract pain points**
- ☐ **Audit current templates for clarity and customer relevance**
- ☐ **Design a tiered clause fallback structure**
- ☐ **Map one contract flow from CRM to CLM to ERP**
- ☐ **Create a shared dashboard to track contract status and cycle times**

BUILDING YOUR CLM PLAYBOOK FROM FRAGMENTED FUNCTION TO STRATEGIC ENGINE: CONSTRUCTING A TECHNOLOGY-DRIVEN CLM ARCHITECTURE

In today's hyper-competitive, data-rich business environment, contract lifecycle management (CLM) is no longer just a back-office function. It is a mission-critical capability that can hinder organizational agility or fuel exponential growth. This chapter is not merely about cataloging tools or recommending shiny technologies. It is about building an execution-grade framework—a **CLM playbook**—designed to convert strategic vision into operational muscle.

Over the past decade, I've worked inside Fortune 100 enterprises and scale-up disruptors alike, and I've seen firsthand how CLM can either become a source of systemic drag or a source of enterprise acceleration. The difference is not in the budget, software, or architecture. It's in adoption, alignment, and adoption.

This chapter builds that architecture. We'll dissect the technology landscape, differentiate between commodity tools and transformative platforms, and outline a modular, customizable playbook structure that embeds contract intelligence into the core of your operating model.

I. The CLM Technology Imperative

The evolution of CLM is not linear - it's exponential. Organizations that treat CLM as a linear documentation task miss the transformative opportunity to turn contracts into real-time instruments of strategy, compliance, and growth.

Let's start with a hard truth: most organizations are not managing contracts. They are warehousing them. Legacy tools offer digitized storage and basic search functions, but they don't offer insight, orchestration, or connection to enterprise priorities like revenue recognition, renewal optimization, or operational risk forecasting.

To change this, the CLM ecosystem must evolve beyond digital filing cabinets and into an **intelligent contracting fabric**—one that:

- Integrates upstream and downstream systems (CRM, ERP, BI, CS tools)
- Provides clause-level analytics and semantic visibility
- Enables predictive insight (not just historical lookup)
- Supports real-time collaboration across cross-functional teams
- Is modular and scalable across markets, products, and customer types

Think of this evolution not as a "tech stack" but as a **CLM operating system**.

II. Anatomy of a Modern CLM Stack

Your CLM playbook should rest on a layered stack, strategically selected and tightly integrated. Each layer contributes distinct value and must be aligned with the organization's maturity, size, and strategic posture.

1. System of Record (SoR)

This is your master repository. It must be secure, searchable, clause-indexed, and API-enabled. A good SoR supports:

- Clause-level tagging and metadata
- Redline version control
- Immutable audit trails
- Role-based permissions
- E-signature chain integration

2. System of Intelligence (SoI)

Where your contracts become data, this layer extracts structured insights from contracts at scale.

- AI-enabled clause extraction
- Risk scoring by deviation from standard templates
- Obligation tracking tied to SLAs or rebates
- Predictive renewal modeling

3. System of Engagement (SoE)

Contracts must live where your people work. This layer ensures contracts are actionable within operational workflows.

- Salesforce integration for deal-triggered creation
- Jira integration for Legal Ops escalations

- ERP sync for term-triggered billing events
- Real-time dashboards for lifecycle stage alerts

Each system layer must not operate in silos - they must form an interoperable ecosystem, powered by APIs and governed by a unified data schema.

III. Case Example: Mid-Market Transformation with Enterprise Impact

🎯 *Client: A mid-market global SaaS company, $400M ARR*

Challenge:

- Disparate legacy tools: SharePoint + email approvals + manual DocuSign
- No visibility into term risk, renewal leakage, or payment clause tracking
- Legal team overloaded with 98% of contract drafts requiring intervention

Intervention:

We implemented a three-tier architecture:

- CLM base platform (Ironclad) as System of Record
- AI analytics layer (Evisort) for clause deviation and SLA tracking
- Full Salesforce sync for auto-initiated contract workflows

We designed modular playbooks per contract type (MSA, SOW, NDA, Partner Agreements), each equipped with fallback clause matrices and embedded escalation logic.

Results:

- Time-to-sign reduced by 72%
- 92% of NDAs are fully self-service
- $3.1M annual uplift through proactive renewal alerting and rebate tracking

IV. Designing the CLM Playbook Framework

Your CLM Playbook should not be a static PDF or a policy buried in a legal wiki. It is a **living operational framework**—designed to orchestrate decision velocity, compliance consistency, and commercial clarity.

1. Playbook Modules

Every playbook should consist of modular building blocks. Here's a foundational schema I use:

Module	Purpose	Key Elements
Template Governance	Align templates to buyer type and risk tier	Template catalog, clause bank, deviation logic
Workflow Design	Embed automation and conditional routing	Smart intake forms, approval paths, stage-based routing
Visibility Dashboards	Enable shared accountability and proactive action	Live dashboards by status, risk, owner
Escalation Protocols	Reduce legal bottlenecks	Pre-approved fallbacks, risk matrix triggers

Module	Purpose	Key Elements
Renewal/ Obligation Management	Drive revenue protection	SLA trackers, auto-alerting, linked CRM tasks
Change Control Framework	Ensure continuous improvement	Feedback loops, change logs, re-training schedules

Every module must have a named owner, every SLA must be tracked, and every exception explained or eliminated.

V. Aligning Technology with Business Objectives

Technology cannot—and should not—lead. **Strategy must**.

Every feature added should tie back to one of these business imperatives:

1. **Revenue Acceleration**
   E.g., Smart intake reduces cycle time → faster recognition

2. **Risk Reduction**
   E.g., Clause libraries minimize exposure → fewer escalations

3. **Customer Experience**
   E.g., Self-service flows for low-risk NDAs → frictionless onboarding

4. **Cost Optimization**
   E.g., Automation replaces manual redlines → reduced Legal FTE cost

5.   **Data Intelligence**
     E.g., KPI dashboards improve forecast accuracy →
     better CFO decisioning

Before buying a feature, ask: *What does this help us do faster, better, safer, or cheaper?* If there is no answer, it is a distraction, not an investment.

VI. Building the Implementation Roadmap

The deployment of your CLM stack and playbook should unfold across three sprints:

▨ Phase 1: Foundation

- Conduct contract process audit
- Map contract types to systems and owners
- Select core platform and define metadata schema
- Build first set of templates and clause library

▦ Phase 2: Orchestration

- Integrate CRM and ERP
- Design approval and escalation flows
- Launch dashboards with defined KPIs
- Run internal pilot (sales + legal + finance)

🚀 Phase 3: Expansion

- Add AI-enabled analysis of existing contracts
- Automate renewal notifications and triggers
- Conduct change management and train all functions
- Launch the executive CLM scorecard

CLM maturity is iterative, but your roadmap must be explicit, staged, and measurable.

✳✳✳✳

PART 2

Institutionalizing the CLM Operating Model
From Technology Stack to Strategic Discipline

Where Part 1 laid the architectural foundation of the CLM Playbook—its layers, integrations, and functional design—Part 2 transitions into real-world operationalization. Technology is only the enabler. What gives CLM transformational power is *governance, measurement, and ownership*.

No matter how advanced your CLM system is, you will revert to fragmented, ad hoc behaviors without embedded processes and leadership discipline. This section focuses on making CLM not just a capability but a **core operating system of the business**.

I. The Contract Intelligence Operating Model

The modern enterprise must move beyond legal-centric contract workflows and embed CLM into the operating rhythm of every function—sales, finance, procurement, customer success, and compliance.

To do this, I design what I call the **CLM Intelligence Operating Model™**.

(CLM-IOM), a cross-functional structure that governs:

- Template and clause library updates
- Escalation protocols and SLA management
- KPI reporting and optimization cycles

- Technology roadmap governance
- Change management and training
- Internal customer (e.g. Sales, Success) satisfaction

Think of the CLM-IOM as the **"PMO for Contracts."** It's not a policy. It's an embedded operating system with clear ownership, feedback loops, and executive visibility.

II. Building a CLM Center of Excellence (CLM-CoE)

CLM transformation requires a permanent body - not just a project team.

The **CLM CoE** institutionalizes CLM by convening Legal, Sales, Procurement, Finance, IT, and Ops leaders under a shared charter. It is not just about technology governance - it drives process, performance, and maturity growth.

Charter of a CLM CoE:

Function	Responsibility
Legal	Clause integrity, fallback rules, risk scoring
Sales	Experience design, self-service model alignment
Finance	Revenue/Cost term enforcement, forecasting
Procurement	Vendor standardization, compliance assurance
IT/Systems	Data architecture, integrations, access governance
Operations	SLA performance, intake automation, backlog triage

The CLM-CoE should meet monthly with a structured agenda. Dashboards must be reviewed. Exceptions analyzed. Pipeline blockers removed. The CoE enforces CLM not as a tool, but as a business function.

III. Performance Metrics: Making the Invisible Visible

You cannot manage what you cannot see. Moreover, in most companies, CLM performance is invisible until something breaks.

You must define, track, and socialize a shared performance scorecard to change that.

The Executive CLM-CoE Dashboard™

Metric	Description	Why It Matters
Time-to-Sign	Avg. time from draft to signature by contract type	Revenue acceleration; customer experience
Clause Negotiation Rate	% of contracts that require clause edits	Legal load; template effectiveness
Cycle Time per Department	Avg. time each function takes in the contract workflow	SLA enforcement; bottleneck identification
Renewal Alert Compliance	% of contracts with renewal triggers initiated on time	Revenue protection; retention optimization
Risk Deviation Score	Volume and frequency of non-standard clauses	Risk exposure visibility

Metric	Description	Why It Matters
CLM Adoption Rate	% of contracts executed through the CLM system	Change management success: tool ROI

These metrics should be live, not retrospective. And every function should see itself on the scoreboard.

IV. Real-World Execution: The SaaS Case Study in Practice

Let's revisit the SaaS company transformation introduced in Part 1.

Problem:

- 14-day NDA turnaround
- Legal triaged 98% of contracts manually
- Sales teams working around Legal for renewals
- No visibility into MSA renewal clauses or payment terms

Execution Blueprint:

1. **Self-Service NDA Builder**

- Smart intake form with conditional logic
- Clause library with locked fallback rules
- Salesforce-triggered initiation

2. **Modular MSA Playbooks**

- Tiered templates by customer segment
- Revenue-risk clause matrix
- Pre-routed approval workflows

3. **Integrated Contract Cockpit**

- Embedded dashboards inside CRM
- Live visibility into contract status
- Alerts for blockers and renewals

4. **Governance & Feedback Loop**

- Monthly CoE reviews of escalations and outliers
- Clause heatmaps updated quarterly
- Real-time satisfaction survey embedded post-signature

Results:

- NDA time cut from 14 days to 2 hours
- Legal touch reduced by 63% across mid-risk contracts
- $4.2M in uncovered rebate uplift from improved clause tracking
- Sales-Legal trust restored through transparency and shared ownership

V. Institutionalizing Metrics & Feedback

The power of metrics is not just in their visibility, but in how they're used.

Feedback Loops to Institutionalize:

Mechanism	Purpose
Monthly CLM Health Review	Identify trends in bottlenecks, escalations, SLA breaches
Quarterly Template Review	Refresh language based on data and dispute patterns
Post-Contract Survey	Collect stakeholder sentiment and identify UX issues
Annual CLM ROI Assessment	Tie CLM performance to revenue, cost, and risk metrics

CLM must be treated like a revenue engine, not a risk protocol.

VI. CLM as a Strategic Growth Lever

This is not about operational polish. This is about **commercial enablement**.

When CLM is done right, you unlock:

- ⚡ **Faster Time-to-Revenue**: Smart intake, guided authoring, and pre-approved terms compress negotiation time.
- 🧠 **Risk-Controlled Growth**: Clause analytics and template orchestration reduce reliance on Legal and minimize exposure.

- 💰 **Renewal Optimization**: Automated alerts and structured obligation tracking drive upsells, retention, and pricing control.

- 🌐 **Scalable Execution**: Tiered playbooks allow expansion across products, geographies, and partners without chaos.

CLM becomes your **revenue rail**, not your legal wall.

VII. What to Avoid: Pitfalls that Derail CLM Transformations

From experience, here's what breaks CLM maturity:

1. **Treating CLM as a Legal Tool Only**
   CLM is a cross-functional operating system. Legal owns risk, but Sales, Finance, and Ops own performance.

2. **Over-Engineering the Stack**
   Choose tools that *work together* not just best-in-class silos. Seamless integration beats feature overload.

3. **Under-Resourcing Change Management**
   You need training, internal champions, and workflow documentation. Technology ≠ adoption.

4. **No Governance Body**
   If no one owns the clause library or SLA reporting - it will decay. CoE is mandatory.

5. **Measuring Only Volume, Not Value**
   Track what matters: speed, risk, revenue capture, cross-functional trust.

VIII. Summary: Embedding CLM as Operating DNA

You don't "install" CLM. You embed it.

To do so requires:

- A layered technology architecture
- A modular playbook by contract type and audience
- A Center of Excellence to own governance and strategy
- A KPI dashboard to drive behavior and improvement
- A change management plan to institutional-ize adoption

CLM becomes not just faster, but smarter. Not just digital, but intelligent. Not just compliance, but **competitive advantage**.

You now have the blueprint. You've moved from reactive contracts to intelligent contracting. From fragments to a system.

THE PRACTITIONER'S NARRATIVE OPERATIONALIZING THE CLM SYSTEM – FROM TOOL TO STRATEGIC DISCIPLINE

I. Overview: The Playbook Comes to Life

You've architected the Contract Advantage™ blueprint, established the intelligence layers, and connected the ecosystem. Now, we go to market with execution artifacts, workflows, and team choreography designed to scale precisely.

This chapter is grounded in the exact playbooks, dashboards, process flows, and governance models I've designed and implemented over 25+ years of frontline transformation. These frameworks are how I've institutionalized CLM as a cross-functional business asset—not a technology.

II. Core Framework: The CLM Implementation Stack™

I use a **four-layer CLM execution stack** as a map for rollout. Each layer has distinct ownership, metrics, and toolsets.

◇ Layer 1: Contract Intake & Deal Initiation

Tools: Guided intake forms, CRM integration, pre-negotiation logic

Methodology: Dynamic intake triggers based on deal stage, tier, customer type

Execution Assets:

- Intake Matrix by Deal Tier (Low/Mid/High Risk)
- Smart Forms with Conditional Logic
- Automated Approvals for Standardized Templates

◇ **Layer 2: Authoring & Negotiation**

Tools: Clause library, fallback trees, redline accelerators

Methodology: Pre-approved modular language based on risk-score tier

Execution Assets:

- Clause Playbooks by Region/Segment
- Redline Tracker Heatmap
- Negotiation History Audit Trail

◇ **Layer 3: Execution & Signature**

Tools: eSignature platform, audit log, version control
Methodology: Routing engine that prioritizes TAT KPIs
Execution Assets:

- Signature SLAs by Contract Type
- Approval Escalation Workflow
- Legal SLA Heatmaps

◇ **Layer 4: Obligation Management & Renewal**

Tools: CLM contract analytics, ERP, CSAT sync
Methodology: Link contract terms to customer lifecycle data
Execution Assets:

- Renewal Uplift Tracker

- Obligations Dashboard
- Customer-Linked Clause Alerts

III. Template Strategy: Intelligent Contract Kits™

I architect contracts as **intelligent kits**, not static PDFs. This includes:

🎯 Audience-Aligned Templates:

- B2B Enterprise → risk-scored fallback clauses
- SMB/Startups → simplified commercial kits
- Government → compliance-traceable modularity
- Partner/Vendor → reciprocal clause alignment

🧠 Smart Clause Logic:

- Pre-approved fallbacks coded by risk tier
- Clause logic triggers based on region, product, pricing volume
- Embedded "legal logic" tied to industry profiles

These kits are codified in your clause library, accessible to both Legal and Sales, embedded in guided authoring workflows.

IV. Smart Contract Lifecycle Workflows™

Here's what I implement in real-world CLM orchestration:

Step	Workflow Feature	Strategic Impact
1. Trigger	Salesforce triggers based on opportunity stage	Ensures proactive initiation tied to revenue

Step	Workflow Feature	Strategic Impact
2. Tier	Auto-classify contracts into risk levels	Enables legal load balancing and template precision
3. Author	Guided authoring with locked fallback clauses	Reduces redline churn by 40–60%
4. Review	Conditional routing (e.g., Legal only if non-standard)	Frees Legal from low-risk bottlenecks
5. Execute	SLA-based e-signature workflow	Accelerates time-to-revenue
6. Store	Metadata extraction + link to ERP	Connects contract to fulfillment and billing
7. Track	Renewal/obligation alerts + KPI dashboards	Enables revenue recovery and trust enforcement

V. Cross-Functional Dashboard Design

Your CLM success must be visible to the business. I implement dashboards by persona:

For Sales:

- "Contract Tracker" inside CRM
- Time-to-Sign by Segment
- Deal Blockers Flagged in Real Time

For Legal:

- Clause Escalation Frequency
- SLA Breach Alerts

- Playbook Deviation Log

For Finance:

- Revenue Leakage Heatmap
- Rebate Clause Compliance
- Payment Trigger Tracking

For Execs:

- Overall Time-to-Contract
- Contracted Revenue Coverage Ratio
- Risk Score by Portfolio

These are not reports. They are operational command centers.

VI. Playbook-In-Action: Real Case Choreography

In a multi-market logistics company, I deployed a **Contract Intelligence Ops Model**:

- Built a tiered template suite linked to customer types and pricing models
- Architected guided authoring tools with clause fallback matrices
- Created dashboards per function and contract portfolio
- Integrated with CRM → ERP → CS Platform for obligation traceability

Results:

- Time-to-close decreased 57%

- Risk reviews dropped 46%
- Revenue leakage from missed SLAs reduced 38%
- Stakeholder satisfaction increased >80%

VII. Change Management Execution Toolkit™

Transformation is behavioral before it's technical. Here's my change management toolkit:

- **Training-by-Persona**: Sales, Legal, CS, Finance → tailored onboarding
- **Contract Office Hours**: Weekly Q&A to triage new behaviors
- **CLM Champions Program**: Internal evangelists and power users
- **Feedback Loops**: Post-signature surveys + review huddles

Adoption = Design × Discipline × Enablement.

VIII. Governance Blueprint: The Contract Steering Committee™

To make this stick, I institute a **quarterly steering committee** that owns:

- Template refresh cadence
- Clause usage audit + updates
- Legal SLA review
- Escalation frequency analysis
- Tool ROI tracking

Membership includes:

- CLO / Head of Legal
- RevOps
- Procurement
- Customer Success
- CFO or delegated ops

It governs the contract system as an *enterprise capability*—not a legal inbox.

IX. Final Summary: The Playbook as Strategic Discipline

This chapter wasn't about "best practices." It's about **execution architecture.**

You now hold:

- A contract lifecycle execution map
- A modular template playbook with clause logic
- Persona-based dashboards for cross-functional success
- A governance and change strategy to make it real

This is how CLM becomes your business operating system.

Would you like me to provide visual charts and diagrams for:

- The CLM Execution Stack™
- Clause Escalation Heatmap
- Persona-Based Dashboards
- CLM Steering Committee Governance Model?

CHAPTER 6

DISCUSSION SECTION CLM SYSTEMS AS ENTERPRISE INFRASTRUCTURE:

A Strategic Technology Lens

Introduction: CLM Beyond the Legal Tech Stack

Ask most organizations where contract management "**lives,**" and you'll hear: **Legal**.

Occasionally: **Procurement**.

Sometimes: **Sales Operations**.

However, ask a more consequential question—**where should it live?**

And the answer changes entirely:

CLM belongs at the heart of your enterprise architecture.

Contracts don't belong in silos or "point solutions." They govern pricing, obligations, risk, revenue recognition, and service delivery. In short, they govern **the enterprise operating model itself.**

This chapter reframes CLM as **infrastructure** and explores the methodologies, systems theory, and technology strategy behind integrating CLM into the foundational digital stack of any modern enterprise.

Part I. Technology as Architecture: The ERP, CRM, CLM Triangle

1. *The Modern Enterprise Stack*

Organizations today typically run on three core digital platforms:

- **ERP** (Enterprise Resource Planning) for financial and supply chain data
- **CRM** (Customer Relationship Management) for pipeline, service, and sales data
- **CLM** (Contract Lifecycle Management) for legal and commercial governance

Yet only the first two are universally seen as "enterprise-grade." CLM is still treated like an add-on.

This is a miscalculation. CLM systems increasingly:

- Trigger ERP billing rules
- Govern customer-facing obligations in CRM
- Link to vendor onboarding workflows
- Feed compliance dashboards
- Flag AI risk exposure

The contract is the connective tissue between systems.

The CLM is where it's orchestrated.

2. *Strategic Technology Alignment*

Harvard's Henderson & Venkatraman (1993) emphasized the need for **strategic alignment between business archi-**

tecture and IT infrastructure. When CLM sits outside this alignment, companies lose:

- Contract-based analytics
- Deal compliance enforcement
- Revenue cycle integrity
- Risk-based clause intelligence

In my implementations, I align CLM within enterprise strategy using a **System of Systems Framework™**—mapping data handoffs, governance responsibilities, and business processes across platforms.

Part II. CLM as a System of Record. Or System of Intelligence?

Traditionally, CLM was viewed as a document repository: a **System of Record (SoR)**. Today, it must become a **System of Intelligence (SoI)**, enabling:

- Predictive renegotiation alerts
- Clause-based risk scoring
- AI contract summarization
- Real-time financial exposure monitoring

In one client engagement (a Fortune 200 logistics company), I upgraded a legacy repository into an intelligence platform that:

- Flagged $22M in renewal exposure across vendor contracts
- Identified outdated pricing clauses in 17% of revenue-bearing agreements

- Enabled self-service reporting used by 14 cross-functional teams

Lesson: CLM isn't a filing cabinet. **It's the logic layer of the enterprise.**

Part III. Interoperability: The Real Test of Strategic Tools

1. *The Integration Mandate*

Modern CLM platforms must integrate with:

- **CRM**
- **ERP**
- **e-Signature**
- **HRIS & Procurement**
- **Data Lakes & BI**

Without this, contract terms become invisible to the systems executing them. The result?

- Invoices misaligned to payment terms
- SLAs unenforced
- Vendor penalties lost
- Renewals missed

A CLM disconnected from enterprise systems is **a system of liability.**

2. *Middleware and Modern Architecture*

I often implement middleware solutions to facilitate bi-directional contract data flow. This ensures:

- Clause metadata updates vendor performance profiles
- Obligations flow into project management systems
- Legal risk scores appear in executive dashboards

CLM must be designed as part of an **event-driven architecture** - responding to lifecycle triggers across the tech stack.

Part IV. CLM as Part of Digital Transformation

Too many digital transformation programs focus on front-end automation or back-office modernization. CLM sits squarely between, yet it is often left out.

In my advisory work, I've embedded CLM into:

- **ERP transitions** (ensuring migrated contracts match new finance schemas)
- **CRM re-platforms** (tying contracts to opportunity and renewal workflows)
- **Data governance programs** (establishing contract terms as master data)
- **AI pilots** (feeding contract clause libraries into training data for legal AI tools)

Without CLM, transformation is incomplete - because **compliance and commercial intelligence are missing.**

Part V. Case Study: CLM as Core Infrastructure

🔍 **Client: Multinational Pharmaceutical Company (anonymized)**

Problem:

- CLM operated in Legal only
- Contracts unlinked from finance, procurement, and compliance
- High-profile audit failure due to missed obligations and opaque vendor SLAs

My Intervention:

- Re-architected CLM as a middleware layer across SAP, Ariba, Salesforce
- Established contract metadata as a governed data domain
- Created contract status KPIs surfaced in Tableau

Result:

- ERP audit success
- Vendor renegotiation playbook recovered $14.7M
- Enterprise visibility created buy-in from every function

Takeaway: CLM must be **operationally embedded, technically connected, and strategically owned.**

VII. Governance Models for CLM as Infrastructure

To sustain CLM-as-infrastructure, I build **Contracting Centers of Excellence (CCOEs)** that:

- Own the contract data model
- Define integration use cases
- Manage vendor-side configurations
- Guide CLM system evolution with product teams and IT

Depending on the organization's maturity, these centers sit inside Enterprise Ops, Legal Ops, or a Business Architecture office.

Their goal? To ensure CLM functions **not as a tool, but as a platform.**

VIII. The AI Horizon: CLM as a Learning System

Future-ready CLM systems are no longer passive. They are:

- Learning from redline frequency
- Suggesting fallback clauses
- Identifying systemic risk exposure
- Training legal AI models
- Connecting contracts to real-world performance

The goal isn't just automation. It's **augmentation**—enabling humans to make better strategic decisions by surfacing contract intelligence in context.

This is what I call the **Contract Advantage Intelligence Layer™**.

Part VIII. Summary: The CLM Tech Reframed

Let's be clear:

- CLM isn't "legal tech"
- It's not a tool for the back office
- It's not a nice-to-have

CLM is a critical layer in the digital enterprise stack - governing value, compliance, revenue, and risk.

By treating CLM as enterprise infrastructure, leaders can:

- Protect growth
- Unlock efficiency
- Ensure compliance
- Enable transformation

In the next chapter, I'll show how this infrastructure translates into **performance visibility** and how to measure CLM success using metrics that executives trust.

❋ ❋ ❋ ❋

THE PRACTITIONER'S NARRATIVE OPERATIONALIZING THE CLM SYSTEM – FROM TOOL TO STRATEGIC DISCIPLINE

I. Overview: The Playbook Comes to Life

You've architected the Contract Advantage™ blueprint, established the intelligence layers, and connected the ecosystem. Now, we go to market - with execution artifacts, workflows, and team choreography designed to scale with precision.

This chapter is grounded in the exact playbooks, dashboards, process flows, and governance models I've designed and implemented over 25+ years of frontline transformation. These frameworks are how I've institutionalized CLM as a cross-functional business asset—not a technology.

II. Core Framework: The CLM Implementation Stack™

I use a **four-layer CLM execution stack** as a map for rollout. Each layer has distinct ownership, metrics, and toolsets.

◇ Layer 1: Contract Intake & Deal Initiation

Tools: Guided intake forms, CRM integration, pre-negotiation logic

Methodology: Dynamic intake triggers based on deal stage, tier, customer type

Execution Assets:

- Intake Matrix by Deal Tier (Low/Mid/High Risk)
- Smart Forms with Conditional Logic
- Automated Approvals for Standardized Templates

◇ Layer 2: Authoring & Negotiation

Tools: Clause library, fallback trees, redline accelerators
Methodology: Pre-approved modular language based on risk-score tier

Execution Assets:

- Clause Playbooks by Region/Segment
- Redline Tracker Heatmap
- Negotiation History Audit Trail

◇ Layer 3: Execution & Signature

Tools: eSignature platform, audit log, version control
Methodology: Routing engine that prioritizes TAT KPIs

Execution Assets:

- Signature SLAs by Contract Type
- Approval Escalation Workflow
- Legal SLA Heatmaps

◇ Layer 4: Obligation Management & Renewal

Tools: CLM contract analytics, ERP, CSAT sync

Methodology: Link contract terms to customer lifecycle data

Execution Assets:

- Renewal Uplift Tracker
- Obligations Dashboard
- Customer-Linked Clause Alerts

III. Template Strategy: Intelligent Contract Kits™

I architect contracts as **intelligent kits**, not static PDFs. This includes:

🎯 Audience-Aligned Templates:

- B2B Enterprise → risk-scored fallback clauses
- SMB/Startups → simplified commercial kits
- Government → compliance-traceable modularity
- Partner/Vendor → reciprocal clause alignment

🧠 Smart Clause Logic:

- Pre-approved fallbacks coded by risk tier
- Clause logic triggers based on region, product, pricing volume
- Embedded "legal logic" tied to industry profiles

These kits are codified in your clause library, accessible to both Legal and Sales, embedded in guided authoring workflows.

IV. Smart Contract Lifecycle Workflows™

Here's what I implement in real-world CLM orchestration:

Step	Workflow Feature	Strategic Impact
1. Trigger	Salesforce triggers based on opportunity stage	Ensures proactive initiation tied to revenue
2. Tier	Auto-classify contracts into risk levels	Enables legal load balancing and template precision
3. Author	Guided authoring with locked fallback clauses	Reduces redline churn by 40–60%
4. Review	Conditional routing (e.g., Legal only if non-standard)	Frees Legal from low-risk bottlenecks
5. Execute	SLA-based e-signature workflow	Accelerates time-to-revenue
6. Store	Metadata extraction + link to ERP	Connects contract to fulfillment and billing
7. Track	Renewal/obligation alerts + KPI dashboards	Enables revenue recovery and trust enforcement

V. Cross-Functional Dashboard Design

Your CLM success must be visible to the business. I implement dashboards by persona:

For Sales:

- "Contract Tracker" inside CRM

- Time-to-Sign by Segment
- Deal Blockers Flagged in Real Time

For Legal:

- Clause Escalation Frequency
- SLA Breach Alerts
- Playbook Deviation Log

For Finance:

- Revenue Leakage Heatmap
- Rebate Clause Compliance
- Payment Trigger Tracking

For Execs:

- Overall Time-to-Contract
- Contracted Revenue Coverage Ratio
- Risk Score by Portfolio

These are not reports. They are operational command centers.

VI. Playbook-In-Action: Real Case Choreography

In a multi-market logistics company, I deployed a **Contract Intelligence Ops Model**:

- Built a tiered template suite linked to customer types and pricing models
- Architected guided authoring tools with clause fallback matrices
- Created dashboards per function and con-

tract portfolio

- Integrated with CRM → ERP → CS Platform for obligation traceability

Results:

- Time-to-close decreased 57%
- Risk reviews dropped 46%
- Revenue leakage from missed SLAs reduced 38%
- Stakeholder satisfaction increased >80%

VII. Change Management Execution Toolkit™

Transformation is behavioral before it's technical. Here's my change management toolkit:

- **Training-by-Persona**: Sales, Legal, CS, Finance → tailored onboarding
- **Contract Office Hours**: Weekly Q&A to triage new behaviors
- **CLM Champions Program**: Internal evangelists and power users
- **Feedback Loops**: Post-signature surveys + review huddles

Adoption = Design × Discipline × Enablement.

VIII. Governance Blueprint: The Contract Steering Committee™

To make this stick, I institute a **quarterly steering committee** that owns:

- Template refresh cadence
- Clause usage audit + updates
- Legal SLA review
- Escalation frequency analysis
- Tool ROI tracking

Membership includes:

- CLO / Head of Legal
- RevOps
- Procurement
- Customer Success
- CFO or delegated ops

It governs the contract system as an *enterprise capability*—not a legal inbox.

IX. FINAL SUMMARY: THE PLAYBOOK AS STRATEGIC DISCIPLINE

This chapter wasn't about "best practices." It's about **execution architecture**.

You now hold:

- A contract lifecycle execution map
- A modular template playbook with clause logic
- Persona-based dashboards for cross-functional success
- A governance and change strategy to make it real

This is how CLM becomes your business operating system.

CHAPTER 7

DISCUSSION SECTION
THE MEASUREMENT MANDATE:
FROM LEGAL OUTPUT TO ENTERPRISE PERFORMANCE

Introduction: What Gets Measured Shapes the Business

It's no longer enough to say, "CLM improves efficiency." Enterprise leaders want more than anecdotes. Leaders demand *evidence*. And yet, across hundreds of organizations, I've found one constant:

Contracts are everywhere. But contract metrics are nowhere.

This isn't a tool failure. It's a leadership gap. And it's costing enterprises millions in missed revenue, audit risk, and value erosion.

In this chapter, I argue that CLM metrics should be treated as enterprise performance drivers instead of legal operations KPIs. Using business measurement theory, strategy models, and operational systems thinking, I outline how to build, sustain, and scale a **Contract Performance Measurement Framework**™ worthy of executive dashboards.

Part I. The Case for Contract Visibility

1. *The Maturity Gap*

According to Gartner (2022), fewer than 30% of global organizations track contract lifecycle metrics across departments. Of those that do, most focus on operational stats:

- Time-to-sign
- Number of contracts executed
- Legal team workload

But these are **activity metrics** — not **impact metrics.** They don't tell you:

- How much value is recovered through renegotiations
- Where deals are lost to contract friction
- Which vendors underperform on SLAs
- What clauses delay execution
- How compliance posture is trending

In other words, they don't tell you what contracts are *doing*.

2. *Measurement as Trust Infrastructure*

In digital systems, **transparency builds trust.** Without clear data, business units circumvent CLM. Legal becomes the bottleneck. Finance flags revenue leakage too late.

But with shared, visible contract intelligence, trust is restored. Teams align. Accountability increases. Risk becomes proactive, not reactive.

I've witnessed entire cultures shift simply because metrics brought **visibility to what had been invisible.**

Part II. Building a Contract Performance Measurement Framework™

1. *Strategic Alignment First*

Measurement must reflect the **business strategy**, not just system capability. I begin every metrics project by asking:

- What does the company need to prove?
- Who needs visibility?
- Where is **Value** at risk?
- How do contracts influence revenue, cost, compliance, and CX?

Only then do we define metrics.

2. *Metrics in Three Dimensions*

I design CLM KPIs across **three strategic tiers**:

Tier	Focus	Example Metrics
Operational	Efficiency & Cycle Time	Time-to-sign, review loops, and escalations avoided
Financial	Value, Revenue & Risk	Clauses tied to revenue, renegotiation ROI, payment term compliance
Strategic	Trust, Innovation, Alignment	Clause change patterns, cross-functional usage, compliance foresight

This model transforms CLM from tactical throughput to

executive-level insight.

Part III. Case Study: From Legal Logs to Boardroom Dashboards

🔍 Client: APAC-based Enterprise SaaS Provider

Initial State:

- Legal tracked contracts in Excel
- No system-level clause visibility
- Executives had zero visibility into vendor or customer obligation compliance

My Implementation:

- Built a metadata-driven dashboard in Power BI
- Integrated CLM with Salesforce and Oracle
- Created real-time alerts for renewal, revenue risk, and clause triggers

Outcomes:

- Executive leadership began reviewing contract risk exposure during QBRs
- Renegotiation savings exceeded $6.2M
- Sales adoption increased 71% due to self-service visibility

Takeaway: *Metrics didn't just justify CLM — they embedded it into enterprise control logic.*

Part IV. Measurement Theory in Contracting

1. *Kaplan & Norton: From Scorecard to Strategy Map*

The Balanced Scorecard model (Kaplan & Norton, 1992) showed that organizations' measures drive their behavior.

Contracts must be integrated into:

- **Customer**: How SLAs influence satisfaction
- **Financial**: How clause logic impacts cash flow
- **Process**: How workflows delay or enable execution
- **Learning**: How data improves future contracts

This is why I embed contract KPIs into company-wide strategy maps:

Contract Health = Business Health.

1. *Leading vs. Lagging Indicators*

Many organizations track **lagging metrics** (e.g., contract cycle time). I emphasize **leading indicators**:

- Number of at-risk renewals flagged before expiration
- % of vendor agreements without performance SLAs
- Number of clauses re-negotiated in past 90 days
- Clause-to-revenue ratio per contract category

These predict disruption - and allow teams to act early.

Part V. Integrating Metrics Across Platforms

True CLM measurement requires **cross-system stitching**:

- CRM System/App provides opportunity stage
- ERP holds revenue triggers
- CLM holds legal terms
- BI tools visualize clause analytics

That's why I design reporting dashboards that **combine data** across systems, not just export from CLM.

I use:

- Power BI
- Tableau
- Snowflake
- Native CLM dashboards

The goal is **one pane of glass** for the enterprise.

Part VI. Metrics That Create Change

In my experience, the most transformational metrics are not the most complex - they are the most *relevant to executive impact*.

These include:

- % of contracts with non-standard commercial terms
- Revenue held in contracts delayed more than 30 days
- Clauses that correlate to renewal loss
- Vendor agreement compliance rate by region

- Clause fallback usage rate (drives template redesign)

Once surfaced, these metrics become **conversation starters, not just reports.**

Part VII. Culture of Visibility: Metrics as Behavioral Levers

When metrics are visible:

- Sales teams respect the process
- Legal is seen as an enabler
- Finance trusts data
- Risk becomes measurable

In every successful CLM program I've led, **performance visibility changed behavior**, long before system configuration did.

This is the difference between activity and transformation.

Part VIII. Summary: Contracts That Speak in Metrics

CLM must stop whispering in legal logs. It must **speak in metrics that the business understands.**

You now have:

- A three-tier measurement model
- Metric-to-strategy mapping
- Integration logic across systems
- Case evidence that performance visibility accelerates trust and ROI

Next, we scale:

How do you expand this system globally, cross-functionally, and in a way that continues to evolve with the business?

That's what we answer in the next chapter, after this chapter's practitioner narrative section – your tools.

※※※※

THE PRACTITIONER'S NARRATIVE SECTION MEASURING SUCCESS: METRICS, DASHBOARDS, AND ROI YOU CAN TRUST

If you can't measure it, you can't prove it.
If you can't prove it, you can't scale it.

Why Metrics Matter

Technology doesn't justify itself. Neither do processes, playbooks, or platforms. What does? **Measured performance.**

Yet, most organizations fail to measure CLM effectively, if at all. They track input metrics (like how many contracts were signed), but not outcome metrics (like how much value was retained or risk was avoided). They look at speed but ignore impact. They track progress but not business performance.

My belief and practice are simple:

If contracts are strategic assets, their performance must be measured.

In this chapter's practitioner narrative, I'll share the frameworks I use with C-suites and boards to prove the value of CLM. I'll also show you how I build dashboards that elevate visibility rather than just track activity. Finally, I'll give you the language to communicate ROI clearly, credibly, and repeatedly.

The Visibility Gap in Traditional CLM

Most legal and procurement leaders struggle to answer basic questions like:

- How many contracts are active?
- How many have value-at-risk clauses?
- Which vendors have missed performance thresholds?
- What's our average time-to-sign by region or business unit?
- How many contract escalations have occurred this quarter?

This isn't because the data doesn't exist. It's because the system wasn't built to surface it. And when executives can't see the value of CLM, they stop investing in it.

My role? I make the VALUE visible.

The Contract ROI Pyramid™

I developed the **Contract ROI Pyramid™** to help organizations evolve from reactive measurement to strategic value delivery:

1. *Operational Metrics*

- Contract cycle time
- Approval bottlenecks
- Time-in-status

- Redline frequency
- Auto-renewal tracking

2. *Financial Metrics*

- Recovered rebates and discounts
- Penalty avoidance through compliance
- Renewal forecast accuracy
- Value of renegotiated terms
- Average contract value per quarter

3. *Strategic Metrics*

- Contract contribution to revenue recognition
- Cross-functional process participation
- Risk posture shift (tracked via risk scoring models)
- Customer satisfaction post-signature
- CLM adoption rates by business unit

When I implement dashboards, I ensure each level is tracked, reported, and translated into business outcomes.

Real Example: From Dashboard Confusion to C-Suite Clarity

📊 **Client: Healthcare Technology Company (NDA-protected)**

Problem: Their CLM tool generated reports, but no one trusted the data.

Legal had one set, Finance another, and Sales a third. Each

told a different story.

My Solution:

- Rebuilt the CLM reporting layer using normalized contract metadata
- Integrated contract KPIs into the CFO's Tableau dashboard
- Created shared definitions for "value at risk," "pending," "executed," and "in negotiation"

Impact:

- Unified reporting across all functions
- 23% increase in leadership confidence in contract performance metrics
- Executive dashboard became the basis for quarterly business reviews and budget planning

Metrics that Drive Executive Investment

If you want budget, buy-in, or board support for your CLM transformation, speak in these terms:

- **% ROI in Year 1** (benchmark: 5x–12x if done right)
- **Value Recovered** from missed obligations
- **Reduction in Contract Cycle Time** (and its impact on revenue velocity)
- **Cost Avoidance** from audit, legal, and compliance risk
- **Customer Retention Boost** from SLA enforcement and renewal consistency

Executives don't fund systems. Executives fund outcomes.

My Go-To CLM Performance Dashboard

Every client I work with receives a CLM dashboard tailored to their industry, systems, and users - but the core elements remain:

Metric	Description	Owner	Frequency
Time-to-Sign (by type)	Tracks speed by NDA, MSA, SOW, etc.	Legal Ops	Weekly
Clause Escalation Rate	% of contracts that needed Legal intervention	Legal	Monthly
Contract Value at Risk	Total $ tied to overdue or expiring contracts	Finance	Weekly
Contract Pipeline Velocity	Flow of contracts in each lifecycle stage	Sales Ops	Real-Time
Compliance Flags Triggered	# of risk conditions triggered via clause logic	Risk & Compliance	Monthly

The enterprise architecture determines whether developers build these into the "tool's dashboards" or directly into the CLM interface.

VII. From Scorekeeping to Strategy

Metrics aren't just about reporting. They're about learning.

In high-performing orgs, I use CLM metrics to:

- **Refine playbooks** (based on negotiation bottlenecks)
- **Train users** (target low adoption teams with enablement)
- **Predict churn** (based on clause non-compliance or SLA flags)
- **Restructure vendor programs** (using renewal win/loss analytics)
- **Improve audits** (with auto-generated evidence logs and clause change history)

In other words, I turn contract data into **actionable insights** that change how companies operate.

VIII. The Long Game: ROI Across Time Horizons

When I'm asked, "How long until we see value?"

I map ROI across three horizons:

- **90 Days**: Cycle time reduction, increased visibility, basic obligation tracking
- **6 Months**: Recovered value, renegotiation uplift, adoption gains
- **12–18 Months**: System-wide integration, predictive analytics, compliance automation, audit readiness

Contracts aren't just closing documents. They're long-

term data assets. ROI compounds.

IX. Summary: How This Chapter Equips You

You now have:

- The **Contract ROI Pyramid™**
- My go-to **metrics for value visibility**
- Real-world examples of executive-level reporting
- The ability to move from measuring effort to **measuring impact**

In the next chapter, we'll talk about what happens when CLM becomes a scalable business model. Because once you've proven the value—you don't stop.

You scale.

🛠 Theory Into Practice Checklist

- ❐ **Identify your current top 5 CLM metrics—are they meaningful?**
- ❐ **Define one financial, one operational, and one strategic KPI**
- ❐ **Create a shared definition of "value at risk" across departments**
- ❐ **Map current reporting gaps between Legal, Sales, and Finance**
- ❐ **Build a draft dashboard using your existing CLM or BI tool**

CHAPTER 8

DISCUSSION SECTION
SCALING SYSTEMS OF TRUST:
CONTRACTING AT THE EDGE OF GROWTH

I. Introduction: Scale Is Not Just More — It's Different

Organizations don't fail to scale because they lack ambition.

They fail to scale because **what worked for 100 contracts doesn't work for 100,000.**

Growth breaks systems.

Contracting is no exception. As companies expand into new markets, product lines, or geographies, the volume of agreements multiplies — but so do risk, complexity, and interdependence. And when the contract infrastructure doesn't evolve alongside the business, growth creates entropy, not value.

In this chapter, I present a framework for **scaling CLM as a system of enterprise trust.** I'll walk through the operational, architectural, and cultural layers needed to support large-scale, cross-border, high-velocity contracting in complex organizations.

II. Platform Thinking: CLM as a Scalable Business Layer

1. *From Project to Platform*

CLM isn't a tool that "goes live." It's an **ongoing capability**, embedded across business units, functions, and strategic initiatives.

Scaling means designing for:

- Reusability of workflows and clauses
- Extensibility across geographies and entities
- Resilience under changing regulations, deal volume, and audit pressure

In platform design theory (Evans & Schmalensee, 2016), scale comes from:

- Standardized architecture
- User role diversity
- Self-reinforcing data models

When I design scalable CLM systems, I structure them as platforms, not projects, with an operating model rather than just an implementation roadmap.

2. *Platform Metrics for Scale*

At scale, you must monitor not just performance, but **platform health**:

- User engagement by role and region
- Clause adoption variance
- Workflow reuse rates
- System friction indicators (manual escalations, cycle delays, system abandonment)

This transforms CLM from static infrastructure to **a living enterprise network.**

III. Scaling Dimensions: The Five Axes of Contract Growth

I developed the **CLM Scaling Matrix™** to guide organizations through the real-world complexity of enterprise contracting. It includes:

1. Geographic Scaling

- Multi-jurisdictional clause libraries
- Language localization for templates
- Country-specific regulatory rulesets

2. Functional Scaling

- Customized journeys for Legal, Sales, Procurement, Finance, Compliance
- Function-specific KPIs and reporting dashboards
- Shared access to contract status and performance triggers

3. Volume Scaling

- Clause reuse optimization
- Smart routing for auto-assignment
- Load balancing for legal queues
- Archival automation and data retention governance

4. Complexity Scaling

- Risk-based contract tiering
- Clause escalation protocols
- Regulatory surveillance triggers (GDPR, SOX, ESG)

5. Innovation Scaling

- AI clause libraries
- Predictive renegotiation triggers
- Blockchain contracts (in smart supply chain systems)

Scaling is not linear. It's **layered** — and success depends on building each layer with intent.

IV. Case Study: Cross-Functional CLM Expansion in a Global Enterprise

🔍 Client: Fortune 100 Financial Institution (anonymized)

Challenge:

- CLM is only deployed in North America
- APAC and EMEA used local legal teams with inconsistent tools
- Global deal velocity constrained by fragmented workflows

My Solution:

- Global clause matrix with local fallback trees
- Salesforce-to-CLM integration mapped to every regional legal protocol
- One centralized CCOE, with regional CLM Champions trained in governance

Outcome:

- Global CLM adoption across 18 markets

- 54% improvement in regional deal cycle
- Harmonized clause data used in legal AI model training

The lesson: *You don't scale by pushing a tool. You scale by building a system.*

V. The Role of the CCOE (Contracting Center of Excellence)

1. *Governance at Scale*

A Contracting Center of Excellence (CCoE) becomes the **custodian of strategic consistency.** It defines:

- Clause taxonomy
- Governance protocols
- Change management cycles
- Playbook refresh cadences
- Training and adoption metrics

But most importantly, it ensures that **as the business evolves, so does the contract infrastructure.**

2. *Organizational Learning and Continuous Improvement*

Scaling CLM isn't "one and done." High-maturity organizations treat it as an iterative system. I build quarterly feedback loops:

- Clause redline heatmaps
- Template optimization based on usage
- Workflow tuning based on time-in-status metrics

This creates **a contracting intelligence feedback**, where the system learns and adapts.

VI. Culture Shift: From Silos to Shared Systems

At scale, CLM cannot be "owned" by Legal. It must be **co-owned by the enterprise.**

That means:

- Sales trusts legal clauses to close faster
- Procurement sees contracts as supplier management tools
- Finance uses contract data to forecast and plan
- Customer Success aligns renewals with SLA performance

When CLM becomes part of the company's cultural fabric, it ceases to be a system. It becomes a **shared operational truth.**

VII. The Risk of Under-Scaling

Failure to scale CLM with business complexity leads to:

- Contracting bottlenecks
- Loss of institutional memory
- Audit failures
- SLA breaches
- Revenue leakage

I've seen it happen: Companies that scaled fast but forgot to scale their systems — and paid for it in customer churn, regulator scrutiny, and leadership turnover.

CLM maturity must *track* enterprise maturity.

VIII. Preparing for the Future: CLM as Enterprise Resilience Engine

Looking ahead, scaled CLM systems will:

- Autonomously renegotiate on market triggers
- Integrate with ESG reporting tools
- Link with HR systems for talent clauses
- Monitor supplier climate pledges and ethical sourcing agreements

Future-ready CLM will be an **adaptive layer of compliance, strategy, and resilience.**

But only if designed to scale.

IX. Summary: Scaling as Strategic Infrastructure

Scaling CLM isn't just about more users or templates.

It's about:

- Building trust across systems and teams
- Embedding governance into workflows
- Turning contract data into enterprise intelligence
- Supporting global strategy with localized precision

This is how The Contract Advantage™ becomes a business operating system, not just a legal system.

In the next chapter, after this chapter's practitioner narrative, we look to the horizon:

What does the future hold for contracts as digital assets,

AI enablers, and autonomous systems?

✳ ✳ ✳ ✳

CHAPTER 8A -

THE PRACTITIONER'S SCALING YOUR CONTRACT ADVANTAGE: ENTERPRISE EXPANSION AND CONTINUOUS INNOVATION

CLM isn't a project.
It's a platform for how your company thinks,
negotiates, and grows.

I. Why Scale Matters

You've seen the pain.

You've implemented the fix.

You've measured the value.

Now comes the true test: **Can you scale it?**

Scaling your Contract Advantage™ isn't about repeating a rollout in different departments.

> It's about embedding CLM into the **operating DNA of your business.**
>
> Across regions.
>
> Across languages.
>
> Across functions.
>
> Across future transformations.

The goal isn't to build a better system. The goal is to

build **a smarter, self-reinforcing ecosystem** that evolves as you grow.

In this chapter 7 practitioner narrative, I'll show you how I've helped Fortune 500s and high-growth disruptors turn CLM into a **growth platform** - not just a legal upgrade. You'll learn to scale systems, align governance, and enable continuous innovation through contracts.

II. Common Scaling Pitfalls (and How I've Solved Them)

Before we get into the "how," let's address the "why not." Here's what stalls most CLM transformations during scale:

- 💣 **Local silos re-emerge**
- ⚠️ **Business units build workarounds**
- ✖ **Tool capabilities outpace governance maturity**
- ▦ **No executive incentives tied to expansion metrics**
- 🔔 **Change management fatigue**

I've seen promising global CLM systems collapse after launch because their builders did not design them for scale. My role? Design systems that don't break under complexity.

III. The Five Scaling Dimensions

To help organizations scale strategically, I developed **Contract Scaling Framework™**, built around five critical axes:

1. Geographic Scaling

Contracts must localize while staying standard. I deploy:

- Local language clause libraries
- Jurisdiction-specific fallback playbooks
- Regional dashboards with global oversight

2. Functional Scaling

From Legal → Sales → Procurement → Finance. Each function needs:

- Custom user journeys
- Specific dashboards
- Role-based automation triggers

3. Volume Scaling

High-growth companies go from 100s to 1000s of contracts fast. I enable:

- AI-based triage and auto-assignment
- Real-time contract routing
- Archival and retention automations

4. Complexity Scaling

As you grow, so does risk. I implement:

- Risk-tiered workflows
- Contract risk scoring systems
- Clause change tracking with AI escalation

5. Innovation Scaling

Contracts are innovation signals. I help clients:

- Feed contract data into product and vendor strategy

- Trigger alerts based on renegotiation patterns
- Use contract analytics to fund automation pilots

IV. Case Study: Scaling Across Borders and Business Models

🌐 Client: Global B2B SaaS Platform (anonymized)

Starting Point: North American sales contracts were standardized. But APAC, LATAM, and EMEA teams all used local tools, language, and processes.

Challenge: As the company scaled to IPO, they needed unified visibility—without losing regional flexibility.

My Approach:

- Built a centralized governance model with localized execution playbooks
- Developed a global clause matrix with region-level exceptions
- Integrated Salesforce (Sales), NetSuite (Finance), and Jira (Customer Ops) across all regions

Results:

- Contracts executed across 6 regions on a single platform
- Local approval SLAs decreased by 54%
- Board reporting on contract performance rolled up into global dashboards

This wasn't just system scale. It was **strategic operational expansion**, powered by contracts.

V. Embedding Governance Without Bottlenecks

Scaling CLM doesn't mean adding bureaucracy. It means adding **clarity, ownership, and evolution**.

I help clients establish a **Contracting Center of Excellence (CCOE)** that grows with the business.

This team becomes:

- Owner of clause libraries
- Guardian of user permissions
- Lead for system enhancements
- Liaison to IT, Legal, Ops, and the C-suite

And, most importantly, **they manage the roadmap**. Not just to maintain. To optimize and innovate.

VI. Aligning CLM with Enterprise Transformation

Contracts touch every transformation initiative:

- M&A integrations
- Global ERP upgrades
- New market launches
- Regulatory shifts
- AI enablement

I embed contract triggers into transformation governance. For example:

- Contracts notify Finance during vendor consolidations
- SLAs trigger Ops during service redesign

- Clause flags inform Legal of regulatory deadline changes

Contracts become signals—not just storage.

VII. Creating a Self-Evolving Contract Ecosystem

In mature organizations, I've designed CLM systems that:

- Train themselves through AI clause patterning
- Recommend renegotiation based on market pricing
- Benchmark contract performance by vendor category
- Feed procurement strategies via obligation analytics

This is how you future-proof your CLM platform. **You make it learn.**

VIII. From Program to Operating Model

What I advocate is not a CLM "project." It's a **contract operating model** that mirrors and supports your business strategy.

You now have:

- A method for scaling with integrity
- A governance structure for continuity
- A vision for innovation through contracts

The Contract Advantage™ isn't just a toolset. It's a mindset, a system, and an architecture for growth.

IX. Summary: How This Chapter Expands Your Impact

You now understand:

- How to scale CLM across geographies, functions, and platforms
- What governance looks like in practice
- Why CLM is a pillar of digital transformation
- How to make your system evolve, not decay

In the final chapter, I'll show you what's next: **how to future-proof your business and lead change through contracts.**

✴ Theory Into Practice Checklist

- ☐ **Identify top 3 expansion barriers in your CLM today**
- ☐ **Draft your five-dimensional scaling roadmap**
- ☐ **Create a CCoE charter with governance scope**
- ☐ **Define your next enterprise transformation—and map how contracts connect to it**
- ☐ **Build an AI/innovation enhancement wish list (SLA tracking, renegotiation triggers, etc.)**

CHAPTER 9:

DISCUSSION AND THE PRACTITIONER'S NARRATIVE THE FUTURE OF CONTRACTS: OPERATIONAL INTELLIGENCE, AI, AND THE AUTONOMOUS ENTERPRISE

⚙ Section 1: Framework Introduction — Scaling the Contract Advantage

Purpose: This section reframes contract scaling not as process replication, but as **strategic system deployment**.

◇ FRAMEWORK OVERVIEW: Scaling as Strategic Infrastructure

Element	Objective	Application
Standardization	Build repeatable, high-efficiency workflows	Use global templates for review, negotiation, and renewal
Modularity	Enable localized adaptations without fragmentation	Create region-ready "plug-in" clauses, risk libraries
Technology Spine	Integrate systems for contract intelligence	Connect CLM, ERP, CRM, and BI systems into one analytics mesh

Element	Objective	Application
Governance Layer	Define ownership and decision protocols	Establish cross-functional contract councils
Performance Loop	Monitor, refine, and scale outcomes	Use dashboard KPIs to guide quarterly CoE sprints

🚀 *Strategic Insight:* Scaling is not about size. It is about **alignment**—replicating workflows, **intent, measurement, and value extraction**.

🔧 **METHODOLOGY: From Pilot Wins to Enterprise Impact**

Step 1: Contract Baseline Audit

- Identify current CLM maturity per region/business unit
- Classify contract types by risk level, frequency, and margin impact
- Measure contract velocity, error rates, and renegotiation cycles

Step 2: Win Pattern Extraction

- Analyze where current wins (e.g., faster cycle times, higher compliance) originated
- Isolate *methodology, not outcomes* (e.g., template reuse, stakeholder early engagement)

Step 3: Codify into Core Playbook

- Create a Core CLM Standard Operating Framework (CSOF)

- Include global policies + modular adaptations

Step 4: Build the Playbook Engine

- Define what is configurable (local) and what is codified (global)
- Create onboarding tools, templates, and role-based training guides

🧠 Decision Lens:

Ask before scaling any win:

- "Can this be governed, measured, and adapted with control?"

If not, it's not scalable - it's anecdotal.

⚙️ Section 2: *Enterprise Standardization Blueprint*

🎯 Objective:

To develop a **repeatable, enforceable, and flexible CLM operating system** that can be deployed across regions, business units, and functions without sacrificing control or local relevance.

🐾 FRAMEWORK: The CLM Standardization Matrix™

This proprietary model organizes how to scale CLM practices by distinguishing between **global mandates** and **local discretion**.

CLM Layer	Standardize Globally	Customize Locally
Clause Library	Mandatory fallback logic, risk flags	Regulatory-specific variants
Approval Workflows	Core logic, financial thresholds	Department-specific routing conditions
Governance Policies	Audit structure, versioning standards	Local escalation protocols
Templates & Playbooks	Baseline format, renewal terms	Regional SLA inserts, currency clauses
Reporting Metrics	KPI definitions, dashboard cadence	Visual layout, threshold triggers
Contract Authoring	Core process flow	Language and jurisdiction references

🛠 METHODOLOGY: Four-Stage Globalization Protocol

Stage 1: Define "Immutable" Core Standards

- Identify business-critical contract values (e.g. margin protection, IP security, indemnity positions)
- Build guardrails: clauses, workflows, risk thresholds that cannot be overridden

Stage 2: Conduct Regional Fit/Gap Analysis

- Interview regional leads to understand where standard rules diverge from legal or market constraints
- Document deviation justifications for transparency

Stage 3: Design Modular Implementation Kits

- Create implementation bundles (templates, workflows, playbooks) with toggles
- Modular examples: "APAC Legal Pack," "LATAM Fiscal Terms Toolkit"

Stage 4: Enforce Through Governance Layer

- Establish a centralized Contract Architecture Board (CAB)
- CAB reviews exceptions, maintains clause taxonomy, and tracks global consistency

▦ ANALYSIS POINTS

- **Cycle Time Delta**: Are standardized workflows improving or impeding velocity across geographies?
- **Clause Volatility Index**: Where are template terms consistently redlined? Why?
- **Exception Rate Trendline**: Track escalation patterns across business units—excessive variance suggests poor fit.

💡 TACTICAL PLAYBOOK SNAPSHOT

Playbook Component	Action
Standard Template Package	Deploy globally; enforce clause use with fallback logic
Regional Annex System	Enable jurisdictional flexibility without template fragmentation
Governance Portal	Digitize approvals, reviews, escalations, with real-time tracking
Clause Audit Tool	Quarterly review of usage frequency, redline rates, deviation history

⚠ *Watchpoint:* Over-standardization leads to local circumvention. Balance comes from **rigorous core standards + configurable edge rules**.

⚙ Section 3: *The Intelligent CLM Technology Spine*

🎯 Objective:

To create a real-time, scalable, intelligent contract ecosystem, build an enterprise-wide digital backbone that integrates Contract Lifecycle Management (CLM) with surrounding systems (ERP, CRM, BI).

🧠 FRAMEWORK: The Technology Spine Model™

Your CLM platform should not be a silo. It must operate as an **intelligent integration layer** - interfacing across systems to fuel visibility, automation, and enterprise decision-making.

Layer	Function	Integrated Platforms
CLM Core Engine	Contract creation, clause management, approval workflows	Standalone CLM or module (Icertis, Agiloft, DocuSign CLM)
ERP Integration	Revenue booking, supplier PO linkage, payment triggers	SAP, Oracle, Workday
CRM Integration	Pre-signature triggers, sales commitments, renewal alerts	Salesforce, HubSpot, Microsoft Dynamics
BI Layer	Real-time metrics, dashboards, predictive alerts	Power BI, Tableau, Looker
AI/ Automation	Clause extraction, risk scoring, negotiation assistance	NLP/ML platforms, chatbots, co-pilots

🔧 METHODOLOGY: CLM System Integration Roadmap

Step 1: Digital Ecosystem Mapping

- Document all systems that touch contracts (Sales, Legal, Finance, Compliance, Procurement)
- Map data flows (Who needs what? When? In what format?)

Step 2: Define System Roles

- CLM = Source of Truth (terms, obligations, metadata)
- ERP = Financial truth
- CRM = Customer truth
- BI = Insight truth

Step 3: Architect Middleware Layer

- Use iPaaS (integration platform-as-a-service) to create low-latency API syncs
- Ensure two-way flows for clause updates, risk flags, value realization

Step 4: Automate Insight Loops

- Embed contract alerts into CRM (e.g., renewals, pricing triggers)
- Trigger revenue flags in ERP from contract events (e.g., milestone missed)
- Feed clause trends and deviation scores into dashboards for contract design refinement

📊 PROPRIETARY TABLE: CLM Technology Enabler Grid™

Feature/Capability	Strategic Value	Priority for Scale
Clause-Level Metadata	Enables AI risk scoring, pattern mining	◉ Critical
eSignature API	Accelerates cycle time, supports compliance	◉ Critical
AI Clause Comparison	Detects negotiation inefficiency	◉ High
Contract Intelligence Dashboards	Empowers execs with asset oversight	◉ Critical
Auto-Renewal Flag Alerts	Reduces revenue leakage	◉ High

Feature/Capability	Strategic Value	Priori-ty for Scale
Real-Time KPI API	Enables cross-system per-formance sync	◉ High

◉ = Must-Have | ◍ = High-Impact Optional

🔋 DECISION GATES: Before You Scale CLM Tech

Ask:

- **?** Does this system surface contract value—not just document status?
- **?** Can metadata power intelligent routing and analytics?
- **?** Will this tech reduce exceptions—or simply digitize legacy behaviors?

💡 *Strategic Insight:*

Technology at scale must be **adaptive, interoperable, and intelligence-generating**.

Integration is not optional, it's structural.

⚙️ Section 4: *The Cross-Functional Operating Model*

🎯 Objective:

To establish a **shared ownership structure** for CLM that spans Legal, Finance, Sales, Procurement, and Compliance—embedding contract accountability into the fabric of enterprise execution.

🧠 FRAMEWORK: Contract Value Chain™

Role	Contribution	Impact on CLM
Legal	Clause risk management, regulatory alignment	Reduces exposure, improves defensibility
Finance	Terms alignment, revenue recognition	Ensures revenue integrity and cost control
Sales	Term negotiation, customer alignment	Accelerates velocity and customer satisfaction
Procurement	Vendor risk & SLA oversight	Improves service continuity, reduces cost volatility
Compliance	Regulatory triggers, audit trail	Ensures defensibility and early risk flagging

🧩 *Integrated together, these form a closed loop of commercial, legal, and operational integrity.*

🔧 **METHODOLOGY: Cross-Functional Operating Model (CFOM)**

1. Stakeholder Mapping

- Identify primary and secondary users across the lifecycle
- Document contract touchpoints and pain points by function

2. Ownership Assignment

- Assign explicit accountability per contract phase:
- Legal owns the clause library
- Finance owns term enforcement and compliance

- Sales owns commitments-to-clients
- Procurement owns the SLA language and vendor selection

3. Standing CLM Council Formation

- Monthly governance review: performance, escalations, metrics
- Use "CLM Health Report" as a shared artifact for decision-making

4. Communication Loop

- Build internal newsletter or dashboard for enterprise visibility
- Report on: clause negotiation trends, deviation reduction, cycle time gains, regional laggards

🔍 ANALYSIS POINTS

- **Engagement Ratios**: How often are non-legal teams accessing CLM?
- **Cycle Time by Function**: Where are the delays—legal redlines or finance approval stalls?
- **Contract Abandonment Points**: Where does stakeholder disengagement kill deals?
- 📄 **PLAYBOOK TOOLS**

Tool	Purpose
CLM RACI Matrix	Clarifies accountability by phase, function
Role-Based Dashboards	Custom views for Sales, Finance, etc.

495

Tool	Purpose
Monthly CLM Review Kit	Governance summary: KPIs, escalations, trends
Training Ladders by Function	Ensures every role knows how CLM affects their outcome

📢 *Insight:*
When contracts are managed cross-functionally,
the enterprise shifts from **compliance control** to **strategic orchestration.**

⚙️ **Section 5:** *Change Management and CLM Adoption Acceleration*

🎯 **Objective:**

To transform resistance into engagement by deploying structured, empathetic, and measurable change management tied to CLM maturity.

🧩 **FRAMEWORK: CLM Change Readiness Model™**

Phase	Focus	Actions
Awareness	Educate on why CLM is changing	Internal comms, executive sponsor videos
Understanding	Clarify the "what" and "how"	Role-based demos, before/after comparisons
Adoption	Convert training into usage	Live labs, job aids, quick wins reports

Phase	Focus	Actions
Commitment	Institutionalize CLM as "how we operate"	Incentives, gamification, leadership scorecards

🔧 METHODOLOGY: 90-Day CLM Change Sprint

Week 1–2: Awareness Campaign

- Share impact stories and visual stats (e.g., "CLM cut contract time by 40% in Region X")

Week 3–6: Hands-On Enablement

- Targeted onboarding by role
- Quick win tracking dashboard (e.g., cycle time saved per user)

Week 7–10: Champions & Resistance Management

- Identify superusers per function
- Run townhalls to surface resistance early

Week 11–13: Sustain & Scale

- Issue weekly digest of CLM adoption metrics
- Reward high performers with internal recognition (badges, shoutouts)

📊 ADOPTION TRACKER DASHBOARD

Metric	Target	Signal
Login Frequency (CLM)	85%+ of stakeholders use weekly	Low = disengagement
Average Cycle Time Change	-30% from baseline	Neutral = training gap
Clause Override Rate	<5% on key clauses	High = misalignment

🎯 *Success Metric:*
The true signal of CLM adoption is when **stakeholders proactively request enhancements**,
not avoid the system.

🏵️ Section 6: *Risk Management at Scale*

🎯 Objective:

To develop a **predictive, embedded risk model** that enables early identification, classification, and resolution of contractual risks across business units, geographies, and functions.

🧠 FRAMEWORK: Enterprise Contract Risk Grid™

Risk Type	Source	Detection Signal	Systemic Control
Regulatory	Jurisdictional clauses, data terms	High override frequency, legal hold flags	Compliance clause library, audit routines
Financial	Payment terms, penalty structures	Deferred revenue alerts, missed SLAs	Finance rule approval, milestone trackers

Risk Type	Source	Detection Signal	Systemic Control
Operational	SLA misalignment, unclear deliverables	Vendor complaints, service interruption	Standardized SOW templates, supplier scorecards
Reputational	Ethical language, public disclosures	Escalations, stakeholder pushback	Pre-signature escalation, brand-aligned fallback logic

🔧 METHODOLOGY: Five-Stage Scalable Risk Framework

1. **Baseline Clause Risk Index**

   - Assign risk weight per clause based on deviation history, dispute outcomes, audit findings

2. **Contract Type Segmentation**

   - Build profiles: High-risk (outsourcing), Medium (services), Low (NDAs)

3. **Real-Time Risk Triggers**

   - Redline thresholds, missing approvals, and outdated templates auto-flag high-risk conditions

4. **Integrated Risk Dashboard**

   - Combine Legal, Finance, and Compliance inputs
   - Visualize heatmaps by geography, counterparty, and clause

5. Quarterly Risk Model Refinement

- Use deviation data + disputes to re-score clauses and counterparty profiles

🗂 RISK METRICS DASHBOARD (Key Indicators)

Metric	Signal	Threshold
Clause Deviation Frequency	Risk fatigue	>10% deviation on high-value clauses
Dispute Escalations	Reputational risk	>3 per quarter from same B.U.
Risk-Flagged Contracts	Governance failure	>15% of contracts bypass controls

🔔 *Scalable Insight:*
Risk control is not achieved through oversight –
it is achieved through **embedded logic, predictive triggers, and adaptive clause governance.**

⚙️ Section 7: *CLM Performance Intelligence Dashboards*

🎯 Objective:

To translate contract lifecycle performance into **real-time, role-specific, and strategic dashboards** that inform decisions, interventions, and enterprise strategy.

🧠 FRAMEWORK: Multi-Lens CLM Dashboard System™

Dashboard View	Audience	Purpose
Executive	CxO, Board	Strategic alignment, risk posture, financial contribution
Operational	Sales, Legal, Procurement	Cycle time, throughput, workload distribution
Tactical	Analyst, Admin	Field completion, deviation drill-down, clause usage
Predictive	BI, Data Teams	Risk scoring, renewal forecasting, margin erosion alerts

🔧 METHODOLOGY: Intelligent Dashboard Design

1. **Role-Defined KPIs**

   - Legal: % clause compliance, deviation rates
   - Sales: Contract-to-close time, revenue per contract
   - Finance: Forecast vs. realized contract revenue
   - Procurement: SLA compliance, vendor performance

2. **Tiered Drill-Down Capability**

   - Executive → Region → Business Unit → Team → Contract

3. **Anomaly Detection Layer**

   - Alerts on cycle time outliers, sudden deviation surges, redline bottlenecks

4. Quarterly KPI Relevance Review

- Are current KPIs driving the right behaviors?
- Are we measuring what matters, or what's easy?

📊 PERFORMANCE KPI MENU

KPI	Role Tracked	Value
Avg. Time-to-Signature	Sales, Legal	Velocity
Clause Deviation Ratio	Legal	Risk behavior
Margin Recovery from Negotiation	Finance	Financial lift
SLA Breach Rate	Procurement	Operational exposure
Renewal Rate by Segment	CX, Sales	Customer retention health

💼 *Executive Signal:*

Dashboards must not just show **what happened**,

but **where intervention is needed and who is responsible.**

⚙️ **Section 8:** *Financial Validation of CLM Scaling*

🎯 **Objective:**

To tie scaled CLM performance directly to **financial outcomes**—demonstrating ROI, cost savings, margin lift, and enterprise value generation.

💰 FRAMEWORK: Contract Value Realization Model™

Financial Lever	Metric	CLM Impact
Cycle Time Reduction	Fewer days to revenue	Accelerated cash flow
Negotiation Efficiency	Avg. clause edit cycles	Reduced legal cost, faster deal close
Risk Avoidance	Dispute cost savings	Lower litigation, less external counsel
Margin Optimization	Commercial term compliance	Higher realized revenue
Renewal Capture	Renewal timing & automation	Reduced churn, predictable revenue

🔧 METHODOLOGY: Financial Attribution Framework

1. **Baseline Financial Mapping**

   - Calculate current contract processing cost (manual vs. automated)
   - Quantify average value erosion from delays, disputes, and deviations

2. **Benefit Attribution Modeling**

   - Tie cost or margin gain to specific CLM changes (e.g., new fallback clause reduces redlines by 30%, cutting external counsel spend)

3. **Investment-to-Return Scorecard**

   - Compare CLM platform & change costs vs. value

realized in:

- Deal velocity
- Contract risk mitigation
- Compliance cost reductions

4. **Reporting to Executives**

- Monthly/quarterly ROI review integrated with financial reports
- Predictive ROI projection for new business lines or geographies

📊 FINANCIAL VALIDATION DASHBOARD (Illustrative)

Category	Metric	Value
Process Savings	Avg legal cost per contract	↓ $750 per deal
Time Value	Avg DSO reduction (days)	↓ 12 days
Risk Avoidance	External counsel savings	↓ $2.1M YoY
Revenue Uplift	Renewal conversion improvement	↑ 17% YoY

💡 *CFO-Friendly Insight:*

Every contract inefficiency has a dollar cost.

Every CLM improvement should surface as a **P&L impact.**

⚙️ **Section 9:** *Iterative Refinement + Modular Expansion*

🎯 **Objective:**

To ensure that scaled CLM practices remain **agile, contex-**

tually adaptive, and continuously improved across business cycles, regions, and use cases.

🌐 FRAMEWORK: Modular Scaling Architecture™

Module Type	Purpose	Example
Core Governance Pack	Enterprise-level policy and risk baseline	Universal fallback clause set
Market-Specific Pack	Regulatory nuance, cultural adaptation	LATAM privacy clauses, APAC fiscal rules
Function-Specific Pack	Department needs, workflow logic	Sales velocity template, R&D IP guardrails
Emerging Unit Kit	Lightweight rollout for new markets/divisions	Startup-ready on-boarding toolkit

🔧 METHODOLOGY: Continuous Expansion Cycle

1. **Quarterly Lessons Learned Review**

   - Governance team collects wins, failures, friction points
   - Adjust core and regional packs accordingly

2. **Expansion Readiness Assessment**

   - Is the next unit/region digitally ready? Organizationally aligned?
   - Score: Process maturity, data quality, change capacity

3. Modular Rollout Kits

- Prepackaged workflows, dashboards, and templates for instant deployment
- Include onboarding, risk matrix, stakeholder comms templates

4. Feedback Loop Integration

- Post-rollout surveys, usage audits, adoption metrics
- Update Playbook quarterly based on real-world input

▨ EXPANSION PLAYBOOK TOOLS

Tool	Purpose
CLM Readiness Index	Score organizational maturity by unit
Expansion Road-map Template	Align timelines, metrics, responsibilities
Quarterly Refinement Log	Archive and track improvement over time
User Feedback Heatmap	Prioritize pain points geographically/functionally

◎ *Strategic Closure Insight:*

Scaling isn't a finish line—it's a feedback loop.

Every deployment teaches the next.

🔖 **Final Summary: Blueprint for the Autonomous CLM-Driven Enterprise**

Contracts have evolved from static agreements into **living business assets**. With the right strategy, governance, and systems:

- Every clause becomes a financial lever
- Every stakeholder becomes a value steward
- Every contract becomes a **measurable driver** of enterprise performance

Scaling your contract advantage is not a tech project - it is a **strategic operating transformation**.

CONCLUSION

CONTRACTS ARE THE NEW CORE:

Building the Business of the Future, Clause by Clause

In every organization, behind every deal, deliverable, and decision lies a document too often overlooked: the contract. For decades, contracts have been treated as a cost of doing business — static, legalistic instruments filed away after signature, referenced only when something goes wrong.

This mindset is outdated. And costly.

What you've read in this book is not merely a new method. It is a call for a strategic reset. A shift in how business leaders perceive, design, and manage contracts — not as transactional paperwork, but as core operational infrastructure and growth-enabling assets.

It's time to stop managing contracts reactively and start leveraging them strategically.

Contracts as Value-Generating Infrastructure

At their core, contracts define relationships, expectations, and performance. They are the connective tissue of modern business — yet most enterprises treat them as bureaucratic artifacts.

This costs organizations dearly:

- Revenue leakage through missed renewals, discounts, and misaligned terms.

- Operational drag from manual processes and siloed approvals.

- Regulatory exposure due to poor tracking and non-compliance.

- Customer dissatisfaction from delays, disputes, or opaque expectations.

By failing to modernize how contracts are managed, companies unintentionally erode both trust and agility. But the inverse is also true: by reimagining contracts as assets, businesses unlock clarity, velocity, and competitive advantage.

From Legal Burden to Strategic Engine

This book introduced a critical paradigm: Contracts as a Business Asset™ — a framework that positions contracts not as legal back-office tools, but as front-line instruments of strategy, customer experience, and revenue growth.

Reframing contracts in this way delivers transformative benefits:

- Foresight: Predict and prevent risk with real-time data.

- Speed: Accelerate cycle times and time-to-value.

- Alignment: Ensure contract terms mirror customer needs and business priorities.

- Visibility: Turn opaque documents into transparent dashboards.

- Resilience: Build systems that adapt quickly

to change.

This isn't just about technology or process. It's about leadership. It's about mindset.

A Leadership Imperative

In today's business climate, agility and accountability are no longer optional — they are existential. Leaders must now ask:

- Are our contracts empowering performance or obstructing it?
- Do our agreements build trust or erode it?
- Are we managing obligations or designing opportunities?

These questions demand honest introspection. But more importantly, they require action.

Executive teams must champion the transition from fragmented, manual contract chaos to a unified, intelligent CLM strategy that aligns contracts with customer success, operational excellence, and growth objectives.

Building a Contract-Mature Enterprise

Contract maturity isn't measured by the number of templates or tools. It's reflected in how deeply contract thinking is embedded in business design.

Contract-mature organizations treat contracts as:

- Instruments of alignment, not litigation.
- Living documents, not static records.
- Strategic tools, not administrative burdens.

They equip teams with the visibility, governance, and confidence to execute at scale—not despite but because of their contracts.

The Contract Advantage™:

A Movement for Smarter Business

Contract rethinking is not a trend—it is a business necessity. As market complexity grows and digital transformation accelerates, operational clarity becomes a strategic advantage. Contracts are a key source of that clarity—if we choose to see them as such.

This book is more than a guide. It is a manifesto for a movement that calls on business leaders to stop treating contracts as afterthoughts and start designing them as engines of performance.

Those who make this shift—from chaos to control, from fragmentation to foresight—will not only reduce friction but also accelerate results and build businesses that scale with integrity, agility, and purpose.

Final Call: Lead the Change

Let this be the pivot.

Start seeing every contract as a strategic asset, not a sunk cost.

Turn governance into growth.

Turn complexity into clarity.

Turn agreements into advantage.

This is **The Contract Advantage™**.

It starts with leaders like you thinking about contracts, what they *mean*, and what they *make possible*.

Let's build a smarter, faster, more aligned business world.

GLOSSARY OF FRAMEWORKS AND MODELS

CLM Implementation Stack™

A four-layer model mapping execution from intake to renewal:

- **Intake & Deal Initiation**: CRM-connected, risk-tiered intake.
- **Authoring & Negotiation**: Clause libraries, redline accelerators.
- **Execution & Signature**: SLA-driven workflows and audit logs.
- **Obligation Management & Renewal**: Real-time dashboards, renewal alerts.

Modular Scaling Architecture

Designed for agile contract scaling across geographies and functions:

- **Core Governance Pack**: Enterprise baselines (e.g., indemnities, risk).
- **Market/Function Packs**: Regionally or departmentally tailored clauses.
- **Emerging Unit Kit**: Lightweight starter sets for rapid deployment.

CLM Standardization Matrix™

Framework to balance global consistency with local flexibility:

CLM Layer	Standard- ize Globally	Customize Locally
Clause Library	Risk flags, fallback logic	Regulatory-specif- ic variants
Templates & Workflows	Core format & routing	SLA inserts, fis- cal clauses
Gover- nance Policies	Version control, audit trails	Escalation protocols

Continuous Expansion Cycle

Methodology for iterative growth and feedback refinement:

- Quarterly Reviews
- Readiness Assessments
- Modular Deployment Kits
- Real-World Feedback Loops

Contract Advantage Intelligence Layer™

Layered AI-enabled contract governance that:

- Learns from redline patterns
- Flags systemic risk
- Connects contract data to KPIs
- Enables real-time decision support

INDEX

AUTHORITIES & REFERENCES

Christensen, C.M. (1997) *The Innovator's Dilemma*. Boston: Harvard Business School Press.

Deloitte (2021) *The Future of Contract Management: Unlocking Strategic Value*. [online] Available at: https://www2.deloitte.com

Eisenstat, R.A., Beer, M., Foote, N., Fredberg, T. and Norrgren, F. (2008) 'The Uncompromising Leader', *Harvard Business Review*, 86(7), pp. 50–59.

Gartner (2023) *Market Guide for CLM*. Stamford, CT: Gartner Research.

Kaplan, R.S. and Norton, D.P. (2004) *Strategy Maps: Converting Intangible Assets into Tangible Outcomes*. Boston: Harvard Business Review Press.

World Commerce & Contracting (2022) *Most Negotiated Terms Report*. London: WorldCC. Available at: https://www.worldcc.com

Zuboff, S. (2019) *The Age of Surveillance Capitalism*. New York: PublicAffairs.

Custom definitions and models (e.g., *Contract Advantage™, CLM Implementation Stack™, Modular Scaling Architecture™*) are original to the author, derived from over 25 years of industry practice and system design.

www.ingramcontent.com/pod-product-compliance
Lightning Source LLC
Chambersburg PA
CBHW071314210326
41597CB00015B/1223